My Story

My Story

BERNARD DUNNE

PENGUIN
IRELAND

PENGUIN IRELAND

Published by the Penguin Group
Penguin Ireland, 25 St Stephen's Green, Dublin 2, Ireland
(a division of Penguin Books Ltd)
Penguin Books Ltd, 80 Strand, London WC2R ORL, England
Penguin Group (USA) Inc., 375 Hudson Street, New York, New York 10014, USA
Penguin Group (Australia), 250 Camberwell Road,
Camberwell, Victoria 3124, Australia (a division of Pearson Australia Group Pty Ltd)
Penguin Group (Canada), 90 Eglinton Avenue East, Suite 700, Toronto, Ontario, Canada M4P 2Y3
(a division of Pearson Penguin Canada Inc.)
Penguin Books India Pvt Ltd, 11 Community Centre,
Panchsheel Park, New Delhi – 110 017, India
Penguin Group (NZ), 67 Apollo Drive, Rosedale, North Shore 0632, New Zealand
(a division of Pearson New Zealand Ltd)
Penguin Books (South Africa) (Pty) Ltd, 24 Sturdee Avenue,
Rosebank, Johannesburg 2196, South Africa

Penguin Books Ltd, Registered Offices: 80 Strand, London WC2R ORL, England

www.penguin.com

First published 2010

1

Copyright © Bernard Dunne, 2010

The moral right of the author has been asserted

Set in 12/14.75pt Bembo
Typeset by Palimpsest Book Production Limited
Falkirk, Stirlingshire
Printed in Great Britain by Clays Ltd, St Ives plc

A CIP catalogue record for this book is available from the British Library

ISBN: 978–1–844–88257–1

www.greenpenguin.co.uk

To my entire family for their constant support and love.
Especially Pamela, Caoimhe and Finnian

Contents

Prologue: Gone in Eighty-six Seconds

They say when you get hit and hurt bad you see black lights – the black lights of unconsciousness. But I don't know nothing about that. I've had twenty-eight fights and twenty-eight wins. I ain't never been stopped.

Muhammad Ali, 1967

25 August 2007
The Point Depot, Dublin

I don't know anything about those black lights either. I've had twenty-four fights and twenty-four wins. Super bantamweight champion of Europe. I ain't never been stopped either. Never had any reason to be anything but supremely confident in my own ability.

I know what this kid is. Twenty-one years old. Sixteen wins and zero defeats. Fourteen knockouts. Unbeaten as an amateur. A phenomenal puncher.

This is boxing. This is my life. I can handle him. You have to think like that. You have to take your opponent's best dig at some stage. The trick is to do it on your own terms. Sugar Ray Leonard turned that into an art form.

It is Kiko Martinez's first professional bout outside Spain. He arrives in the ring ready to fight. No robe. No frills. Just his squat little frame and all those muscles. Pacing back and forth like a caged animal.

I do my usual entrance. High-voltage stuff as 'The Irish Rover' cranks up the volume. Hood up. Eyes blazing.

Just before the bell, my coach Harry Hawkins repeats his mantra of the past five weeks: 'Keep your hands nice and high for the first couple of rounds. Pick your shots and keep it long distance.'

I don't like watching videos of my opponents, but Harry was

pushing me to sit through a few rounds of Kiko obliterating chumps.

Yeah, Harry. The big overhand right. Got ya. I can handle him, Harry.

I start well. I don't follow Harry's instructions to stay out of range in the early going. I fire off a flurry of punches. Left lead and a right cross followed by two left hooks to the body. No damage inflicted so I stand tall and wait for another opportunity. This is my town. My ring.

I throw a left. Kiko is waiting. He counters with a right followed by a savage left uppercut.

Down I go.

Dazed, I jump up. I claim it was a slip. It wasn't a slip. I look to the corner. I can't make them out. On the count of seven I nod to the referee, Terry O'Connor, that I am fine.

The end is coming just after the beginning.

He hits me a right hook. I am back-pedalling. My guard is wide open. He sets himself up with a right hand over the top. It whizzes past my left eye. He steadies himself and lets it go again. It connects with the top of my temple.

It ruins me.

I use the ropes to pull myself up and immediately start protesting to the referee. I am in serious trouble and glance desperately to where I think Harry might be. He urgently puts his fists up to his face but he knows I have left the building. This is when a coach is powerless. He can see my glazed eyes as well as anyone else ringside.

The referee gives me a mandatory eight-count but he has to tell me four times to put my hands up. I look through him. Eventually, I comply.

There is blood in the water and a killer shark is circling back around for the final frenzy. Kiko walks in like a fin cutting through a wave. I see him but then he slips from view. I should be running, but a left hook to the chin takes the decision out of my hands. I am not hurt. Just stunned.

I try to stand and trade. It is a natural reaction, but it opens my chin again. I try to finish a three-punch combo but my left arm goes limp. The room is spinning. Everything goes dark. Hammer blows rain in. I regain consciousness and I am on one knee staring at the canvas.

Harry climbs into the ring and hugs me but I break loose. I am rambling.

'Is it over or wha'?' I am confused. Not hurt, confused.

They get me onto the stool.

'The first one wasn't a knockdown,' I keep repeating.

Harry holds a bottle of water to my lips, 'Drink, drink, drink. First round. Always a disaster.'

I get to my feet. Only when Dad is by my side do I realize what has happened. Martin Donnelly is also beside me now, 'He caught you cold.'

Fuck. I'm embarrassed.

'I just got caught but my legs were fine.' I look around for someone to agree with me.

Harry delivers the truth with parental certainty, 'Aw, Bernard . . .'

The punters in the Point Depot are from all walks of life but they have that same astonished look on their faces. Most of them are half-way up the quays when Marty Morrissey puts the microphone under my nose. Marty is just doing his job.

'What went wrong, Bernard?'

'I . . . I got caught cold . . .' I apologize to the crowd.

My pride demands the lie. All this stuff about being caught cold is bullshit. I don't believe there is such a thing. You get hit and the guy knocks you out or he doesn't.

We are in the dressing room now. It is like a morgue. No one knows how to react. This is unfamiliar territory. Harry, Pamela, my cut man Benny King, Brian Peters and Martin. Other family members are in and out. I am naked. Someone throws a towel over me. It covers my face.

Reality comes as a chill up my back. Bernard Dunne, former European super bantamweight champion, gone in eighty-six seconds. He hasn't hurt me – not physically, anyway – but the knot in my stomach is tightening. I come out of most fights in bits. This time there isn't a mark on me. Eighty-six seconds isn't a fight.

I also lied about the black lights. Ali probably did too. I had seen them before. 'Mighty' Mike Anchondo shone them in my eyes one day in Freddie Roach's gym in West Hollywood. Lots of things happen in the gym but it is only what's on paper that counts.

I go into the shower room and curl up on the floor. Finally alone, I cry. Brian Peters follows me in. I tell him to get away from me.

I am talking to myself.
How the fuck is that after happening?

I never once consider Kiko to be the end, although to everyone else it seems like the extinguishing of a flame that flickered for a brief moment. Good man, Bernard, but there will be no boxing revival in Ireland led by you. I am not, as it turns out, the answer. Brian Peters steers his promotional ship towards the middleweight division where Andy Lee, John Duddy and Matthew Macklin have, overnight, become more promising headliners. Irish boxing is not all about Bernard Dunne, he explains to anyone who will listen. For nearly three months he refuses to return my calls.

Others reach out. Michael Carruth calls down to the house. Harry Hawkins stays in my corner.

If Harry was in the mafia he would be a consigliere. We have only arrived at base camp and there is some serious altitude training to be done, he tells me. Kiko was kind enough to show us that. Scaling my personal Everest seems such a long way off now that I have been so easily dismantled. But Harry still believes in me. He always has.

I need more power to fend off these little tanks, he says. I am not a big puncher. But I am a boxer. Born into it.

A meandering route is mapped out: Castlebar for redemption, one last return to my beloved National Stadium on Dublin's South Circular Road – the scene of my greatest amateur scraps – and, finally, a return to a remodelled and rebranded Point Depot to plant my flag on the mountaintop.

The climb would be difficult; the descent would be worse. The black lights would come again, but not before I had sucked in the rarefied atmosphere only world champions get to breathe.

I am Bernard Dunne and this is my story.

1. The Playground of My Youth

The fight is over, but I am too sore to go home tonight. We are back in the Burlington Hotel and there is a party in full swing to celebrate the delivery of the European super bantamweight title to the city of Dublin.

'Christmas has come early, lads!' I yelled into the microphone earlier. It is November 2006. I feel unbeatable.

It is late now and all I want to do is retreat to my room with Pamela, eat some shite food for a change and ice my broken hands. My head is bruised but the problem is always those three little metacarpal bones in my right paw that I damaged by slamming it into Mick Roche's bony Cork elbow six years ago.

I am exhausted but I'll never sleep. The adrenaline coursing through my body will see to that. Though with the EBU belt glistening at the end of the bed, the long wait for morning will not be so bad.

My mind is racing. I desperately want the sanctuary of my room. Pamela can see that. She stays close so we can make a quick exit. I don't know the people around me – happy fight fans. The handshakes will hurt more than Esham Pickering's right hook. The back-slapping is rattling my swollen brain.

My people, the Neilstown crowd, steer clear. They know how I feel. They know I will make time for them tomorrow. And the day after that. Generally, I round up the old reliables about twenty-four hours later to sup a few pints. Maybe a bellyful. I would be thirsty after months of sacrifice and hard training but I never drink on the night of a fight. I just want to disappear upstairs.

Yeah, my family and friends know to wait until the pain subsides. They are all from boxing stock, you see. It is part of who we are.

I love telling people I'm from Neilstown. It's my badge of honour. Loved growing up there even though there were moments I could have done without it – like the time I was electrocuted by the lamp post outside our house or the time I was run over by a horse and cart at the dump behind our back wall.

My dad describes young fellas from Neilstown and O'Devaney Gardens, where my parents were reared, as 'rough and ready'. We are street-smart and if enticed early enough, like I was, can be moulded into seriously efficient boxers.

Boxing hasn't exactly thrived in elite circles now, has it? You can't bring the silver spoon into the ring with you. Your gut must be hard, formed in a harsh environment.

I was born in Neilstown on 6 February 1980 and I grew up instinctively knowing how to fight, whether in the schoolyard or over a football match with rival lads from around the area. It came naturally for Clondalkin young fellas. You stand your ground or they will always come looking for you. I stood my ground.

It seemed like everybody around Clondalkin boxed at some stage. Nearly every family on Neilstown Avenue had sons boxing. My older brothers William and Edward were decent – Willie won two national titles and Eddie was a big heavyweight. The next-door neighbours were the Jenningses, and Paddy, Andrew and Brian all boxed. That was three out of seven boys. Number 33 had the Baileys. John boxed. Mark came down a few times and trained. Next door again were the Doyles – young David boxed – and then the Byrnes: Shane boxed for Neilstown. Then there were the Drumms. Three of them boxed: Keith, David and the older brother Jason. The door beside them? David Kelly boxed. The Moores were next and on it went.

Neilstown Boxing Club was right beside us. Kenny Egan is their most famous son, a ten-time national champion who won the silver medal in the light heavyweight class at the 2008 Olympics in Beijing. But I always trained out of the CIE gym in Inchicore because Dad coached there. Paddy Jennings followed me down. The Drumms were also there. And the Baileys, David Doyle and the Kellys. All because of us Dunnes.

My old man was right, the conditions are naturally in place to shape a Neilstown boy into a fighting machine.

'And with skills like you have, Bernard, the world is your oyster. Once it is channelled correctly. Right?'

Right, Da.

He would put his palms up. I would unload.

And he thought I wasn't listening. Brendan Dunne doubled up as my coach, you see. And he knew a thing or two about this boxing business, having fought at the Montreal Olympics in 1976. He always said I was merely developing something that I was born with. I was never concerned about getting hit. That's partly due to the environment I was brought up in, and partly because for most of my life I saw them coming, in the mind's eye, usually before my opponent knew what he was going to throw.

I had a gift. It helps that my dad was a thoroughbred – the first light flyweight to represent Ireland, though he is no more a light fly these days, I can assure you – and my ma's brother Eddie Hayden was a genuine light middleweight contender.

So, I come from boxing aristocracy.

Neilstown and O'Devaney Gardens are important starting points as these are the places that first moulded me for the road ahead. Both these places flickered into my mind as the curtain fell and a delirious Dublin crowd welcomed me into the ring to fight Ricardo Cordoba for the WBA super bantamweight title in March 2009. My home gives me strength.

I don't consider Neilstown a bad area. When you have grown up there the neighbours become your family. They have cared for me all my life, even during my darkest hours. Despite all the bad press the area received over the years there was a real sense of community to Neilstown that outsiders could never see. That's the kind of place it was. Not the unsavoury reputation created by a few bad seeds and enhanced by the media caricature.

I have done some travelling in my time and I consider Neilstown the greatest place on earth. How many people can say that about their own neck of the woods?

Boxing and Neilstown Avenue are my childhood. Whether it was football matches against other tiny pockets or whatever, everything I did around Clondalkin was representing 'The Avenue'. We are a proud bunch.

Everyone saw the problems, but they were prevalent throughout west Dublin and the inner city. Although the cars were being stolen by local lads who flashed them on the hot corners, thinking they were great, the drug epidemic was mainly brought by outsiders coming into the area. But boxing saved me from all that. I was a junkie all right but my fix was easily found within the confines of the CIE gym.

A lot of the lads we played against in the Neilstown Avenue versus Neilstown Drive derbies got sucked into drugs; be it dealing or using. They'd still be friends of mine now. They went through their problems but most of them grew up and worked it out. Some didn't, but that's the way life goes. Who am I to judge other people's choices? I look after my own.

I still spend more time up in my ma's than anywhere else. Still get fed there on a regular basis. I have got more support around home than anywhere else over the years. So, I'm a mammy's boy.

When people ask me where I'm from now I would never say Palmerstown, where I live with Pamela and our kids Caoimhe and Finnian; no, I'm a Neilstown native.

I remember the street parties when I came back from Multinationals with a medal. It was brilliant to see our neighbours take so much pride in the achievement. When I beat Pickering for the European title in November 2006 there were banners all down the Avenue. Number 30 was the centre of festivities. For our little pocket of Ireland, it even topped the Italia '90 celebrations.

Even if they leave, families tend to migrate back to Neilstown. I bought my first house on our road because I knew it was a good place to start a family. I have two other friends who did the same. You could always walk through neighbours' unlocked doors.

Ask Paddy Jennings.

Every Sunday morning without fail there would be a big fry-up in our kitchen. Paddy would get the smell of rashers and sausages from his couch or, more likely, his bed. Just as everyone was sitting down to dig in, Paddy would leap over the back wall and present himself at the table.

Paddy is still my best mate. For better or for worse, richer or poorer, in sickness and in health. Butch and Sundance, that's us. He came to visit me in Los Angeles when I was fighting out of Freddie Roach's Wildcard gym. He was supposed to stay for a fortnight. Pamela finally kicked him out of the apartment three months later.

A good lad is our Paddy. Another proud son of Neilstown Avenue. I got my fingers melted together on that very strip of concrete when barely out of nappies. Myself and Paddy were out catching bees. The cover was taken off a lamp post and I heard a buzzing sound. Genius that I was in the mid-1980s, I presumed it was the queen bee and stuck my hand in without a moment's consideration. I felt a buzz all right. Got jumped out of my socks. The doctor said if I hadn't been wearing rubber soles it could have been fatal. Instead of my obituary in 2062 reading: 'Dr Bernard Dunne – author, renowned fight promoter and former world champion dies at the ripe old age of 82,' it would have stated: 'Bernard Dunne – Neilstown urchin (6) fried chasing bees.'

I've never tended to do things by halves. Paddy, aka Butch Cassidy, scarpered for help. A junior doctor made a bollix of it by bandaging up the hand so when I returned to have the dressing removed a few days later the fingers had welded together. They had to slice them apart with a scalpel. I may have screamed. Such pain revisited me in 2008 when my old friend Dr Joe McKeever put seven stitches into my forehead without an injection after the Cristian Faccio fight on that Road to Damascus evening down in Castlebar. I screamed like a girl when the needle made contact. For a boxer, I don't like pain too much.

The 'sticky fingers' incident might have been the beginning of my dodgy hands. Don't mind me, I'm just another fighter with arthritis in the post.

The bee episode wasn't Angela Dunne's only trip to A&E with her youngest boy. I was never seriously injured, but I was flattened by a horse-drawn cart as an eight-year-old. It was tied up at the dump in the field behind our house. Me and Paddy went for a look. The owner foolishly went into the shops so we immediately climbed aboard. We gave the horse a belt and away he went. Paddy Jennings and Bernard Dunne: horse rustlers. Yee-haw!

When your man gave chase we jumped off but a rope got caught around my foot. The horse stepped over my stranded body but the cart was not so considerate, its wheel running over the back of my thigh. Fortunately the muscle prevented it crushing the bone. Very hard to have a boxing career with a gammy leg.

Paddy, again, escaped without so much as a scratch. His scars have always been more psychological anyhow. Basically, he would have kissed any young one, or auld one for that matter, growing up.

We were Neilstown's finest all right, but we still persecuted some neighbours. Just being young fellas, really – creating havoc and causing mischief.

We had Mrs Duffy on the corner. Everyone has a Mrs Duffy on their road growing up. She didn't like people shorter than five foot and she had a particular dislike for me and Paddy. One of the poles we used to play football against was outside her garden, so she gathered a collection of balls to compare with any national soccer team. You would swear we were standing in her doorway selling drugs or petrol-bombing her gaff. Well, we may have sneaked in one night and cut the heads off all her roses. I can see her perspective on that now.

Mrs Duffy was the caretaker at my primary school, St Peter Apostle in Neilstown, and I saw her recently when I came back to visit the principal, Mr Pat Burke-Walsh. She still hasn't forgiven me for the roses. Many of the same people are still around. My daughter Caoimhe has the same playschool teacher, Ann Quinn, as I did.

I still have a good relationship with St Peter's and with Collinstown Park Community College. Believe it or not I was a fairly decent student. When I won the world title Collinstown threw a big reception for me. Every student was there, all the teachers, and even a few retired ones came back to see me.

Boxing, increasingly, became a priority while I was at college. The teachers understood this and accommodated me. Still, I held my own in maths, biology, chemistry and business studies. When I beat Joe Burke for my first senior national title my teacher Ms Duffy (not the same lady from our road), who is now Collinstown principal, rushed down the National Stadium steps and planted a kiss on my cheek. Half my class was there. I had to go into school on Monday and take a rake of abuse. And me an Irish champion!

Every morning before school I hit the road – around the park and back again. About four or five miles. Coming up to championships I would do an extra lap to ensure I made the weight. That's how my Irish suffered. It's the only school subject I failed because it was the first class of the day and I usually snoozed until about half nine. The Irish teacher, Maura Griffin, cut me some slack and that's why she is teaching me the language today. Better late than never.

Going hungry is another torture fighters must endure. We are like middle-aged housewives trying to shake the pounds for our beach holidays. Ma would buy chocolate every week. Coming up to the Nationals, I would land into the kitchen for my cut. Into the thin box and under my bed they would go so I could gorge after my weigh-in. The cruel thing about the Nationals was they took place around Easter. Not being able to eat my egg on Easter Sunday, while my sister Deborah scoffed hers, was tough. The temptation was always there, but with resistance comes the discipline.

Neilstown has been a huge influence on my whole life, but so has O'Devaney Gardens. In the summertime, straight after school on Fridays, myself and Willie would head to the North Circular Road. Aunt Betty is now in Montpelier Drive, the houses beside the flats – just off Infirmary Road near the Phoenix Park. Not many Dubliners know about it. It is easier to forget about such places.

Three generations of families can still be found there. Dad was from Dominick Street originally and the Haydens lived on Hardwicke Street but they both moved up to O'Devaney before my ma was born. This was my parents' home and where they met. They moved out to Neilstown in 1977 when my brother Willie was three.

Although many left to take up council housing in Crumlin and Neilstown in the late 1970s and early 1980s, they will still tell you they are from O'Devaney first and foremost. That's what roots are all about, I guess. The affiliation cannot be broken easily. Most people moved there from condemned tenement buildings in the 1950s. There are 276 flats or houses and four shops.

The people from the community can do little as they watch history repeat itself. In the 1950s the developer went bust, forcing the local authority to step in and finish the job. O'Devaney is now in desperate need of regeneration, but the project stalled in 2008 when a public-private partnership deal with Dublin City Council went belly-up. At the last check the Council were considering asking for a €50 million government grant from the National Treasury Management Agency.

The people of O'Devaney are not holding their breath.

My dad used to box out of Phoenix down the hill. My uncle Eddie Hayden boxed for Arbour Hill.

My brothers, Willie and Eddie, are both five years older than me, and Deborah, my sister, is two years younger. Eddie is not my biological brother, he is actually my cousin. He is Eddie Hayden's son. Uncle Eddie was shot in 1982 and Eddie Jr's mam died not long after, so he moved in with Aunt Betty in O'Devaney. My granddad, Willie Hayden, also lived with them. Betty adopted Eddie, though he lived with us during the summer months.

Dad remembers Uncle Eddie used to have some vicious tussles with Christy Elliott and Terry O'Riordan back in the day. Elliot fought at the 1972 Olympics. My dad came up behind him, but they went to a few European championships and Multinationals on the same team.

Although Eddie is my cousin, I have only ever known him as a brother and he's always been treated as such. Granted, we get a laugh when I introduce him: he is six foot three and twenty stone. A brave person might make a smart comment. Our mammy gets some dirty looks!

Granda William was a charmer – an old-school Dublin gentleman, good-looking and a prince of the old inner-city ballrooms and snooker halls. He always dressed impeccably, in the old-style suits. His sense of style has supposedly rubbed off on me: Ma says I'm not happy unless I look immaculate.

He died the night I came home from the Olympics in September 2000. On my return home he was, thankfully, one of the first people I called.

'Granda, it's Bernard.'

'This is a great line from Australia, Bernard.'

'Ah, for fuck's sake, I'm in Neilstown, Granda, and I'll be in to you tomorrow with Pamela.'

He was pleased by the news. He loved Pamela as well.

That evening a call came through from Ma. She told us that Granda had gone out to his car to drive home from his girlfriend's (I told you he was a charmer) and suffered a massive heart attack.

Losing him so quickly put everything that was happening in my life into perspective. He was one of my best friends and loved me unreservedly. I never got to see him again but at least I talked to him that day. And, thankfully, I was home.

Willie Hayden used to walk tall beside his little boxing champion grandson. One time I was coming into the ring at the National Stadium, barely a teenager, and he described me as a 'walking robe and headgear' because I was so small. He started humming the *Rocky* theme tune.

'Will you shut up, Granda!'

But we understood each other, and he was always proud of my achievements. When another club would come down to CIE for a match he would say, 'Will I call the ambulance now, Bernard, or wait until they are all mown down?'

He came to all our fights. Brought me down to the club every Sunday morning and stayed to watch training.

Our family has always done everything together. And still do today. Deborah bought the house on Neilstown Avenue from me and Pamela. It meant she was close to home as well. We kept it in the family. Dunne territory.

Any fellas interested in Deborah while she was growing up got a hard time. Daddy made sure us boys watched over his princess. We made sure lads knew not to mess her about. Imagine ringing the doorbell to take out a girl who has three brothers and they are all boxers. And, of course, my auld fella was known to swing a punch when he was younger as well, so there were four of us. We would just sit and stare.

Ironically, Deborah ended up marrying one of my best mates from school, Derek Maher. I was away when Mahersy asked her out for the first time – he timed it to perfection. They have two great kids now, Amber and Maddison, so we have forgiven him.

We did get a laugh out of him coming to the house to ask Dad for permission to marry his daughter. Mahersy was shitting himself – who knew what my dad was going to say? Me and my brother Willie were rolling around the kitchen as he went out to the pigeon loft.

'Eh, howya Brendan . . .'

Willie and Eddie used to call me The Stalker. Willie used to pay me to stay away from him and his stuff. But I still followed them everywhere.

Willie had a bird back in the gaff one afternoon when my parents were away. They were up in his room. Myself and Paddy Jennings emerged from the underbrush and slipped upstairs to investigate. We were bored stupid and the risk of a serious beating was outweighed by the chance to see a naked girl. In our house there are glass panels above the doors and Paddy gave me a leg up so I could look down. There was your one lying half naked on the bed. She looked up and saw my evil eyes glaring down at her. She let out a scream. We were gone before Willie could pull his jeans up and do some damage.

It must have been a nightmare for him and Eddie, especially when they became teenagers, but they put up with their little brother. They would be pissed off, but it wasn't as if they had a choice. Maybe they knew I would become a world champion some day. Smart lads, are my brothers, and still thick as thieves today.

Inevitably, following Willie and Eddie led me down to the CIE gym in Inchicore. I was five years old when I first walked through the doors of Peter Perry's kingdom.

I was too young to be there but I was Brendan Dunne's son so I got a free pass. They had to do something with me when he was training other young boxers so I was put on a chair to thump the floor-to-ceiling ball. That initiation served me well. Not too much time elapsed before they started taking notice. Put a child that young in that environment and the stance, the head movement and the combinations won't be long following.

'Jesus, Brendan, look at your youngest.'

They moved me on to pads. I was delighted as it meant I got to be closer to me daddy.

I had my first fight when I was six years old up in Drogheda. I was small enough but did grand. The lad I was against was ten or eleven, so it was just like taking on a smaller version of Willie or Eddie. My first competitive (and legal) fight came when I was eleven, so I was already a veteran when my peers were only lacing up for the first time. Hardly fair, now, was it?

I never got into fights outside the ring. Well, everybody has the occasional tiff when they are younger, but nothing major. Maybe because I ended them quickly. I was never afraid of a scrap. Boxing was what I was good at. The training was hard but I didn't mind, and although, like most boxers, I experienced pre-fight nerves, I never feared an opponent. I trusted my ability.

By the time I turned pro I knew enough to realize that, by the time you step into the ring, the hardest part is over. You have ticked all the boxes. You have done everything you possibly can. All you need to do now is go out and perform.

I was very disciplined when I trained. I did everything that was ever asked of me. Sometimes I probably over-trained. It took a while for me to learn the importance of listening to my body. Okay, you are exhausted today – stop and rest. I only really learned that in the last two years of my career. Short, sharp stuff was best.

I was always big into soccer and I'm a Liverpool nut to this day. One of my earliest sporting memories is Michael Thomas scoring that poxy injury-time goal at Anfield on the last day of the 1989 season to give Arsenal the First Division title. And then we signed him!

I played for Neilstown and Quarryvale. Eventually I joined Palmerstown Woods. They used to harass Dad coming up to the National Championships because he would call a halt to my football season in case I got injured and couldn't compete. I was a hatcher. Top goal scorer. That said, I was no Ian Rush or John Aldridge. It got to the stage where Dad said, 'Look, you are sixteen, you can be good at any sport but it is time to pick just one.'

It wasn't a difficult decision. I liked my team sports but I was a boxer. My heroes were never Liverpool players or Dublin GAA men. They were Wayne McCullough, Michael Carruth, Sugar Ray Leonard and Mike Tyson in his prime. That's why it was an easy choice to quit football.

Wayne paved the way for what I wanted to do. The 1992 Olympics in Barcelona, where Wayne won a silver, unfolded in our living room. Me and Da may as well have been ringside for every second.

I sparred with Wayne as a teenager. I had just won the National Youths title and Wayne was training out in Luttrellstown Castle. It was 1996, just before he fought the Mexican José Luis Bueno at the Point. A young Meath publican named Brian Peters was co-promoting the event with an American named Matt Tinley. The great Eddie Futch was also in Wayne's corner at the time.

Straight after my fight one of McCullough's people came and asked me if I'd like to spar with the current WBC bantamweight world champion. I didn't even change out of the gear I'd just won my title in. 'Yeah, let's go!'

To get into a ring with someone of his calibre left a huge impression. I was never a person to be overawed, but it was a thrill of a lifetime.

Matt Tinley thanked me for the spar afterwards. 'He is working on moving his head with the punches,' he told me.

'Yeah, right. His head was moving because I was punching it, pal.'

I was a cocky little kid but Wayne and his wife (and manager) Cheryl found it funny. Good people.

We are still good friends, despite the numerous times he tried to goad me into fighting him. We met up in 2009 when he was over in Dublin in his capacity as an Ultimate Fighting Championship ambassador.

It made sense for Wayne to chase the fight but I told him I had no interest. It was a lose–lose situation for me. He was pushing forty and hadn't won a fight since 2004. I told him straight: 'Wayne, we are friends first and foremost but that wouldn't stop me. I have boxed friends' lights out before. But I'm going down another road and you ain't on it.'

'But it is the fight people want to see,' he said.

'It may well be but I don't want to fucking see it!'

There is a great picture of the two of us together outside the O2 Arena. Two ships passing in the night unfortunately. Sorry, Wayne.

I also became good friends with Michael Carruth, who won Ireland's first-ever Olympic gold boxing medal in Barcelona, at a very young age. He had a genuinely positive influence over me. I sparred with him down in Drimnagh a few times and he was always good at whispering the right stuff in your ear afterwards. Words that would stay with you. He was an army man and I fed off that military discipline. The man was purpose-built for the amateur game. Get in, pick off your points, and back behind your guard. Repeat process.

These were my local heroes, but Ray Leonard was my idol when I was growing up. I have all the old tapes and *Boxer* magazines full of his great fights. When I was younger I dominated my age group and weight class in Ireland, so Sugar Ray's 'bolo punch' came out a few times. Spinning right arm and, just as your opponent was about to burst with rage, Pow! Nail him with the left. Did it in some big fights, at the Nationals even, and the crowd loved it. I was enjoying myself. Becoming the entertainer. Switching to southpaw. All Sugar Ray's doing.

I admired the way he went up eleven pounds from welterweight to middleweight to fight Marvin Hagler in 1987. For me that was like going abroad as an amateur. Taking on the best in the world. Just like Sugar Ray.

I have met them all, I suppose. But the biggest influence on my career was me da. I wanted to emulate Brendan Dunne and then better everything he had achieved. He finds that amusing. I never did follow him into the Olympic arena, so to keep him quiet I had no choice but to win a world title.

Pound for pound, the greatest boxer in the world today is Manny Pacquiao. I sparred with him numerous times in LA and he still loves to play basketball between sessions, much to his trainer Freddie Roach's frustration: while it's good for conditioning purposes the chances of picking up a niggly injury that will ruin a big pay-day – or back then, for me, a national title – is an unnecessary risk. That's why I stopped playing soccer for Palmerstown, even though I was top scorer. Dad never forced the discipline aspect on me. He knew I had to develop it for myself. Don't get me wrong, there were times when I hated him because I felt he was stopping me from living my life. I believed I was missing out on the things that other teenagers look forward to.

During what for most kids would be a guaranteed drinking session, like your Junior Cert results night, I would be training, although I didn't really care by then. Halloween? I would be woken up by the fireworks. Next morning on a training run I would jog past the charred remains of the massive bonfire. Cans everywhere. A shell of a car.

Looks like a good party was had by all. Bet they are all dying now, though, I'd think as I pumped my legs for home.

Living with your coach isn't the easiest arrangement in the world. Dad couldn't help but watch what time I came home on the rare occasions I went off with my mates for a night out, watch what I was eating.

We used to train in the house. Sometimes that drove me mad. For a young boy it seemed like there was no escaping it.

I wanted to emulate Brendan Dunne but I also wanted to be like all the other young fellas from Neilstown.

I resented him for a long time. Now, I am eternally grateful. It was hard being a teenager: I thought I was missing out on chasing girls and having a few drinks but when I look back I know I missed nothing.

I would turn to him sometimes and say, 'I don't want to fuckin' box any more.' He would say, 'If you don't want to box, don't box.' He was great at coaxing me into doing things – just had a great knack of encouraging me to keep doing what I wanted to do, even when I didn't know it myself. I would sleep on it and then almost as a reflex go jogging the next morning. Sometimes I did it out of pure frustration. But he knew his own son.

I didn't realize it at the time but he used to have three jobs on the go at any one time to keep food on our table, yet he'd resist what must have been an overwhelming urge to sleep just to spar or do pads with me in the kitchen.

He did the same with Willie and Eddie, but at about seventeen they simply stopped. There were two fundamental distractions: women and drink. Like most normal people, they allowed these other interests to take over their lives. Don't get me wrong – when I got the chance to enjoy myself, I did. There just had to be a time and a place. Once we were into serious training everything else became secondary.

I see the similarities between my relationship with Caoimhe nowadays and mine with my dad. Basically, we do everything together.

That's what really got me down to the gym, the curiosity to follow him wherever he went.

He retired from coaching as soon as I hung up the gloves. Job done, he felt. Peter Perry had him down in CIE for years and then he went to St Matthew's when I turned pro. He put so much into my career. Time to take a break and focus on the pigeon coop in the backyard. Andrew Jennings, Paddy's younger brother, is his chief second.

It was tough on Da when he dropped me off at the airport to go to America when I turned pro in 2001. Mainly because we had gone through so much together and now he had to let go. It was the end of our boxer–coach relationship and we both knew it. I could see him welling up.

'Okay son, I'm going to go.'

He walked away.

Seeya, Da.

Years later he admitted to breaking down as soon as he walked away. I had to keep my tears inside as I turned my back on Neilstown and the playground of my youth.

Time to grow up.

2. Peter Perry and His Enforcer Rasher Dunne

That's it, Bernard. Left jab, Bernard. Do it again, Bernard. Through the middle.

I can always hear my dad. And Peter Perry. Everyone else gets shut out. Every other sound, even the crowds that are baying for blood, become like the humming of a fridge after a while.

I can watch fights back now from any time in my career, amateur or professional, and hear my dad or Peter shout something from the crowd and I instantaneously carry out the order.

Left jab, Bernard.

That's it!

It is the 1992 Juvenile Championships and I am giving the first young fella they put in front of me a lesson. This was my introduction to competitive boxing in an official capacity. I am eleven but already a veteran of CIE trips to Drogheda and various Dublin haunts.

The left jab is never for show. It is thrown as often as possible to entice my opponent into a wild retaliation. Then a right on the inside. Bam, bam. Blink and you'll miss it, sucker. I have watched the videos at home. I am Sugar Ray. Ali. Super confident in my natural environment.

Peter Perry is angry with me again. I have abandoned the fight plan and started trading punches. The Neilstown boy loves a scrap.

It is my dad's fault really. Brendan Dunne was a fighter, not a natural technician like his son. That instinct has been passed down, and while it serves me well this evening, it will become a weakness when I run into some brick walls later on. But I can't resist testing my opponent on the inside. He misses me every time. I am invisible.

My jab breaks the next kid's nose. Never for show. I don't feel the need to brawl with this fella. We are back on our stools and he is crying. Always a good sign. That standing eight-count brought the water-works. His corner tried to say it was a slip but I caught him flush with a left uppercut. It is stopped. I'm as cocky as they come but I never gloat. I'm excited to get my gloves off and take the plaudits, though. Peter has the same old grumpy pout. He flips off a glove and lets his prodigy salute the crowd. I hug the defeated and thank the opposing corner. Take my pat on the head. 'Well done, Dunne.' Respect is paramount, I figure out quickly, because in a boxing life what goes around comes around as sure as a counterpunch.

The next guy insists on going toe to toe. I grant him this wish.

Keep boxing, Bernard. Keep boxing!

Dad is exasperated but he has accepted that I'm going to handle this one my way. Really, it is my opponent's fault. He asks for it. The fight quickly becomes about who wants to win more. It was always going to be me. No one could love boxing as much as I do. To attack me wildly is probably the best tactic but it rarely works.

The other kid is regretting it now. I can see that. I slip to the right after landing a crisp left-right-left combo. He stumbles headlong into the space I just occupied but I'm gone. In complete control now. Moving backwards at an angle and picking him off. We swap a flurry of blows but mine are the only ones connecting.

Ahhh, that's beautiful.

I can always hear my dad.

Peter Perry is raging. His cheeks are redder than usual and his bulging eyes are inches from my face. It was common enough for Peter to throw me a harder slap on returning to the corner than I had just received in the ring. He grabs me by the chin, sponge on my neck. Need that sponge but feeling sharp.

That's not what we talked about!

I'm listening, but I know I am winning. The kid wanted to go. So we went. I peek over Peter's round shoulders and see the opposing coach doing helicopters with the towel as my victim gasps for air. The bell goes. I'm already in my stance. Left hand high. Bobbing, no weaving, just bobbing. Soak up his desperate last flurry and then go for the kill.

Left. Left. Then a lovely right cross. He catches me with a counterleft. I admired my right too much there. I stand tall and show him my hands again. Held up high. *Come on!*

I let him fly past and through the ropes. Complete control again. Invisible.

Dad has gone silent. That is either a good sign or a really bad sign. I know this time it is a good sign. Peter is less urgent now. I go back out for the final round. My first national title in sight. Eleven years old but I have been doing this for as long as I can remember. I finish the lesson. My opponent's courage gets him a standing eight-count. Then he walks straight into my jab. He will always remember my jab.

I'm dancing now. Ali shuffle. Even the ancient guys ringside are smiling.

'National Boy 1 champion. 31 kilos. The blue corner.' They don't know my name yet. They will.

Arms raised. Hug my opponent. Visit the red corner for a pat on the head, pick up my medal from Felix Jones (got lots of medals off Felix) and back to Peter – who knows by now he has a natural-born pugilist under his wing. Back to CIE we go.

Peter always knew. Peter Perry sent me where I needed to go. Places like Holy Trinity in Belfast. Other kids can cry in defeat or become ecstatic in victory. I just wanted to know who or what was next.

The 1993 Juvenile Championships are a repeat of 1992. My opponent in the final gets disqualified for throwing himself at me in a last act of desperation. Pat on the head. Back over to Felix.

Go on, Rasher!

They used to call me Rasher. I settle for Ben now. One time up in Drogheda I was doing my Sugar Ray Leonard impression. Bolo punches and the sneaky left. I had the whole place swaying to my rhythm. I was ten years old. By the end of my bout even the locals were calling me Rasher so I knew it would take a while to shake that nickname. It was better than 'Skinny', I suppose.

All the hard work was done in the CIE Boxing Club off Granite Terrace in Inchicore. Rough terrain, a concrete jungle. A perfect environment for my kind. There were others like me.

Jim Rock was there when I was coming up. 'The Pink Panther', as he is known today, remains a decent middleweight from Blanchardstown who ended up featuring on a number of my undercards when I returned from America in 2005. Like many before him, Rock honed his craft under Peter Perry. So did Paul Stephens.

Peter had two prodigies at the same time. I lived in the shadow of Paul Stephens. Paul was a year older and two weight classes up but he also boxed out of CIE. For my two European bronze medals, Paul had a pair of golds. I always seemed a step or two off his brilliance and yet it would have been detrimental for my progress not to have had him around. I got to spar with a brilliant southpaw on a regular basis. It meant the lefties never confused me because most of them were inferior to Paul. His was a superb talent and there was pedigree as well. He is related to seven-time national champion Glen Stephens.

But this is where the discipline comes in. Paul had everything I had, and that little bit extra, but I guess I wanted to be a boxer just that little bit more than he did while he wanted to enjoy his life. One day he just stopped coming to training. Dad swears if Paul had stayed at it he could have turned pro and even become a world champion. Peter Perry loved him as he did me; like a son.

Life intervened for Paul, but I refused to let that happen. No time for girlfriends. No drinking on Junior Cert results night or any other night when a tournament was looming. My discipline was always my greatest attribute. Nothing was more important to me than chasing my dreams. I kept it simple: Olympic gold and then champion of the world. Didn't want to start thinking about Inter-Galactic domination just yet. Too distracting.

Dad and Peter complemented each other in the gym. Peter could read any fighter and develop a method to counter his style. He would observe and intervene when necessary while my dad was great at the hands-on coaching. The combination served me nicely.

'You are twitching your left elbow when shaping to throw a left hook. If I can see it some fighters might and some coaches definitely will,' Peter would say.

He would bellow when I did it again.

'Don't twitch that elbow!'

It would eventually compute in my brain. Camouflage the dig. Little intricacies.

'You are dropping your left hand, Bernard!'

He was always giving out to me about that.

'Listen, son, he is dropping his right hand when throwing left hooks. As soon as you see that, you want to be capitalizing.'

This is where I learned about timing. I listened. Really, I did. An overhand left would be the medicine. I caught on quick.

Peter excelled in two pursuits: the sweet science and giving out to people! But one thing he always gained from me and all other young boxers was unwavering respect. He was well known around Inchicore, not just boxing circles, and he managed several junior football teams up in St Patrick's Athletic. His son Gerry was a respected League of Ireland referee and became an instructor at the FAI school of excellence for referees.

Peter instilled the importance of never giving my opponent an inch. When other clubs came down from Mount Tallant or Drimnagh or, my favourite, from Neilstown, Peter would be there, 'Okay, I'm shouting in take it easy but I mean *fucking wipe him out*.' That was Peter. This is our club and they are coming here so we need to show these boys what it is all about.

His was a tough love. You knew not to mess around with Peter. He developed a subtle system to deal with the undesirables or supposed hard lads who would inevitably wander in from St Michael's estate around the corner, or anyone that landed in with the intention of messing about. They had to be weeded out quickly as they were wasting the valuable time of us serious boxers. You would spot them after a few days. Peter would pick the biggest one and tell him he was ready to spar.

'Bernard, get your gloves on.'

He would tell me all I needed to know with his eyes. *Make sure he doesn't come back.* I'd go to town on him. That would be the end of that lad and his mates wouldn't be long following him out the door. If the lads were significantly bigger or older than me, Paul Stephens would do the job. We were Peter's enforcers.

Paul was not the only other decent young boxer in the club. The Maughan family – there were about six of them – contained at least three national champions: Francie, Martin and Patrick. The twins –

Francie and Martin – were always trying to knock you out. We were all close mates but once you stepped in the ring it became deadly serious. And our ring was tiny with literally nowhere to run, never mind hide. You learned to fight against the ropes. We had some great digging matches in there.

Peter and Dad were constantly telling me that, technically, I was better than anybody else and to stick to boxing rather than brawling, but I always wanted to mix it up.

The 1994 national final was supposed to be my first defeat. So everyone kept telling me. 'Don't worry,' they said. 'There's no shame in being beaten by Robert O'Connor. You learn more from a loss, anyway.' Did they not see that I was improving; gathering more and more advanced weapons? Learning to think a safe route out of trouble. Fighting my own fight but tweaking when necessary or altering the point of attack against a crafty opponent.

Robert O'Connor was from Cork's Sunnyside club, which is home to the famous Joyce boxing clan. Jaysus, he was tall. This time I was in the situation most of my opponents had experienced. No option but outright aggression. The knowledgeable observers in the National Stadium were predicting a rude awakening for the cocky Neilstown kid.

Seconds before the opening bell: loosen my shoulders, touch my headgear, glance a glove off my nose. Relaxed. I'm supposed to be beaten here. Will I accept that? Touch my headgear again. Calm. Feet planted. Robert is skipping.

Come on, Robert!

Come on, Bernard!

Ding! I barely get two paces out of my corner and he is on top of me. Will I accept this? He's a southpaw just like Paul Stephens, but smaller. Less power, I presume. He hits me a left. Yeah, less power. I nearly tear his head off with a counter-right. Bloody nose for Robert. Every weapon in the arsenal on display. Left, right, left. No option but outright aggression? Mandatory eight-count isn't long coming for Robert. I'm supposed to lose this? You learn more from a loss? Fuck that.

My ring alter ego is born. The animal. Bernard Dunne, the good-humoured kid from Neilstown, is no longer with us. I am a vicious dog of war. His head is up in the clouds so I land a big right to his chest instead. He blocks his body so I reach up and clock his head. A vicious Neilstown dog. Like the one my granda used to own. That dog liked me.

The bell comes to Robert's rescue. He can hear a few bells ringing now, I imagine.

Peter is as close to smiling as I have ever seen him. Surely he must have handled a few boxers like me in sixty years sending kids out of his corner? Robert cannot touch me. Simple instructions from Peter to close it off. Jab. Jab. Left, right. Robert's head is snapping skywards. The referee has seen enough.

One of the Joyce brothers gives me a gentle slap on the face. 'Well done, Bernard Dunne.' Respect.

Applause.

Collect medal off Felix and back to Peter Perry. Through the ropes and off we go.

That was the first time I really thought, *Right, I'm up against it here*. Robert had been impressive throughout the championships. I had been watching so I knew I needed to dominate. Jump all over him from the opening bell. Not let him use his reach advantage against me. He had stopped everybody else coming through the ranks. He had three national titles at different weights. I stopped him in round two.

My dad liked that one. He described it as my most competent under-age display. I won the boxer of the year award that year but I told him to give the trophy back.

'Da, I don't want that bleedin' trophy.'

'Why, son?'

'Da, I'm Bernard Dunne and that trophy says Brendan Dunne. Give it back.'

He had already won that trophy as a juvenile and again as a senior over thirty years ago. He wasn't getting any silverware off my performance. Coach or not! Brendan Dunne, sniggering, happily pointed out the error to the IABA officials and got the name changed.

I start picking off my dad's records – winning six national titles to his five, from age eleven to sixteen, puts a smile on his face. I can make a life from boxing, I begin to tell myself. The Olympics in Sydney. Maybe Athens as well. Michael Carruth. Wayne McCullough. 'We won't be jumping around the living room, Da, we will be jumping around the Olympic village.' I feel like Al Pacino in *Scarface* – looking out that window at the Goodyear blimp that reads: *The world is yours*.

I can become champion of the world. Emulate Brendan Dunne and then surpass him. Six national titles to his five. An Olympic medal and world title are next. I walk into the living room of number 30 Neilstown Avenue. 'Ma, go in and pick your husband off the floor,' I tell her after a particularly vicious session in the kitchen.

It is 1995. I am rocking opponents backwards with the jab. It opens everything up. It makes them miss. They can never see my right coming with that jab in their face. Eight-counts are mandatory. So are busted noses. Always listening to Peter. I weigh 36 kilos and counting. Happy with my medal and certificate from Felix Jones. Peter is holding the ropes for his prize fighter to exit. Back to CIE we go with the spoils.

One time we almost didn't make it to the National Stadium. Dad loves his motor bikes. I can picture him back then with the Tom Selleck moustache on his Honda 50. I can also remember falling off the back of the thing on the way to a weigh-in on the South Circular for the National Juniors. There were a load of cars parallel parked along the road. Some woman pulled out, I swear she saw us but panicked and jammed on the brakes – there was nowhere to go but straight into her. I hit the top of the roof and flipped over. Dad was on the bonnet. She was in a rush to work. I wrecked my already cursed right hand and left knee. I had the knee heavily bandaged and was in no condition to box. Strolled through it, though. I was invincible back then. No pain. *The world is yours*. Something like that merely concentrates the mind.

A year later I had a touch of pneumonia. Peter Perry had me covered up in blankets just moments before entering the ring. Somehow I got it done again. Once the adrenaline kicked in I didn't need my right hand or left knee and forgot that I was death warmed up. Whatever was called for; I could brawl or box.

My first trip abroad with the Irish amateurs was to Turkey. I was showboating at home but Clive Smith was another tough nut that needed cracking in order to maintain progress. He was a year older than me so the IABA organized a 'box off' to see who went to the European Juniors. There was plenty of hype about this one. High stakes. His dad would have been good friends with my uncle Eddie so there was a rivalry there. Clive was coached by Philip Sutcliffe of the Crumlin Boxing Club. The Crumlin fellas really fancied their boy's chances against me. I gave him a boxing lesson.

Still only fifteen but they gave me the opportunity and I took it. I would be in against foreign sixteen-year-olds.

They didn't like us much in Istanbul. I was up against a Russian in the semi-final. I remember this guy with a beard staring at me in the changing room. 'You are fighting him, Rasher.' Jesus, he looks like Ivan bleedin' Drago from *Rocky IV*.

Me and the alter ego had a brief conference. 'Howya, once the bell sounds I'm off, so look after this big Russian block for us, okay?' said Bernard Dunne, carefree teenager from Neilstown. My alter ego sheepishly agreed.

Making our way to the ring I experienced another first: I was intimidated. Not so much by the sight of the bearded one waiting for me but the Turks baying for my Irish blood to be spilt on the canvas. They were pro-Russian and spitting abuse in my face. The place was a kip. Ivan was clearly stronger than me and dominated the opening round, cutting off the space.

I could live with that. I was no longer in Istanbul. I was at home. In the ring. This is where I always wanted to be. There were a few things I was going to try before he could get hold of me.

I got inside and landed some sledgehammers. He didn't flinch. I tried again. *I'll put you down.* I dropped a left hook into his nuts. Nothing. He didn't even complain to the referee and I clonked him, deliberately, below the belt. Frankenstein just kept plodding forward. Stand up Russian-style. Bang-bang combo. Time to stick and move,

Bernard. No joy with that either. Not much of a lesson either. What can you learn from a freak? Don't get hit. I knew that in the changing room. I get beaten officially for the first time in my life.

I deal with it and move on to the Gaelic Youths tournament in Canada. Some local chap named Su Ki something or other is up first. My amateur record is 60–1. Irish cap flipped backwards as I bounce into the ring. I get warned by the referee for doing my Sugar Ray Leonard impression in the opening seconds. No bolo punches? Okay Su Ki, have a standing eight-count instead. Right uppercuts are the order of the day but a left cross brings the referee back between us. No warning this time, just some respite for Su Ki. He is whimpering. I go on to claim the gold.

Next stop on my world tour was Michigan for the Junior Olympics. Robert O'Connor had moved up in weight so he joined Dermot Hamill and myself on the team. The coach was Billy McClean. I boxed Brian Viloria, soon to be known as the Hawaiian Punch, who went on to win the WBC light flyweight title when he knocked out Eric Ortiz in 2005. He was a class act. I lost on points. We renewed our rivalry during sparring sessions in the Wildcard gym several years later.

All this time Peter Perry is trying to decide what to do with me. He knows I am outgrowing CIE. I am guided towards someone he trusts, not just as a coach but as a man. That is the stamp Peter Perry put on Harry Hawkins.

I first came across Harry when I was fourteen years old. Two experts in the same field, Peter and Harry were friends. Plenty of mutual respect. It also made sense to keep communication lines open between Dublin and Belfast, where Harry coached. I was sent up to the Holy Trinity Boxing Club in West Belfast to harden me up some more with a new experience. Due to Peter's persistent alerts, Harry had followed me through the age grades. He liked my killer instinct. If I was on top of someone I wouldn't let up. I went up to Holy Trinity again before my first tilt at the National Seniors.

I was still a teenager in 1998 when I moved up to senior at 54 kilos. The national final was against Joe Burke, who was trained by Billy Walsh. Peter had had a knee replacement so getting up the steps to the corner was proving difficult. He swapped roles with Dad – but I could still tune in to his voice. Jesus, I would hear him in the rafters of a packed Point Depot. I beat Joe Burke and became the bantamweight champion of Ireland.

Harry was back on my radar a few months later as Ireland sent a three-man team to Minsk in Belarus for the European Amateur Championships. I was the baby on the squad alongside Eugene McEneaney from Dundalk and Brian Magee of Holy Trinity, who was the best amateur prospect in Ireland at that time. As Brian's coach, Harry came with us and looked after me. I was sent back up to Belfast for the training camp.

I came up against Reidar Walstad of Norway. Reidar was a fully developed twenty-year-old and he picked me off, winning 10–2, though I would settle that score nine years later.

The pro game is so different to the amateurs. The amateurs is a race. Four two-minute rounds. Get your point off and move. In the professional ranks it can be twelve rounds of three minutes. It is more calculated, setting yourself up for shots, working your angles and breaking guys down rather than outpointing them. In the amateurs it is more like fencing. I was still an amateur; still learning.

Brian Magee lost in the final and took a silver medal back to Belfast. That's what I wanted. Medals and recognition for my talent. Brian had already been to the Atlanta Olympics in 1996, losing his third bout to Algeria's Mohamed Bahari, and he was destined to become a professional.

I also liked the way Harry Hawkins went about his business. You can have the best coach in the world but unless you get on with him you won't listen to a word he says. Me and Harry clicked. Every team leaving the country during this time wanted me on it. Harry thought it would be better if I stepped back and rested more so I was better conditioned for the really big events, but the IABA had other ideas. I loved representing my country so I never contemplated taking a rest. We had a great team spirit. Especially when I reached the senior squad. Once the boxing was over we quickly became a bunch of young Irish lads in a foreign land. We made like our fellow expatriates and went on the piss. It wasn't like it is now where team members have to sign abstinence contracts.

I travelled the world before I left my teens. Not many kids from Clondalkin can say that. In Halle, Germany, I remember getting drug tested after my last bout. Before taking my urine sample they pointed at this huge fridge and told me to drink as much liquid as I needed. Half the fridge was filled with water, the other half with German beer. I looked at the guy and he didn't seem to care so I had a bottle of beer. And then another. My sample wasn't long coming and he still didn't mind so I took as many bottles as I could carry back in my singlet to the changing room. The lads were impressed.

We were walking into a pub later that night when some local guy coming the other way produced a knife. There were seven of us, Irish national champions every one, and all he had was this puny little East German switchblade. Not the poor chap's brightest move. Our heavyweight, John Kiely, was nicknamed 'Two-Shoes' because that's the sound he made when he punched. Like a reflex jab, Two-Shoes grabbed the guy's blade hand, bounced it against the wall and, without breaking stride, held the door open for the rest of us. 'Enjoy your night, gentlemen.' He even bought the first round. John was a bouncer back home.

I made some lasting friends and there was a genuine feeling of being part of a team – that is, until the bell rang. But the lads were with you. Those amateur trips were as close to a team sport experience a boxer can find. Some names I'll never forget: Áodh Carlyle, Alan Reynolds, Stephen Reynolds, Francie Barrett, Seanie Barrett from Kerry, Michael Roche, Conal Carmichael, Kevin Cummiskey, Darren Campbell, Marvin Lee, Harry Cunningham and Kevin Walsh from Cork, whose dad, Maurice, coached us a couple of times. Maurice is a true gentleman of Irish amateur boxing.

We are in Washington State. Ireland versus the United States of America. The previous night it was San Jose, California, where I beat Saul Perez. The bouts are televised live on Fox Sports. Bagpipes precede the Irish team's entry to Spokane Arena. Some ridiculous American pomp and ceremony. A seventeen-year-old Bernard Dunne is smiling into the camera while he loosens up. The twenty-two-year-old Cornelius Lock gives it up hip-hop style. Black fella from

Detroit. Carved out of muscle. We start trading early and neither of us lets up until Lock runs out of juice in the last round and I put him on one knee with a straight left, right uppercut to the body. After that he is looking to slow dance so I fling him to the canvas with ten seconds remaining. I've turned the battle back in my favour after a tough second round. He stuns me with a straight left just on the bell to end the fight.

Always defend yourself.

The referee, Philip Rooney, had travelled over with us. He was a member of St Matthew's, where my dad was a coach, yet at the end of a desperately close bout he starts a standing eight-count!

'1, 2 . . .'

Disgusted, I walk back to my corner but Maurice Walsh sends me back over to Rooney. Just as the scorecards are being finalized.

'3, 4, 5 . . .'

'Well done, you just cost me the fight, dickhead.'

'. . . Eh? . . . 6, 7, 8.'

Unbelievable. I glare at him. He might as well have kept counting.

Lock went on to win the WBO NABO featherweight belt after stopping Orlando Cruz at the MGM Grand in Las Vegas in 2009.

Terry Carlyle was a man. I was still, in body shape anyway, a boy. Terry had won the featherweight national title in 1997 and lost in the final the next year by a single point. This meant everything to him and he was gunning for me. We both knew he had the power.

There was a genuine animosity to the whole build-up. Last year's bantamweight champion against the best featherweight in Ireland. Two neighbouring tribes – Clondalkin and Tallaght – sending their best gladiators into the Colosseum. Well, the National Stadium.

I was enjoying the hype even though I thought it was all a bit ridiculous. This is what happens in boxing. The featherweight final of 1999 was also the beginning of a year that was supposed to end in qualification for the Sydney Olympics. Everything was building towards that now.

I had never lost to an Irishman and I had never lost on Irish soil. I desperately wanted to keep those records intact.

Sacred Heart Boxing Club is out in force but so is the whole of

Clondalkin with the Neilstown Avenue lads at their core. The place is buzzing; people getting involved all over the shop. The national media are ringside. I should probably introduce myself to those not paying attention these past few years. I'm Bernard Dunne.

Sadie Duffy is the first female referee to take control of a men's senior final.

Terry is as big an opponent as I'm ever likely to meet. Some serious muscle is evident. He must have almost killed himself to make weight. Four two-minute rounds will not be a problem to him, however. I know his brother Áodh very well. We used to travel together in the national squads.

There is pandemonium all around me so I turn the volume down. The gentle humming of a fridge at night.

'All right?'

'Yeah Da, I'm all right.'

Gumshield in. Terry is skipping away on an imaginary rope. His back is turned. We come together and touch gloves. I bless myself and tip the red corner with my right glove.

How the hell did he make the weight?

He turns his back again. In we go. Caution. My technique can win this. Terry looks to rough me up. I react. Sadie warns me early for use of the head. What the fuck? This is a brawl. The first round is over in an instant. I have no idea who won it. Dad is in my ear to move more. I am staring at Terry. Dying to get back out there. *I have never lost to an Irishman.*

In the second round Sadie warns me about going below the belt but I touch gloves with Terry at the bell. There is respect between us. We are just trying to tear each other's heads off.

In the last round Sadie gives me a two-point deduction for head-butting that squares up the contest. It was too obvious to be called a headbutt. Terry locks my arms so I rub my head up his chest and into his face. Let go, you fucker. Sadie intervenes.

What the fuck are you doing, you stupid fucking bitch?

Sadie didn't deserve the abuse and she is still working away as a referee but it was Tallaght against Clondalkin – who in their right mind would want to be reffing that!

The place goes bananas. The Tallaght crowd know they are back in it. My lot, eh, disagree.

We both celebrate at the bell. Dad seems pleased. Always a good sign – if he thought I lost it would show on his face. Clondalkin prevails, but only just. It was 7–7 and I beat him on the countback for landing 44 punches to his 34. I flick the sweat off my eyebrows in mock relief and quickly, without thinking, raise Terry's arm in the air. This immediately ends any further shite talk about a grudge match. This was two Irish champions slugging it out. Then I let out a roar to the lads in the crowd as Terry disintegrates, understandably distraught. A proper boxer is Terry Carlyle.

Boxing can do strange things to the psyche when you least expect it. I am lucky in that fighters were never able to get inside my head but I know I've done it to enough opponents.

I have been shaken, though. I saw a Macedonian guy die in the ring over in Greece. I was eighteen. One minute he was standing there and the next he had collapsed. Something was wrong with his heart, they told us later. To top it off, the ambulance crashed, with him in it, leaving the arena. I watched it all unfold. No warning. Dead. It shook me to the core. Mercedes Taff and John McCormack from St Saviour's were our coaches and, to their credit, they noticed some of us were struggling to deal with what happened. I was scared shitless, to be honest. We took a vote and ended up being the only nation to withdraw from the competition. Some were unhappy with the decision but I know I was in no condition to box.

I remember crying down the phone to my dad. It took a while before I went back training after that but Dad eventually came and said, 'Look, you have to make that decision again. Do you want to box?' I went back running the next morning before school. Back around the park and then off to Irish class for a snooze.

Tá mé tuirseach, múinteoir . . .

In 1998 I left secondary school and a year later went to Trinity College to do a diploma in Enhancing Performance and Monitoring Training in Sport. It was a one-year boxing scholarship. I studied anatomy. Dan Curran was and still is the Trinity boxing coach. He also

used to train up in CIE and was a former heavyweight national champion. He never actually coached me but I would go in and do
exhibitions for the other students. I did fight in the Inter-varsities – just
to make it all official – but the guy I was up against, from University
College Cork, was only in his eighth or ninth fight; I had over a
hundred amateur bouts and thousands of rounds sparring. He got
going in his late teens; I first had my hands wrapped as a five-year-old.

Moments before the bell their coach, one of the Joyce brothers from
Sunnyside, walked across the ring, looked me dead in the eyes and told
me to take it easy.

'No problem,' I smiled.

So, I danced around the Cork boy. Let him off with a few taps. A
cat teasing a trapped mouse. I gave him one stinger near the end just
so he understood what he was missing out on. Stick to the books, son.

A year in Trinity was also an opportunity to come under the influence of the great Fred Tiedt – a silver medallist from the Melbourne
Games in 1956. Tiedt's story is that of an Irish boxer cruelly denied a
gold medal. Those present vehemently believe he was robbed by a split
decision in the final against the Romanian Nicolae Linca. Tiedt had
more points than Linca but lost by majority verdict, 3–2. I saw myself
following in the great tradition Fred had helped to create for Irish
boxers at the Olympics.

My last national final was in 2000 against James Philips from Athy
Boxing Club. It was my third senior title but by that stage I was already
struggling to qualify for the Sydney Games.

I won every amateur accolade going in Ireland. Eleven national titles
– six juvenile, junior, intermediate and three senior. I won 119 fights
and lost 11, all on the road. I never did get beaten on Irish soil as an
amateur. That was the career of Bernard Dunne in a vest.

But what sticks in my memory from my amateur days is working
alongside me da. And Peter Perry in his 1970s Ireland tracksuit. He
would be snapping at you one minute, hugging you the next and then
throwing you out of the club for the day. I would curse him as I disappeared out the door onto Granite Terrace, but Peter was okay. You
knew what you were dealing with. He had lived long enough to behave
any way he pleased. CIE was his kingdom. Only recently, while

researching for this book, I found an interview he gave to the *Irish Examiner* on the eve of my world title fight against Ricardo Cordoba:

He was never a huge puncher but that boy had class. He had skill, he could throw punches from every area, his head movement, his shoulder movement and his foot movement was just dazzling. He was almost impossible to hit. I know he is up against it with the Panamanian because any boxer who ever came out of Panama was good. The fact that Cordoba is a southpaw makes it even more difficult.

Having said that, I think Bernard can win this one. He has all the credentials. During my time with him if he had one failing it was the fact that he did not always listen to his corner – sometimes he would go out and do his own thing.

But you must listen to the corner. They are the ones who are looking at the fight. They can see the things you don't so you must listen to what they are telling you in between the rounds.

I always knew Bernard was destined for great things but I never thought I would see him fighting for a world title in Dublin. Brendan came around with my ticket yesterday and I am really looking forward to it.

For once, Peter wasn't ringside for that fight. He was too ill. But I bet he had a smile a mile wide when it finished.

Peter Perry died on 29 January 2010, aged eighty-four. I'm thankful he lived to see my whole career unfold because he deserved the plaudits that come to a world champion as much as I did. He was still coaching just before he passed on. (Stephen Sherlock runs the place now.) But sure, wasn't he an old man when I first came down to CIE as a five-year-old!

His greatest strength was that he demanded only the highest standards from his young boxers – I'll always remember the slaps on returning to the corner after failing to carry out orders to perfection.

The standards he instilled in me from early childhood helped create the hunger to succeed. I have carried his lessons with me all my life.

3. Olympic Nightmares

I'm Brendan Dunne from O'Devaney Gardens. Near the Phoenix Park, you know it? Didn't think so. It is 1976. I'm twenty-two years old and on my way to the Montreal Olympics with the Irish squad – Davy Larmour, Gerry Hamill, Brian Byrne and Christy McLoughlin. We mean business. Gerry Storey is our cornerman. Gerry is from the Holy Family Boxing Club in North Belfast.

Aw, what a send off I got the morning I was going. Everyone from the flats was out on their balconies. So proud just to see somebody get out and do something of this magnitude. It was some achievement considering where we come from.

Angela and our baby boy William were there too. Her brother Eddie Hayden is a fighter as well. She's also from O'Devaney. We are married barely a year. I had done a bit of travelling with Irish teams but this is the first time I am away for a good while. Very homesick. Ah, Jesus, I miss them something terrible.

It is an eye-opener out here, training and sparring with fighters from all over the world. I sparred a guy from Papua New Guinea called Tumat Sogolik. He was a bantamweight, I was only light fly, but I knocked the crap out of him.

'Hope I get someone like him!' I said to Gerry.

But my first opponent was Japanese. Noboru Uchizama. He came out with a right hand in the first and I knew I was in trouble. He could hit. Believe me, he could hit. But he kept wading in and milling me with his head. Never a good idea to clash with my thick Dublin skull. That's what bashed him open. We clashed again and I stepped back and dinged him a left hook. There was blood everywhere.

Holy shit! I thought I was badly cut but it was only a little nick under my left eye. Turns out he was split open. That was that.

The Puerto Rican that beat me was Orlando Maldonado. I was hard done by there. Boxing well, won the first round. Coming out for the second he hit me a low blow. I went down holding me town halls as one does. When I got up the referee just stopped it. No way back. Olympics over. I wasn't even hurt at all.

I tried to tell the ref as he was leading me to the corner. Boom. Gone. Olympics finished. Gerry Storey couldn't believe he stopped it so quick.

The Cuban Jorge Hernández took the light flyweight gold.

We met the Americans in the Olympic Village. Shared a laugh and a bit of banter.
They were real flamboyant, so they were. Cocky bunch of so and sos, especially that
light welterweight kid, 'Sugar' Ray Leonard – 'I'm gonna drop that guy in the second
with a left hook.' In fairness, he went out the next day and he did drop that guy in the
second with a left hook. Smooth operator, especially when you consider it was for a gold
medal and that the 'guy' was the Cuban wrecking ball Andrés Aldama, who had
knocked out five opponents to make the final. Ray's left hook dropped him all right, but
Aldama kept coming so Leonard dropped him again. And a third time on the buzzer.

Real cocky. But the Americans didn't do too bad for themselves. Ray Leonard beat
his Cuban. The Spinks brothers, Leon and Michael, also won gold.

I didn't win a medal but I wasn't too disappointed. After all, I'd boxed in the Olympics.
Not bad going for an O'Devaney boy, eh? They can never take that away from me.

Yeah, boxing was my life, but I have other priorities now. Family life. But that's
not why I never went pro. I had got to the Olympic Games and that was me finished.
I'd got everything I wanted out of boxing. Still can't believe it ended so quickly, though.

Who knows, maybe I'll go down and help coach in Phoenix with Peter Glennon
– one of the greats. He trained five senior champions, all in the one year.

Anyways, my name is Brendan Dunne. Time to go home and raise a family. I'll
get back around to boxing whenever I can, maybe when my kids start sprouting up.

★

It's going to be very difficult for our boxers to qualify for the Sydney Games.

IABA President Brendan O'Conaire, June 1999

People tend to forget I boarded the plane bound for the Olympic
Games in 2000. Never so much as laced up my gloves for a bout yet
still came home with deep-rooted scars. One is in plain view across
my left eye; the other is a permanently damaged right hand that seriously reduced my punching power. But the deepest wound left no
physical mark.

My belief in the IABA was shattered during those six weeks in
Sydney. The Olympic Council of Ireland? Never met any of them.
Granted, they probably had plenty of plush functions to attend. I don't
know if they even realized I was representing them.

Oh, I went to the Olympics, same as my da. But mine is a slightly ridiculous tale – almost an out-of-body experience – that needs retelling to ensure the IABA never makes the same mistake again. If I had been treated like an Irish representative should have been and looked after as a twenty-year-old three-time national champion deserved, I would have parked my intention to join the pro ranks until after the Athens Games four years later.

I'm not interested in having a go at the governing body of amateur boxing in Ireland but, really, they left me no choice. Basically, they clean forgot about one of their own stranded on foreign soil. If not for the generosity of Mick Roche, his wife Lorraine and the O'Driscoll family from Cork I might still be stuck, living out the surreal existence that unfolded in my time Down Under. No, that is not true. I would have eventually swum home.

To understand the pain inflicted upon me in Australia I must catalogue how I became so obsessed with getting there. It wasn't even my fault as it all started before I was born. My idol had trodden that path back in 1976. Not Sugar Ray Leonard but a rough-and-tumble Dublin scrapper named Brendan Dunne. All I wanted to do was emulate me daddy. The pictures of him exchanging blows loomed over my childhood days.

Even when I was a teenager and he was annoying me about training that feeling drove me on. For 'Brendan Dunne – National Champion' read 'Bernard Dunne – National Champion'. That was the road I was following. The next step on it, I presumed, was to emulate him by becoming an Olympian.

It was the original dream.

My dad was born in Dublin's inner city in 1954. He boxed out of the Phoenix club. In 1973 he became the first light flyweight to represent Ireland (the weight division was only introduced in 1970) and in March 1974 he captured a senior title by beating Paddy Aspell.

Stories of my dad's achievements didn't lead me down to the CIE Boxing Club, but they kept me there; it meant I was on a path to the Olympics before I knew it. Dad wouldn't be so forthcoming himself, but the more I immersed myself in the sport the more others would inform me of Brendan Dunne's exploits. I loved hearing about him, knowing I wouldn't get the full picture at home. He wasn't one for blowing his own trumpet.

He was earmarked for Montreal from a long way out and achieved every vest-wearing boxer's dream gig by banking his second national title after beating Belfast's Jimmy Carson in the spring of 1976.

Gerry Storey had them in training camp down in Kerry. There was no headgear back then. Just to look at him you can tell he ain't soft.

Noboru Uchizama felt the full impact of his noggin in the opening bout and was forced to retire with a bad wound above his right eye, but Orlando Maldonado figured out a good way to stop him.

Like his, my path to the Olympics was mapped out from my teens. Now twenty, I was maturing as an amateur boxer. Hit and move. Invisible to most of my home-grown opponents.

How was it, then, that I had to witness the opening ceremony from an Irish pub down the road from the Olympic stadium before finally realizing I wasn't going to be following in my father's footsteps?

Nicolas Cruz Hernandez was the Irish amateur coach, yet between sessions he was sweeping the floor beneath our feet while we were eating dinner. Honest to God, he was the National Stadium cleaner. That was part of his job. We would train, go across the road for food and Nicolas would follow us over and clean up after us. That's no way to treat your national coach. What sort of message was that conveying to us?

He was living in makeshift quarters behind the gym on the South Circular Road – just like the Morgan Freeman character in *Million Dollar Baby*. With a temporary bed and stove. It was a joke. But that was Irish amateur boxing. Half measures.

Nicolas lived a lonely existence. He was a Cuban exile who came to Dublin in the summer of 1988. The Cubans remain the aristocracy of amateur boxing and Cruz was head of their Higher Institute for Physical Education. He wasn't paid a single penny for helping Wayne McCullough to silver and Michael Carruth to gold at the Barcelona Games in 1992. The IABA eventually put him on the payroll, but I couldn't believe it when he told me his annual salary was only €15,000.

Nicolas is a good coach but an eccentric one. You had to be clever enough to take on board the necessary information and discard the rest when it came to a fight. The man knew the boxing game though.

The other coaches were volunteers, so most gatherings were on weekends. If you didn't show up no one seemed to notice. There was no national gym. Before the Olympic qualifiers we went down to Athy and were put up in B&Bs. The assistant coach to Cruz was a clever man named Billy Walsh. Billy quickly realized how inadequate the whole situation was and moved us to the University of Limerick, where we stayed on campus and had access to better facilities, though finding opponents to spar against remained a serious problem.

We got an insight into just how far we were lagging behind the leading nations on a visit to Crystal Palace near London to work alongside the British team for a fortnight. On our first day I did a job on all their featherweights. I may have been a little too triumphal because they sorted me out the following afternoon by putting me in against their light welterweights.

There were four weeks of pre-Olympic preparation scheduled, but the qualifiers were divided over six countries so the team and coaches had to be split up. John Duddy, Paul McCloskey and Francie Barrett all failed to make it through the qualifiers, so there was certainly talent in the team. It just wasn't harnessed correctly.

The preparation of our team may have been horribly inept but that's not why I didn't make it. I was good enough; I just didn't qualify. I am not complaining. I came within seconds, but two bronzes were worthless from three qualifying tournaments as I needed at least one silver. It never happened.

The build-up began with a trip to New Zealand in the summer of 1999. A journey to the far side of the world to condition the mind for what I would be doing just over a year later. I boxed the same guy twice – Jo Jo Tipace. I remember a few Maori warriors doing the Haka in the ring. Ultra aggressive, nasty crowd. I punished him for their behaviour. They have some decent boxers in New Zealand but no one like me. The Haka is an incredible thing to witness at close quarters but, while it may intimidate some rugby players, it is rather pointless putting on a war dance in a boxing ring. After all, it's already established why we are there. Still, they put on their war dance so I gave them a war. All instructions from the corner were ignored. Peter Perry would have been boiling.

The first card was in Auckland and we were sponsored by a pub. That meant breakfast, lunch and dinner in the bar and booze on tap. We boxed on the Friday and spent the next four days sampling our sponsor's products. The security in the pub stayed close to us and anytime the Irish coaches came to check on us the doormen would radio down and our drinks would be swooped up. Clean table. Cans of Coke and Fanta appearing as if by magic. As soon as they left, our real drinks would be back in front of us. Usually they would have been topped up behind the bar by our hosts.

Things became more serious come the World Championships in Houston that August. Muhammad Ali was there for the opening ceremony. They wheeled him in and wheeled him out. Jesus, look at him. I'll never box past thirty.

It is high noon. What are the Irish boxing team doing for training? Playing football under the blazing Texan sun. Two cops come over to inform our coaches that somebody will keel over from heatstroke. Next goal wins! We seek the coolness of the shade.

In the ring I beat a Dutch guy but it proves a failed venture as I then lose to a Czech and don't feature anywhere near the medals. I bury the disappointment and move on.

In October we arrived in Tampere, Finland for the European Championships. This was where I thought I would secure my Olympic ticket. Tampere is about 200 kilometres north of Helsinki; good thing my focus was on the sunny climes of Australia in eleven months' time.

Right out of the blocks I had another bloody Russian, Alexander Kozlouski. Typically durable, but I figured him out, winning 4–2.

It all fell apart against Falk Huste, a powerful German, who stopped me for the first time with a smashing straight left that scarred my cheekbone. (I am forever grateful for that scar as it led me to a young lady from Ballyfermot named Pamela Rooney. Well, eight pints and the wise decision of the Coco's doormen to grant us entry played an equal part.)

I remember looking at Huste beforehand with that old feeling in my gut, 'How the fuck are you making weight, buddy?' He was six foot and a featherweight. I'm five foot seven and considered tall. He

didn't just have a killer reach, he was a puncher as well. A perfect speci-
men for the amateur ranks, Falk made it to Sydney but he was beaten
in the second round by eventual silver medallist, the American Ricardo
Juarez. No shame in that. It was his second Olympics as four years
previously in Atlanta he lost in the third round to the Bulgarian Serafim
Simeonov Todorov who controversially beat Floyd Mayweather Jr
10–9 in the next round. That's the last man to beat 'Money' Mayweather.
You could join the dots in boxing all day. Everyone is related by six
degrees of separation. In boxing it is usually about three.

Anyway, the following Monday's *Irish Times* made for uncomfortable reading as it became apparent the IABA were fuming at the lack
of return from their investment:

Central council delegates at Saturday's meeting of the IABA had to face up
to the embarrassing possibility of not being represented in the ring at next
year's Sydney Olympics. Senior officials expressed concern with the amount
of money and energy that has already gone into affording their boxers opportunities to clinch Olympic places at various qualifying tournaments around
Europe with no success.

'No other association has handed out so much money or sent so many
boxers around Europe in order to win places at the Olympics as we have,'
said president Brendan O'Conaire.

An original squad of 12 boxers selected to compete at qualifiers in Istanbul
next month has been reduced to three, Liam Cunningham, Bernard Dunne
and John Kinsella.

The IABA were over budget and had no boxers booked on the plane to
Sydney. They were relying on me and a few others to deliver. I knew
that on my day I could beat anybody, but a close amateur fight comes
down to the strange whims of elderly judges. I knew it was a lottery in
these foreign tournaments. I needed my day to come and fast.

I was comprehensively defeated by the Turk Ramazan Palyani in
front of his home crowd. Palyani was European champion and he
proved it. We were one-all after the first round but the judges wouldn't
give me a point after that. In fairness, I was well beaten but I did land
some more shots. Once you are chasing in the amateurs your style has

to change and you don't box your natural fight. It finished 10–1. He was big and strong. Palyani was denied a medal in Sydney in agonizing circumstances when eventual gold-medal winner Bekzat Sattarkhanov of Kazakhstan beat him 12–11 in the quarter-final. Sattarkhanov died in a car crash the following New Year's Eve.

Mick Roche qualified in Halle, Germany. Dad was there. I was drawn against the Russian Kamil Djamaloudinov, whom I had beaten before. Then they came back in and said there was a mistake made in the draw and it had to be done again. Djamaloudinov disappeared into the other half and qualified, going on to win a bronze medal in Sydney. 'There was always a lot of politics in the amateurs,' grumbled Dad. I got the Hungarian southpaw Janos Nagy, who beat me 12–2. Nagy went on to win the IBC super featherweight world title.

Finland, Turkey and Germany failed to yield the golden ticket. This was turning into a nightmare. My last chance came in Venice, in late March 2000. I went to Italy with a serious burden on my shoulders. No mistakes, no margin for error and it felt like fate was pulling against me. I couldn't believe I was in such a perilous position but I was prepared to do anything to qualify. I arrived with a positive outlook. At least everyone already qualified wouldn't be there. The standard of opponent wouldn't be as strong.

It was one of those tournaments where nothing was coming my way so I went out and took what I felt was rightfully mine.

I stopped the Czech Konstantin Flachbart in the second round. That wasn't a sign of intent. I was just disgusted to learn I was behind on points after the first, despite landing some clean shots and getting no points for them. I went out and dropped him. They can't dispute that. The same thing happened in the quarter-final when I was trailing 3–0 to the Armenian Artyom Simonyan after the first. I stopped him in the third. Again, I had no choice.

You can't rely on the judges. One of the worst decisions I ever had was at the Junior World Championships in Argentina in 1998. Armando Bouzan beat me 10–8 in the quarter-finals despite the fact I had him on his backside twice. Two standing counts for those shaky Cuban legs. The second one was so clean that I had to step over his body to get to a neutral corner. And I still couldn't win the fight.

Don't give them the chance to snatch your dream away.

The semi-final in Venice was the biggest moment of my short life. Everything I had done up to that moment rested on my beating Joni Turunen of Finland. I knew the gods were working against me. Yet again, I was trailing after the first so I went chasing, leaving myself open for some cheap points. But I still should have won. With seconds remaining in the third I nailed him with a right to the chin and down he went. He rose on the count of six. My right was cocked but I was going to feint and throw a left hook to the body. The bell saved him. He was all over the shop. He must have loved the feeling of that stool being placed under those jelly legs.

The result came back as 7–5. That's how close it was. I felt physically sick when Turunen's hand was raised. I walked straight out of the arena to a pay phone across the road and called home.

Dad answered after the first ring. He would, of course, be sitting there waiting.

'That's it, Da. It's over. I'm not going.'

I can't remember what he said. Numb. My world was caving in but a chink of light shone from above. Turunen won the final. The Irish management of Mercedes Taff and John McCormack quickly informed me that I was the first reserve in my weight class. They must have seen my expression in the ring and wanted to give me something to cling to. The IABA would send me to Sydney.

I needed one of the European featherweights to get busted up before September. I was depressed but I refused to let the dream fade. I refused to wake up.

In Sydney, Falk Huste looked after Joni Turunen in the first round, 10–6. My mate Falk Huste, unknown to him, had played an instrumental role in creating the next generation of Dunnes.

I came home on 2 April. The lowest moment of my existence quickly turned into the defining night in the lives of Bernard, Pamela, Caoimhe and Finnian Dunne – the latter two can thank Falk for their very existence – because that was the night I met Pamela. The welcoming party was all smiles on my arrival into the house. I knew what was coming. There was no 'Aw, poor Bernard didn't qualify for the Olympics.'

They just started ripping into me and enquired about getting locked down the local. I kindly accepted the offer. Shower, shave, shirt on and off to the pub just like any other young fella.

We had a couple of pints in Finches and wandered down to Clondalkin village. Myself, Willie and Derek Maher – who is now my sister Deborah's husband but back then he was just 'Mahersy'. We ended up in Coco's nightclub in Tallaght. That's where I met Pamela. On the bleedin' dance floor.

Pamela had gone to see a fortune teller that week and I was described to a tee as the man she was going to meet very soon: her soul mate. I would have a scar on my cheek and she would be introduced by a family member. And that's the only reason she married me. I was a boxer. Half the lads in Tallaght and Clondalkin had scars on their faces!

She knew Willie and his girlfriend Sandra and was out dancing with Willie, who was looking over at me.

Pamela asked, 'Who is that?'

'My brother, Bernard.'

'Well, bring him over.'

She got a shock when she saw me up close. She told her friends later, 'I knew it was him.' I knew straight away as well. I had been with a couple of girls before that but I'd never had a solid long-term relationship. I was a boxer. Life sentence. I was just out on temporary release for not keeping my hands up in the ring, otherwise I would be nowhere near Coco's. I would be where I always was when other lads were out drinking and chasing birds. In bed.

There was a silver lining after all for winning bronze medals. On one of the rare occasions I go on a bender, I meet the girl of my dreams. I can't help it if I'm lucky.

I found out from Sandra that Pamela worked in the jewellery store in Liffey Valley shopping centre. I went up to see her. The following week we went out with Eddie and his girlfriend Debbie for a drink in Tim Youngs in Ballyfermot. Eddie used to be a bouncer there. It was a Thursday night. I was nervous. Pamela didn't like 'Big Eddie' the bouncer until she met Eddie the brother. He used to stop her at the door and she was not too impressed. They buried the hatchet and thankfully not in Eddie's back.

We never looked back. A year later we were living together in Santa Monica. When you know, you just know.

I kept training away in CIE with my dad and Peter Perry as if I was gearing up for the Olympics. It was difficult to keep focused. At least Pamela quickly became accustomed to the life we were going to live. She understood immediately, which was great, because it is not easy to partner a boxer. One minute I am playing the role of the romantic boyfriend, and eventually husband; the next I am an unresponsive monk, focusing only on my next opponent. The hours spent away at training camp quickly turn into weeks and months. Pamela, to her eternal credit, understood what I was trying to achieve. She would have followed me to China in the morning.

The smallest ever Irish Olympic boxing team headed to Australia five weeks prior to the opening ceremony. It comprised our sole qualifier Michael Roche, coach Nicolas Cruz and manager Martin Power. Oh, and first reserve in the 57 kilograms division, Bernard Dunne.

The afterthought.

We set up camp in Newcastle, about a hundred miles up the coast from Sydney. Nicolas was doing his job but none of the boxers had a clear idea of what Martin Power's role was supposed to be. He had no boxing input, he was an administrator, and we didn't exactly click on a personal level. It would have made more sense for the IABA to send another coach in a managerial capacity, or at least someone with the fighters' best interests at heart. I know Martin had some family out in Sydney so that was nice.

That was the IABA's first big mistake. The second was to use local Aussies as sparring partners. Mick needed experienced opponents to spar against, not local novices – one of the Aussie lads was only sixteen. This was a disaster for Mick. He was a light middleweight, but in the end I essentially became his primary spar.

I wasn't much help, though, as I had my own priorities. Mick understood this and we tried not to put each other out. Mick Roche is as sound a man as you could meet. The challenge is understanding that thick Cork accent. He might say the same of mine.

Everything that could go wrong, did. I smashed my right hand, fracturing three metacarpals, by catching Mick's left elbow one day in the ring. I said very little about the pain, wrapped up my hand and kept on training. Kept on hoping. There was a constant throbbing from my injury but I told myself I could still box and I would keep boxing until I was told I couldn't.

Martin Power was getting on both my nerves and Mick's. One day Mick lost it with him. We were sparring in the gym with some locals and obviously they were trying their best against the Irish Olympians. You had no choice but to hit them back. Mick was dealing with a big lad who had caught him a few shots. Martin shouted in for him to take it easy. I couldn't understand why the Irish manager would say such a thing. Where did his priorities lie? Mick fended the guy off and walked over to him. 'Do you know anything at all about boxing, Martin? This guy's trying to decapitate me. What am I supposed to do?'

Mick had the perfect amateur style – hit and move – but he never got to box his own fight in the opening round against a Turk named Firat Karagollu. Mick is a counterpuncher but he let himself get into a scrap. He lost it 17–4.

To have any chance of making the opening bout I needed to spar one of the other featherweight Olympians and bust him up. A knockout means concussion and that means an automatic twenty-one days out of the ring.

A guy fittingly named Somluck Kamsing from Thailand agreed to a session in Jeff Fenwick's gym in Sydney. It all went horribly wrong but, Christ, did I go down swinging.

It was a great spar. We were going at it and I was trying everything to take his head off. I knew I had to think my way inside and do some damage. Open him up. Fight my way into the opening ceremony in a few days' time. With one hand – the one I hadn't busted on Mick Roche's elbow. As soon as I unloaded with my right it began to sting, as it would for the rest of my career. I wasn't accustomed to the pain yet, so I had to set him up for a big left hook. I needed a head shot so I walked in. If I'd known he was the defending Olympic champion I might have been more careful.

Somluck caught me a blow to the top of my head. We had bought new head guards when we got to Sydney and the leather was still hard and coarse. When he landed the punch the guard ripped into my left eye and pulled all the flesh off with it. You could see the bone. I needed fifteen stitches inside and a trip to a plastic surgeon. It didn't bleed that heavily but it was an ugly-looking wound. It would be nine years before I received a worse one.

That cut slammed the door shut on my Olympics. The initial plan was to travel back up to Newcastle that day but naturally I wanted this horrible cut dealt with immediately. Martin thought it could wait. There was a blazing row about it – I felt I needed a surgeon and he didn't seem to give a flying fuck. In my opinion, a genuine team manager would care more about his boxers.

Clearly I wasn't going to box in the Olympic Games, so there was no bed for me in the Olympic Village. I was still a kid, albeit with plenty of street smarts, but I was in a foreign place with no money or support. No one seemed to know what to do with me. Surely either the IABA or the Olympic Council of Ireland should have provided accommodation or sent me home, but their officials didn't even seem to know who I was or why I was out there.

Twice I asked to be sent home. I might be dead weight, but don't just cut me loose. The first time was up in Newcastle the day after I was stitched. I wanted to see my family.

'No, we can't break tickets,' I was told. The same answer was given in Sydney.

Even simple things highlighted my Invisible Man status. When the suits we had been measured up for arrived, I never got mine. Rochey saw it still wrapped up when he was collecting his gear.

I remember Mick's kindness. 'Don't you worry, Bernard boy. There are greener pastures over that hill there. I can see them because I'm taller than you.' He came up with the idea of putting me up with some Cork people he knew.

The O'Driscoll family were my saviours. I had met their son Des when we sparred at Fenwick's gym. They had the thickest Cork accents you will ever hear. Proud rebels, but Des Sr and his wife Margaret treated me, a Dub, just like one of their own. Such generosity is very humbling. I was a complete stranger to them but I was a stranded Irish kid so they looked after me. No questions asked.

Young Des was around my age and a bit of a rogue. A good lad, though, and a reliable drinking partner. I needed one.

We watched the opening ceremony together in an Irish pub. What else could I do? Where else could I go? I remember talking to Mick on his mobile as he walked into the stadium. That was the worst moment. I downed my pint and ordered another. And another.

I only made it into the boxing arena because RTÉ's Jimmy Magee secured me media accreditation to commentate on radio for Mick's fight. RTÉ were up with us in Newcastle. That's where I first met commentator Darragh Moloney as he filmed a piece with us on the beach. I had been friendly with Jimmy for years and he'd heard about my situation. We had been talking and I told him I didn't even have a ticket to get in, so he called in a favour.

I have tried to pay Jimmy back in the twilight of his career with a few decent gigs to commentate on. The man has done and seen it all in Irish sport and I'm grateful his was the voice that resonated over my finest, and worst, nights in the ring.

It got to the stage where I was relying on the O'Driscolls for food and board as I had nothing to pay them with. I got a pass for the Village from Mick and managed to track down Martin Power. 'No one is looking after me here moneywise,' I told him. 'I've no food and no accommodation. At least the O'Driscolls should be reimbursed for taking care of me. You just don't give a fuck.'

I told him there had been a couple of media guys sniffing round. 'I don't want to talk to them, but if I'm not looked after I'm going to tell them what's going on here.'

The threat at least produced some money for me to live on, though it was sickening that I had to force it out of them. I felt as though the IABA had treated me like a piece of discarded meat. I knew the situation going out there, but it was a traumatic experience for a young fella just out of his teens.

Once I knew I wouldn't be fighting, training came to an abrupt halt. I socialized a fair bit in Sydney. I drank myself into a happy or sad state. I'm not sure which. I can't really remember. I was on the phone back home the whole time. I wanted to be back with my family and friends. I missed Pamela.

'Look, son, this clearly wasn't meant to be.' Brendan Dunne was talking sense again.

I went back to the pub. Really I was just behaving like most twenty-something Irish kids in Sydney. There were enough of them.

Mick's wife Lorraine was easy to get on with. She got me home. When Mick was beaten we all hung around together for a week. Then Lorraine came up with the idea of swapping her airline ticket with mine so she could stay on and fly home with her husband. It was that simple in the end.

As I've said already, my granddad William died the night I got home. If I had missed his funeral I would have never forgiven the IABA. Never forgotten. As it was I had no desire to box or train. I felt betrayed. I took a few months away from the gym and began behaving like any other twenty-year-old.

Clearly, no one in the IABA or OCI had thought about Athens while they were hanging me out to dry in Sydney. My plan had been to remain an amateur until 2004. I would have boxed at the Athens Olympics and then turned professional. I had been one hundred per cent committed to the Olympic experience. I wanted it so badly. But now – why should I waste another four years of my life after being treated like that?

Even after I arrived home there was no contact from anyone for weeks. The most ridiculous aspect of it all came a few months later when the 2001 World Championships in Belfast were looming. Suddenly I was back in vogue, the IABA presuming I would lead the Irish team. I went to a meeting with the IABA. We regret what happened, they said. I wouldn't be treated like that again, they said. It is easy to say sorry, though. I got my opinion across. I told them about *my* Olympic experience. I asked them about theirs. I took on board what they had to say and went away to think about it.

What I thought was, I'm not going to hang around for the Worlds in Belfast because I'm not going to be around for Athens. They'd forced my hand. Time to look after number one. Simple. They'd have to get another Bernard Dunne to kick around. It was a shame, but it was their own fault. I can't see my treatment in Sydney being repeated.

I let go of the anger once I turned pro. New start. Fresh beginning.

O'Conaire's successor as IABA president, Dom O'Rourke, thought Ireland had only one representative in Sydney because the break-up of the Soviet Union meant that eleven more countries were competing for the European qualifying spots. Twenty-four of the forty-eight boxing medallists were from former Soviet states, so the excuse carried some weight.

That said, Ireland is a proud boxing nation and Irish amateur boxing was in serious trouble. Improvements were desperately needed. They arrived in the form of the high-performance systems introduced in 2003 by Gary Keegan, who acted as director of coaching, and head coach Billy Walsh.

There are now programmes for both women's and men's teams. There are three full-time coaches and ten part-time. The Irish training camps are as good as those in Russia, Britain or Cuba. The senior team is conditioned as professionals would be, with access to world-class training facilities and specialists in psychology, nutrition, physiology, physiotherapy and sports injuries.

As a result, the sport has recovered dramatically. That was evident at the 2008 Olympic Games in Beijing and again at the European Championships in 2010. Ireland is a major force again, and that is down to preparation. These are great days to be a talented amateur boxer in Ireland.

In 2000, though, my options were not unlike my dad's had been in 1976. Go pro or quit boxing. I didn't weigh it up for too long. I'd known for a while that I could do something with my talent.

The professional ranks were my realigned destiny. I could handle that. Now I just needed to dive in.

When I didn't weigh in for the Nationals in January everyone became aware of my decision.

I began talking seriously with Harry Hawkins in Belfast. He was going to be my coach. I was going to train with him. I was going to be promoted by Panos Eliades, just like Brian Magee had been before me, and be managed by Frank Maloney. It was all lined up by Harry through his old promoter/manager friend Pat Magee (no relation to Brian).

But there was a problem. Something that threatened to derail the train before it could leave the station. Something that changed the whole course of my career.

Something the size of a pea.

4. Cavum Septum Pellucidum

DOCTOR #1: *Because of the continuous violent blows to the head you have developed a condition particular to boxers called cavum septum pellucidum – which is a hole in the membrane separating the ventricles. The brain surface neurons in this area have also been traumatized.*

DOCTOR #2: *Simply stated, Mr Balboa, it means you have suffered some damage to the brain.*

ADRIAN: *How long until he recovers?*

DOCTOR #1: *The effects are irreversible.*

ADRIAN: *Oh. Rocky, you have to retire.*

ROCKY: *But Adrian I don't want to retire. This ain't the time to retire. Not in here. Not in no office. I just fought the best fight of my life. All we need is a couple of easy ones, right?*

(Director's note: While in Russia fighting Ivan Drago, Paulie had frittered away all their money.)

ADRIAN: *No, Rocky, you suffered severe brain trauma. You can't get a license in any State. He can't get a license anyway, Doctor?*

DOCTOR #2: *That is correct.*

ADRIAN: *No one has to know, Doctor, right?*

DOCTOR #1: *It will be strictly confidential.*

Scene from Rocky V, 1990

I have cavum septum pellucidum, or CSP. It is a cyst on the brain in everyday language. Rocky Balboa was forced to retire although by *Rocky VI* – sixteen years later – another brain scan scene was conveniently left out of the script.

I had no choice but to become an expert on this particular topic.

The cyst is located in the middle of my brain – not in the substance of the brain but between the two halves. It is about six centimetres behind my eyes in the frontal half of my skull. It doesn't cause any compression or distortion of the brain and does not interfere with any vital structures. It has been loosely associated with schizophrenia, post-traumatic stress disorder and chronic brain trauma, so be careful – I could lose it at any moment!

It is estimated that about fifteen per cent of the world's population have CSP but most people never have a brain scan so they go through life unaware of the problem.

CSP is not brain damage. I have not been hit hard enough or often enough for that. Boxing has not ruined my life, but this little cyst almost did.

Twice.

Turns out Angela Dunne dropped me on my head as a baby. Fractured my skull. Changing my nappy in our Neilstown kitchen, she took her eyes off me for a split second to grab the milk and turned back to witness her little boy roll off the counter and hit the deck. There was no canvas to cushion that knockdown. No ropes to fall against.

Sweet suffering mother of Jesus, Bernard!!!

So my CSP is Ma's fault. Well, that's what we always told her.

The brain scan is a routine occurrence for any boxer entering the professional ranks. So long as they don't find something wrong in your noggin you are good to go.

Bernard Dunne, just out of the amateurs and ready to take on the best English featherweights, was about to run foul of the British Boxing Board of Control.

Brian Peters had been calling non-stop to sign me up but I was ignoring him. I was ready for a big-name promoter and manager. Peters was small fry, a Meath publican, and unable to lure me away from the London-based Panos Eliades. Harry sent Panos my best amateur highlights and he was impressed enough to put £50,000 on the table. In 2001 that would have bought me two houses on Neilstown Avenue.

Everything was in order. All the details had been worked out. A chance to fight live on Sky Sports and opportunities on major undercards were promised.

Harry Hawkins and Pat Magee had arranged everything with Panos and I was to be managed by Frank Maloney. Panos and Maloney were involved with Lennox Lewis, amongst others, so that was good enough for me. (How was I to know that Lewis would eventually brand Panos a 'racketeer' after being awarded $8 million in damages by a New York judge following fraud proceedings in 2002?)

I was fully aware that I was just a small fish diving into shark-infested waters – little did I realize I would be swimming the Atlantic ocean before I could start knocking fellas out.

Panos had already signed up Brian Magee and Damaen Kelly from the Holy Trinity club in Belfast. As it had for them, Holy Trinity was to become my base leading up to fights that would, initially at least, take place in England.

This was the beginning of my pro career.

I looked at Brian Magee. He was undefeated in twelve fights and was being guided towards an eventual title shot. Just as when I watched him win his European silver medal three years previous, I saw what Brian was doing and wanted something similar.

They had me over for Magee's fight against Neil Linford at the Bushfield Leisure Centre in Peterborough. It was January 2001. Harry was in Brian's corner while I was ringside with Panos and Maloney – getting my first taste of the glitz and glamour associated with the British boxing game.

This will do me nicely.

A boxing life can be very fickle. I have learned that the hard way. I was about to be stripped of my chosen livelihood and my natural talent made redundant before I had even signed my first professional contract.

And yet, there was never a time when I felt something was wrong with me. It was the first brain scan I'd ever had, since I was a child anyway, as I had never been hurt badly in the amateurs. I had been cut, but nothing serious.

The eminent neurosurgeon Professor Jack Phillips has been conducting brain scans on Irish boxers for the past thirty years. This was the result of a sensible decision by the Boxing Union of Ireland president Mel Christle, whose ideas were light years ahead of the British way of doing things.

Originally from Ballina in County Mayo, Professor Phillips studied medicine in Cork and was trained in Boston, as well as Oxford and

Cambridge universities. He has also written a great deal on head injuries; all told, he is one of the most respected neurosurgeons in the world.

We should really have very little in common, then, but I would have no hesitation about spending an afternoon in Jack's company.

Jack is my kind of person – a straight-talking, no-nonsense individual who judges others on their personality and behaviour, not on where they are from or their appearance. He called me with the results of the scan, asking me to come into his offices in Dublin's Beaumont Hospital.

All I needed was a green light so I could sign the Panos deal. That document is still gathering dust in Harry's drawer at home. My philosophy has always been that everything happens for a reason, even the stuff that comes around the corner and knocks the wind out of you.

Professor Phillips sat me down. He said that there was a cyst on my brain. (He also said it was unlikely to be due to a childhood fall so that lets Ma off the hook.)

'Bernard, it has never actually been demonstrated that these cysts are caused by boxing, but they are more common in boxers than in the general population.'

What is the problem, then, Professor? He could have dismissed me at this point but he explained my condition in basic terms. 'There are various cysts you can have on your brain and various boxing associations take different views on them. This is an innocent cyst that causes few consequences for your brain and there are many boxers in your category.'

This all sounded fine, with several British and American neurosurgeons agreeing with his opinion. 'We're talking about something so small that it is causing no pressure to any surrounding brain structures. It is the size of a pea.'

I left Jack Phillips's office looking forward to signing with Panos the following week. I was perfectly calm. The Professor had been very reassuring. It didn't seem serious. I remember Jack's parting words, 'Look, there is a bit of an abnormality here. Nothing to worry about. You are perfectly healthy.'

I phoned Harry in Belfast and told him what had just transpired. I told him I had a pea in my head. He was a wee bit apprehensive, to say the least.

'Bernard, don't joke about something this serious.'

'I'm not, Harry.'

Silence down the other end of the line.

'Okay, Bernard,' he finally replied. 'I'll talk to Professor Phillips myself.'

He phoned me back a few minutes later. 'Look, this is worse than you think. If this becomes common knowledge, your boxing career could be done.'

Jesus! You think nothing outside the ring could stun like a clean blow and then you hear something like that.

Harry didn't take too well to the 'various boxing associations take different views' line. Harry Hawkins was all too aware of his recent boxing history.

The British Boxing Board of Control (BBBC) has developed a zero-tolerance policy when it comes to any brain abnormalities and they have a very good reason. They consider it a survival measure.

Michael Watson fought Chris Eubank at White Hart Lane in September 1991. It was the second meeting between the two Englishmen in three months, Eubank winning the previous encounter on a majority decision. This fight was for the vacant WBO super middleweight title. It was a grudge match and the blows were brutal. Watson was ahead on points when Eubank forced a stoppage in the twelfth round. Watson collapsed. There were no paramedics or official doctor at ringside. It is now part of boxing folklore that it took eight minutes, without any oxygen for Watson, before doctors wearing dinner jackets climbed into the ring and a further six minutes before he was stretchered out. Michael Watson remained in a coma for forty days, requiring six operations to remove a blood clot from his brain. After six years in a wheelchair he eventually regained his speech.

Only four years later the reputation of British boxing took another hammer blow.

Gerald McClellan was primed to become one of the great American middleweights. In February 1995 he challenged Britain's Nigel Benn for the super middleweight world title in London. Having dropped Benn in the first and eighth rounds, McClellan ('He is blinking heavily – I've never seen that from him before,' noted the commentator) took a knee in the tenth, in obvious discomfort, after another vicious assault from Benn. He took an eight-count but within seconds he went down on one knee again and was counted out. He walked back to the corner, collapsing soon after. He suffered extensive brain damage, losing his eyesight amongst other disabilities.

The media put British boxing on trial. Calls for the sport to be banned became louder so the BBBC did what they believed was necessary to get through the media storm. They did everything in their power to ensure a third such incident was avoided.

I had just turned twenty-one. My cyst was the equivalent of boxing leprosy, in Britain, at least.

Two of Jack Phillips's sentences repeated over and over in my head:
The size of a pea.
No pressure to any surrounding brain structures.
But the public perception would drown out these facts.

Mam and Dad were thinking brain tumour. That was an indication of what the general reaction would be. That made me worry even more.

Harry and my ma came with me for the next visit to Beaumont. 'The curious thing is, some boxing unions only employ general practitioners with an interest in the sport,' explained Professor Phillips. 'If something is described on the scan as being abnormal the commissioners are entitled to deny the boxer a professional licence. I have always thought this was an over-reaction, and indeed it calls for a more professional assessment of the findings.'

Professor Phillips passed the scan results over to Mel Christle but Mel didn't release them to the Boxing Union of Ireland board: they would almost certainly have been leaked to the media, and that would have started a round of Chinese whispers that would soon have had me on my deathbed.

If the story broke I would be blackballed. That threat still loomed over me in 2009. I never appeared on a professional fight card anywhere in the UK, Belfast included.

CSP isn't necessarily a dangerous condition. In my case, the key to boxing with it was constant monitoring to ensure that the pea-sized growth I have doesn't develop into something more serious. As far as the BBBC were concerned, however, a cyst of any nature that was anywhere near the brain meant an immediate refusal of a licence to box.

Everyone seemed to be saying they would know more over time. After Sydney I was determined not to be forced into another period of inactivity. The thought of having my gift from God ripped from my grasp was a scary prospect. But that was the reality I was forced to deal with.

We knew from Wayne McCullough's experiences to tread carefully. Wayne had his licence revoked by the BBBC when he attempted to return from America to fight in Belfast in October 2000. Despite further tests in UCLA and a US neurosurgeon stating his cyst was in a harmless space between the skull and the brain, the British authorities refused to bend for two years. He went on to fight three times for a world title, losing to WBO featherweight champion Scott Harrison in 2003 and twice to WBC super bantamweight champion Oscar Larios in 2005.

The case to deny McCullough a licence unravelled because Wayne could refer to previous brain scans which showed his condition had not deteriorated as he continued to fight. With me, there was no point of reference.

I went missing on Panos. I could hardly call him up and explain. We had to keep it all quiet, so no warning, nothing. I heard he went nuts when he found out I wasn't signing for him. He had no idea. All he heard was that I'd signed a better deal in the States. He wanted to make a counter-offer but I just ignored him. He has never spoken to me since. I don't blame him, but it was never personal – it was simply about self-preservation and finding the best alternative. I had no choice but to go to America.

I told everyone who asked that I was going over there to serve my apprenticeship. That part of the story was true enough: there is no better place to learn the boxing trade than in America. It just wasn't my initial plan.

Harry acted as my representative. He spoke to the established US boxing manager Cameron Dunkin about signing with Bob Arum and Top Rank. Arum is the leading promoter in the world – the dream ticket. Dunkin had seen me fighting in San Diego in an international amateur contest and there seemed to be genuine interest on his part.

If Harry was going to send me off to America he wanted to ensure I could focus on my fights and not worry about anything else. His proposal included a signing bonus of $25,000 but he also insisted on a retainer of $2,000 per month as well as $2,500 per four-round bout – of which he wanted Dunkin to arrange eight in my first year. In the second year I was to get six fights at $3,500 and up to $5,000 for eight rounds. There was a clause that stated I could return home three times a year and I would eventually come back to Ireland permanently. He asked for an apartment and guaranteed top-class training facilities nearby. Las Vegas or the east coast were the suggested locations. It was all about finding the best environment.

But Dunkin was taking his time coming back with a firm offer from Top Rank, so we decided to make other approaches.

I flew out to New York to meet the Wexford-born agent Martin Sommers, who had come over to watch me in the amateurs. I went with a Belfast boxer named John Lowey who had fought Erik Morales for the WBC super bantamweight title in 1997. Morales stopped him in the seventh round. Lowey had been out of the ring from 1991 to 1994 after falling foul of the BBBC's interpretation of brain scans. It was worth the trip just to check out the famous Gleason's gym in Brooklyn. But nothing else came of it.

On the way back to Belfast from the Nationals in Dublin, Harry stopped into the County Club to see what Brian Peters could offer from his American contact Matt Tinley at America Presents. Tinley and Dan Goossen had set up America Presents in 1996 and signed Mike Tyson, Bernard Hopkins and Wayne McCullough, amongst others.

We hadn't told Peters anything at this stage. Harry was still talking to Dunkin but Peters was keen to become my manager. I had no intention of letting him, but we began to realize he might prove useful if I moved to America. I was willing to talk to anyone at that stage.

I first met Peters when Peter Perry sent myself and Paul Stephens up to Belfast for a training session with the great Eddie Futch. Peters set it up. Futch trained Joe Frazier (calling to a halt the most famous fight ever when he kept a practically blind Frazier on his stool before the fifteenth round against Ali in Manila – Frazier never spoke to Futch again) along with Ken Norton and Larry Holmes.

Peters had been involved in the boxing game for a few years but he had done nothing that impressed me. He had Jim Rock – the only boxer ever to hold the Irish professional title at four different weights – headline two bills, but the gates flopped. He had the heavyweight Cathal O'Grady, who was a European champion as an amateur but his pro career had never gone anywhere. He had been a co-promoter for both McCullough and Steve Collins – most memorably for the world title fight against Eubank in Millstreet, Cork in 1995 when Steve won the WBO super middleweight title. He was not involved in the rematch but was a co-promoter again with Frank Warren when Collins fought Cornelius Carr at the Point Depot the following November.

After Harry's initial approach to Peters, I went to see him myself. We met in the County Club. We sat at the first table on the right as you walk in the doors. We've held most meetings at that table since.

'Look, Brian, this is how things are . . .' I explained the brain problem and the concerns with the BBBC. 'I want to fight professionally. America looks like our best option. I need the opportunity to go to the States and this is where you come in. Are you interested?'

Peters was interested. His business mind started clicking into gear. We both knew there were rumours about the instability of America Presents, but I was getting desperate.

Peters made the deal.

We jumped.

Compared with the Panos deal, Peters was offering me significantly less. But it made sense from his perspective, so I have no problem with that. I signed a manager's contract with him. To be honest, he could have offered me nothing except the opportunity to fight in the States and I would have signed. I had no choice. I needed a chance and, in fairness, Brian Peters gave me that chance.

Harry wasn't looking for anything out of the situation; he was only interested in getting me up and running. He proved as much when Peters asked him straight out what he wanted from the arrangement.

'The best deal possible for Bernard,' Harry replied. You know you can trust someone when they say that. Harry wasn't looking for a cut. Like Peter Perry before him, Harry was looking three or four steps ahead to see what was best for me.

I would need a new coach in America. Harry was with Brian Magee and he was never going to leave the Turf Lodge area of Belfast, where he is a central figure in the community. He also had his plastering business to run.

Peters put us on to some Boston connections through the brother of Eamon Gilligan from Dunboyne Boxing Club. I was to share accommodation over there with three nurses. Explaining that to Pamela was going to prove difficult!

Fortunately, I didn't have to as the opportunity came up to go and train with Freddie Roach at the Wildcard Gym in Los Angeles. After that, all other options were shelved.

It was Brian Peters who made the initial contact with Freddie. Both had worked with Steve Collins.

'We have Bernard Dunne here . . .'

They gave him videos of some of my amateur fights but he didn't feel the need to check me out in person.

'Send the kid over and we'll see how he goes.'

And that was it. I had a promoter, a world-famous gym to train in and a coach to work with.

But one of them wasn't going to last.

5. Wildcard Boxing Club, 1123 Vine Street

Wildcard – An unknown or unpredictable factor.

My flight touched down at LAX on 9 November 2001. Macka Foley was there to meet me. Macka is part of the furniture in the Wildcard Boxing Club in West Hollywood. He and Freddie Roach go way back – to the south Boston days. He was a journeyman pro in the 1970s. He loved that I was this Irish kid coming over to California in pursuit of the ultimate boxing dream. He carried the Foley name around like a badge of honour – Irish people who have never been to Ireland tend to be especially proud of their heritage. Freddie was off working Manny Pacquiao's corner in San Francisco for the Agapito Sanchez fight so Macka made it his business to come get me off the plane.

Only problem was that neither of us knew what the other looked like. He was looking for an Irish featherweight. I was to watch out for a long-since-retired heavyweight. My scrawny limbs and flat nose gave it away.

'Are you Dunne?'

'Yeah, I'm Bernard Dunne.'

'BerNARD.'

'It's BERnard.'

'Okay, BerNARD.'

'Call me Ben.'

'Ben. Why didn't you just say so?'

Only Freddie could pronounce 'Bernard' correctly. It used to drive me mad. Ben quickly became my new name for a new life.

Macka owned a big brown Lincoln. So, this is an American car. Five-litre engine. Jaysus, the joy riders would love a go of this.

I knew absolutely nobody. I was put in the hotel beside the gym, aptly named the Vagabond Inn. It was a run-down squat on the corner of Hollywood and Vine. Ghetto town. There was a Taco Bell for some

Mexican food, a Chevron garage, the Vagabond and then, above the laundromat, up these rickety black steps and through a fortified steel door, the Wildcard. Like all the great boxing gyms, it is a simple place. I felt at home as soon as I got in the door.

West Hollywood is a dump, with prostitutes openly selling themselves all night long. Drugs are freely available on most corners and there are hobos living outside almost every door.

Eddie Murphy was stopped outside the Chevron garage in 1997 with a cross-dressing hooker in his car. It was a known transvestite area. Eddie claimed he was just giving him a ride. Now I was new in town, and a little wet behind the ears, but I knew the score even though there are not too many transvestites on Clondalkin Boulevard. They were everywhere. It was an eye-opener. The most depressing aspect was to look up Vine Street and see the famous HOLLYWOOD sign up in the hills. There's me, having just turned pro and come to America to make a name for myself, heading up to my peachy-coloured room in the Vagabond. The contrast in fortunes, and wealth, in America is vast.

Those first few weeks in the Vagabond Inn were excruciating. Going to the gym only passed a few hours each day. Coping with loneliness is the hardest part of a boxer's life. It is unavoidable. When preparing for a fight you cannot expect to function in a normal environment. A monastic lifestyle becomes essential. That usually means solitary confinement. Running alone. Sleeping alone. Abstaining from basic instincts that a man naturally craves. Your trainer is there, but they can go home. The fighter must never switch off.

I knew I was in the right environment, working with Freddie Roach, but the sounds outside my window at night were crazy. I loved when morning came. Anyone who has ever been alone in a foreign land will know about those seemingly endless nights. Eventually the mind starts playing tricks. Especially in the wee hours.

What the fuck am I doing here?

Freddie was the first to notice I was going a little insane so he sent me down to Santa Monica to look for an apartment. Walking the streets, I got lost fairly quickly. A typically beautiful California day, so I was fairly chilled out about it all. I stopped this fella to ask for directions and, of course, 5,000 miles from home, he was Irish. An actor. I can't remember his name. I haven't seen him in anything since. When we stopped laughing I told him what I was at and how I needed to get out of West Hollywood fast. He was off home for a few months so he sub-let me his studio apartment on 7th and California. I never met him again. The landlord was weird – always knocking on the door. I nearly lost it with him on a few occasions. Pamela came over just before New Year's Eve and eventually she took control of the domestic aspect of our life.

There were some memorable moments in our little studio existence. For our first Valentine's Day I took over the apartment block's communal kitchen to cook Pam dinner. It was all going fine until I tried to transport the gourmet meal up two flights of stairs. The Pyrex dish was so hot it was burning through my glove, so I put it down and let it burn a hole in the carpet instead. The food in it was cremated. I was just standing there scratching my head. We ate what we could salvage. Thankfully, she agreed it was the thought that counts.

I developed a routine. Leave the apartment at around 9 a.m. and if I got the blue express line on Santa Monica Boulevard I would be in the Wildcard by 10.45. Most guys would arrive in their slick convertible or whatever but I was on the number 4 bus. Every morning. That emphasized my hunger. I was never embarrassed about telling people I couldn't afford a car.

My bus journey was never short of entertainment. The people who take the bus in LA tend to be down and outs – hobos, transvestites, drunks, junkies or just plain odd fish. A fight would spark off because someone opened the window. People were talking to aliens. God regularly came aboard for a chat with some of them. I'm just sitting there watching this unfold. Smirking to myself. Wackos. You would see guys unloading on the bus driver over a quarter. Regularly the journey was stalled so the cops could get on and haul off some lad in handcuffs, but I never once had an ounce of trouble. I never bothered them, either. Just sat there and let it all wash over me. Maybe I just have one of those faces.

My dad came to visit not long after Pamela had upgraded us to a decent apartment on 7th and Washington, so he was our first guest in the spare room. There followed a flood of friends and family over the years. Pamela's sister Debbie came next and then her friend, another

Debbie, who married her fella Casso in Las Vegas. Willie and Sandra were there at the same time. Eddie was there for the Sugar Ray signing, of course. Paddy Jennings rolled in for a holiday with another mate, Gerry Desmond. Ma, Aunt Betty and my sister Deborah with her six-week-old daughter Amber arrived in July 2004. There is a good picture at home of Sugar Ray and Amber in her Celtic FC gear.

But in November 2001, that was all to come. At first the homesickness was terrible, and the only way to deal with it was to go training. The walls of the gym were plastered with pictures of fighters and famous actors. I wasted no time, sparring on my first day against a Mexican featherweight called 'Speedy' Gonzalez. I got hit a good few times but that was more down to jet lag. I needed to get hit, anyway.

Two days later I went with Macka to pick up Freddie from the airport. The Pacquiao–Sanchez bout to unify the IBF and WBO super bantamweight belts went to the scorecards when the fight was stopped after six rounds due to a cut above Pacquiao's eye. When not landing low blows, Sanchez delivered two tasty headbutts that were deemed accidental. Freddie was understandably pissed off with a draw in what was only Manny's second fight since moving from the Philippines to America.

Freddie and I instantly hit it off. Like Macka, he liked the idea of a young Irish amateur champion coming all the way over to train in his gym.

Freddie really is the closest an American can get to being one of us. He's from Dedham, south of Boston, which is really an extension of Ireland with third- and fourth-generation immigrants populating the area. Like me, he grew up in a boxing family although under a far stricter regime than Brendan Dunne's household. We didn't have to box; Freddie was told to fight or take a beating. No harm to learn how to defend yourself under those conditions.

Before I'd left Ireland I'd got hold of a documentary called *The Freddie Roach Story* and spoken to Steve Collins. Freddie had worked with Collins for six of his seven world title defences including the Chris Eubank and Nigel Benn epics. He described Freddie as a Dubliner in spirit and I couldn't agree more. (Freddie just liked Steve's chin.) We Dubs have a certain way about us. We are sometimes perceived as over-confident, from a culchie's point of view anyway, and then there is our particular sense of humour. I'm a proud Dubliner.

I also called Wayne McCullough for advice and he said I should catch the next flight out to LA, adding that he was on the other end of the phone in Las Vegas if I needed anything. Wayne knew all about Freddie through Eddie Futch. Both Collins and McCullough said he was a great trainer and easy to work with. They were the only words I needed to hear. Say what you like about Steve Collins, but when he talks boxing, I'm tuned in.

Their careers even briefly overlapped. Collins's debut saw him knock out Julio Mercado on the undercard of a bill in Lowell, Massachusetts, on 24 October 1986 that featured Roach's last ever professional bout, against David Rivello. Collins recorded a third-round TKO. Long past his best, Roach lost a majority decision after ten rounds.

Freddie understood what made me tick. He got my sense of humour. I'm not alone in this as he possesses the rare knack of being able to treat everyone he meets the same. A hobo off the street gets the same respect as a Hollywood A-lister or the seven-weight world champion in Freddie's gym. He has that rare ability to listen to what people are saying and react accordingly.

He loves his fighters enough to tell them when they have taken sufficient punishment. He knows better than most when the petrol tank is empty. He will sit the guy down and tell him to quit. If the guy insists on continuing, Freddie won't train him. This is just how Eddie Futch treated Freddie after Greg Haugen knocked him out in 1985. It was his forty-eighth pro bout. Eddie advised him to quit but, like most boxers, Freddie was unable to accept the hard truth. He fought five more times, losing four, including one more KO after a gruelling ten rounds with Andy Nance. Boxing takes its toll.

Still, he had been a decent lightweight (thirty-nine wins, fifteen by way of a knockout, from fifty-four professional fights). A contender. Then it was gone. A hard head that took too many blows. After a year of solid drinking, he found his way back to Futch as an assistant trainer based in Las Vegas. He found his life's work.

A friendship with the actor Mickey Rourke brought Freddie to Hollywood, where he eventually set up the gym, but it was the guidance of

Virgil Hill to the WBA world light heavyweight title in 1987 that put
Roach on the path to becoming one of boxing's all-time great trainers.
Freddie was still only twenty-seven but already following the footsteps
of his mentor. Since then a steady stream of legendary fighters have
continued to show up at his door.

The irony is, boxing keeps Freddie's illnesses at bay.

Freddie suffers from Parkinson's and another neurological disorder
called dystonia, which have become progressively worse over the years.
Even back in 2001 he had a limp in his left leg from tearing a calf muscle
that never fully healed. He would get the shakes real bad if he forgot
to take his medication, but once those mitts are slipped on the trans-
formation is fascinating to witness. The tics and spasms immediately
disappear and he becomes miraculously fast, adapting to the rhythm
of his boxer and talking him through each combination – be it the
lightning hands of Manny Pacquiao or the reflexes of James Toney.

Freddie trained Tyson for the fight against Englishman Danny
Williams in 2001. He tried playing the greatest boxing wild card of
them all. Just like every other fighter, Freddie wrapped Tyson's hands
before each session and unlaced his gloves after. I never spoke to Tyson
in the gym. Nobody did.

But there were no restrictions on who could train in his gym. Pay
your ten bucks and go do a session with Macka. There was a hobo who
also lived there called Shane Longford. The guy used to come in every
day when I was there and now he works in the gym.

Freddie trusted me enough to look after his cottage up in the Hollywood hills when he was away with his girlfriend Sheila Hudson, who
had competed at the 1996 Olympics as a triple jumper. I didn't have a
US driving licence but he threw me the keys to his big Chevrolet. All
I had to do was feed and walk Sheila's Alsatian. It was a savage dog that
barely put up with Freddie. For whatever reason, it stayed calm around
me. This was a dangerous animal. I was out walking it one day and a
woman, despite my warnings, tried to pet it. He got down to the big
yellow fat tissues of her arm.

I arrived in the Wildcard at around eleven every morning. Freddie
would wrap my hands. Taping me up was always a process that required

a gentle touch because of the damaged metacarpals. Freddie was like a mother cleaning her child's grazed knee. There were half a dozen coaches in the place but I always worked with Freddie or Justin Fortune. The gym would be fairly empty at that time in the morning. Freddie, Macka and Bo – a big black guy who made his few bob training walk-ins – would all be there and, of course, Peppa Roach – Freddie's brother. Peppa fought ten professional fights in the early 1980s, losing only two before a period of incarceration halted his genuine prospects as a featherweight. An absolute head-banger, Peppa also had a limp, but I think his was from a gunshot wound. To survive prison life in America you have to join a gang. The big swastika tattoo on his chest gave me a fairly good idea which group he affiliated himself with. Strange, then, that Bo is one of his best friends. Peppa would be walking around *heil*ing Hitler, but if anyone slagged off Bo, or any other buddy of Peppa's for that matter, black, brown or white, he would open them up without warning. Bonkers – they are hard men in this gym.

I would shadow box for fifteen minutes each morning, then stretch out and switch to mitts with Freddie. On Mondays, Wednesdays and Fridays we would spar. I was fortunate to spend over three years in the Wildcard when super bantamweight and featherweight world champions flooded the place.

For the first year it was myself, Israel Vazquez, Willie Jorrin and Manny Pacquiao. At the time, Pacquiao was just another three rounds to me. Nowadays he is considered pound for pound the best boxer on the planet, having won world titles at seven different weight divisions from flyweight (he actually started at light fly – a wafer thin 106lb) up to welterweight. He weighed in to retain his welterweight crown at 145¾lb when defeating Joshua Clottey in March 2010. When we sparred together he was the IBF super bantamweight world champion so I was heavier than him, a featherweight, tipping the scales at 129¼ at one stage, while Manny never exceeded 126 until losing to Erik Morales for the super featherweight title fight in 2005. This was the period when he really started moving through the ranks, adding incredible power to an already frightening repertoire of natural boxing ability. In 2006 he stopped Morales twice, the second time by an emphatic third-round knockout that began his mind-blowing climb to the top of the boxing tree.

Manny is astonishingly gifted – so quick with both hands. Trading blows with him is a mistake simply because he can take your best shots and land more. He has an abundance of energy, relentlessly coming at you for twelve rounds.

Freddie said I was the only man able to handle him in the gym and repeated as much on Sky Sports when I was no longer with him. I always felt comfortable in against Pacquiao, not overawed by his speed, and enjoyed the hundreds of rounds we sparred together. I'm not saying I could knock out Ricky Hatton or anyone else on the long list of quality boxers he has dispensed with. I just held my own, that's all.

Shifting through seven weight divisions and initially refusing calls from Floyd Mayweather for a blood test has to put a question mark over his recent achievements. Mayweather had no right to ask for the test so close to a fight but can Manny be that afraid of needles?

I have never been offered performance-enhancing drugs. Not in the Wildcard, not anywhere. I gave a urine sample after every title fight but I was never approached for random dope testing while in training camp. That said, I don't think doping is a major problem in professional boxing. I have not seen any evidence of it.

Israel Vazquez was another super bantamweight world champion, although not until 2004, while Willie Jorrin held the WBC super bantamweight belt while he was around the gym.

Willie didn't like getting hit. He hated it, in fact, but there was no messing in our sessions. Everyone got dinged about the place. Freddie was never a fan of the 'bitch bar', as he called it: the head guard that covered the nose. Maybe Willie, who was into his thirties at this stage, didn't like getting tagged by an up-and-coming nobody from Dublin who failed to see the sign entering the ring that said 'I am a world champion; show me respect'. My idea of respect was to give him my best effort. I didn't see a world champion, just a man who didn't like my body shots. Freddie didn't seem to mind me laying into him. Jorrin lost his title to Oscar Larios in 2002 and hasn't fought since losing to Cristian Favela in 2003.

Looking back, Freddie obviously saw the benefits of bringing me along as I was always useful to have around his more established guys. That said, I did get sacked as five-time champion Johnny Tapia's sparring partner.

Big Bear Lake is a popular altitude training camp in the San Bernardino mountains about fifty miles from LA. I got brought up there ahead of Tapia's fight with the legendary Marco Antonio Barrera. I saw it as a huge opportunity to let off some steam but also remind everyone what I was capable of. Basically, I didn't read the script. Sparring partners are there to play a cameo role with a few specific lines. But I was landing a bit more than a good dig when I was supposed to be doing my best Barrera impression. It is crucial to bring in obedient and disciplined guys ahead of a big fight and if not, they have to go. Later in my career, I would have sacked me as well.

Freddie told me on the way up to say I was five foot six, no matter what, because that was Barrera's height and Tapia was a temperamental fucker.

'He's nuts,' Freddie warned.

I was an inch too tall, but Freddie knew it would be a good spar for both of us.

We were working away in the ring and it was going well. He started to unload. When a fighter does that with a sparring partner it is usually a clear signal that they can defend themselves! It is an invitation to simulate a fight scenario. I accepted the challenge and I could see he was getting agitated that I was handling him. I flipped out a jab that watered up his eyes. *Couldn't give a fuck if you are nuts, Johnny.* Tapia went into a rage so I stepped back and clonked him with a left hook to the ribs. My signature punch. Johnny was winded and held on, but when the air flooded back into his lungs he was suddenly back in his corner. I was schooling him and he didn't want any of it. I didn't break any unspoken rules or anything, but that was still the end of me. Next day I was sent back to LA.

I never gave Freddie any problems. If he told me to spar James Toney or Mike Tyson I would jump into the ring without any headgear. If he told me to go running at 4 a.m. and be in the gym by 7 a.m. I would do it. When he wanted me to practise double left hooks to the body, and dip in at a certain angle, I would repeat it for hours on end. I had faith in him. I never had any reason to question his methods.

Freddie tailors his coaching to each fighter. He studies your strengths and weaknesses before helping you to improve. He has no set formula for what a boxer should be doing. That's what makes him so refreshing, he is always learning himself.

It had nothing to do with me but Barrera beat Tapia by a unanimous decision at the MGM Grand in November 2002. Pacquiao did Barrera a year later with an eleventh-round technical knockout and again in 2007 on points. One of Freddie's current stable, Amir Khan, was fed the aging Barrera, the perfect foil for a young pretender, in March 2009. Khan won off a cut.

There were two aspects to the Wildcard – the serious fighter leaking blood on a daily basis and the wannabe boxer rubbing shoulders with the former. Both had to train equally hard when they stepped through that narrow door as it is first and foremost a boxing club. Any confusion with that and Freddie would supply clarity much like Peter Perry did with the young lads wasting our time in CIE. Again, I happily became the pit bull who provided the lesson.

The actor James Caan's son Scott got to spar with me one day. I'm sure he remembers it. Scott Caan is a tough guy, probably like his father before him, and a decent actor in his own right, but he is not a full-time boxer. There is a significant difference, as he found out. I was in the ring sparring away and Scott was over whispering in Freddie's ear when he said, 'Fuck it, I'd love to get in there against Ben.'

'All right, put your gloves on.' That was Freddie all over.

Scott hesitated.

'Get them on so. Now!'

He was in the ring before he knew it.

I dart in like I would against any opponent but really I'm only tip-toeing around the guy. I get on really well with Scott, so no need to bust his nose open. He is a well-made lad so I know he can take the light stuff. He is even having a couple of swings. Back to the corner I go and Freddie is pissed off.

'That's enough messing, Bernard. Go out there and show this guy what being a boxer is all about. These are your sparring minutes being wasted. You won't get another session today.'

That was all I needed to hear. I thought I was just dancing with one of the famous pictures on the wall.

For the next three minutes I emptied the full bag of tricks on Scott Caan. I caught him clean a few times but when he started to fall I held him up and gave him some more. Battered. At the end of a long three minutes Freddie asked Scott, 'Wanna go another three?' Scott took his medicine like the decent skin that he is. 'No Freddie, I'm good.'

We both went back to training.

After any sparring session Freddie pulled out my gumshield and I hit the floor-to-ceiling ball followed by ten minutes on the speed ball and another ten skipping. Then it would be body and core work with my Australian buddy. At just five foot seven, Justin Fortune was too small to be a serious heavyweight but he is a powerful man and a serious conditioning coach. He acted as chief second whenever Freddie was off in a champion's corner.

Anyone could stroll in, sit down and watch what was going on. It was a small place so you became accustomed to Mickey Rourke, John Travolta, Denzel Washington or regulars like Mark Wahlberg and Cuba Gooding Jr. The television personality Drew Carey and producer Sam Simon, a creator of *The Simpsons*, used to come in all the time, as did Mario Lopez of *Saved by the Bell* fame.

I actually helped Simon out with a promotional gig to advertise mobile vet clinics around LA. On the billboard was Drew Carey, Ben Dunne and a giant Irish wolfhound.

You can feel the buzz of excitement when James Toney arrives. Toney is the most naturally gifted boxer I have ever seen. He is also half mad.

He strolls in with a slur of racist remarks for the 'Spics' and 'Niggas' training away. No one gives it back. 'Where's your passport, Oreo?' he asks an Asian boxer. No one is going to turn on James 'Lights Out' Toney. The man knows only one way, the 'Detroit Way'.

He comes past me and Justin. 'All right, Irish?'

A few days earlier I had busted the five-weight world champion's nose in a sparring session but he seemed to appreciate it.

Toney makes it all look so easy. He spreads his ever-expanding frame on the floor (he began his professional career at 157lb in 1989, clocking in at 237 for the 2006 bout with Hasim Rahman) as somebody stretches him and Freddie wraps his hands. He gets into the ring, spars a few rounds and leaves. It might be no more than a half hour but it is priceless – he is conducting a boxing seminar that forces the rest of us to stop what we are doing to watch a master craftsman. He did stuff than none of us could replicate. Not Manny. Not Israel. James Toney had it all.

Unfortunately, he gave it away. His is unfulfilled talent. Greatness was laid before him but he never reached out and grabbed it. He lost his super middleweight title in 1994 to Roy Jones Jr on a unanimous decision. It was the fight that launched Jones into the stratosphere as Toney was fast approaching 'best pound-for-pound boxer' status. Roy Jones took that mantle off him. It was his first defeat and last time at super middleweight as he wandered into the no-man's land of cruiser and light heavyweight.

A still exceptional career peaked when he beat John Ruiz to claim the WBA heavyweight belt in 2005 only for the New York State Athletic Commission to forever tarnish his legacy by stripping him of the title and changing the result to a 'No Contest' after he tested positive for the anabolic steroid stanozolol.

Toney had a dark side that wasn't too far from the surface. He was in a nasty tussle with this big African dude one day. Elbows flying. Yer man loses it, steps back and throws a spinning kick that whizzes an inch past Toney's nose. The 'Detroit Way' meant there could be only one reaction.

There are very rare occasions when the constant hum of a boxing gym goes completely silent.

Toney discards his gloves, climbs out of the ring and heads for the door. He stalls – 'I'm going to shoot you, motherfucker' – then disappears into the light. Jesus – he's off out to his car to get his gun! Freddie and Peppa intercept Toney on the way back up the steps and talk him out of the idea. It takes several minutes, just enough time for the African guy to disappear.

Toney has gone to the other side recently and is due to make his mixed martial arts debut. That wouldn't put Freddie off training him as several of the top Ultimate Fighting guys have been welcomed into the gym, including Anderson Silva. I've been to see UFC and, for entertainment value, I can't see it being a long-term threat to boxing. They hit the deck after a few seconds and it gets boring. You can't see anything. They are just hugging each other.

The Wildcard was like attaining a PhD in boxing to rival the qualifications of Professor Jack Phillips. James Toney would leave and 'Sugar' Shane Mosley would arrive. Shane is a gentleman. I sparred over 150 rounds with Shane before his second meeting with Oscar De La Hoya. I was preparing for Adrian Valdez – my last fight in America, as it turned out – and Freddie saw an opportunity. Get me used to mixing it with a bigger man and let Shane utilize my size and speed. I was always useful to welterweights for technical preparation. Mosley beat De La Hoya at the MGM Grand in September 2004 on a unanimous decision.

With Pacquiao, Vazquez and Jorrin I had my group of sparring partners and there was no ego involved. Nobody saw themselves as the priority, unless it was leading up to a major fight, but when big names visited from other gyms it was different. I was at the centre of several wars in the Wildcard that proved helpful later on. This was my education. This was the real value of the place for me: I took some heavy beatings but I kept coming back for more. Boxing operates on the same fundamentals whether you are in the CIE in Inchicore or the Wildcard in West Hollywood. Other guys come in and it is about letting them know this is your place of worship. It's the same all over. 'Take it easy, Bernard' meant 'Let him have it!'

'Mighty' Mike Anchondo was put in against me one day. Freddie didn't like what was coming out of his trainer's gob so he cut me loose. Freddie was good at getting me going.

I won our first battle hands down. Anchondo didn't expect much from me but they were dying to come back for revenge. A week later I stood tall in the rematch but I took some heavy blows. Standing in the shower afterwards I couldn't work out who was my promoter. Am I still with Matt Tinley or had I signed for Sugar Ray Leonard? Who should I be calling tonight to see about my next bout? Water beating down on me, I was out of it. It had to be Sugar Ray because America

Presents collapsed before I met Leonard. This happens. Anchondo went on to win the WBO super featherweight title. I went home with a thumping headache.

Someone recorded my sparring sessions with Nate Campbell, labelling them 'Bad Blood I' and 'Bad Blood II'. We didn't get on from the moment we saw each other and it got really messy. Nate was talking shit before we started. It's not my style but I gave it back on this occasion.

Who's this skinny white kid, uh? He's too small for Nate Campbell.

I give a polite reply.

Wha' you say, boy?

I repeat my initial courteous comment.

I'm gonna whip your motha . . .

Again, I keep it simple.

Campbell presumes he can play about for a bit and then teach me a lesson. We meet in the centre of the ring. Right-hand feint, left hook to the body. Shakes him straight away.

This drives him insane. Elbows, headbutts, digs in the balls follow – sometimes it can get out of hand in the gym. A coach might let this happen so his fighter is ready for a dirty opponent when a referee is out of his depth.

All hell breaks loose the second time we spar. No talking this time. Again, Nate is a bigger and stronger man, on the verge of unifying the lightweight world championship belts. He shades it but I refuse to back down.

At the peak of his powers Campbell's arrogance got him knocked out. In 2004 against Robbie Peden he was in control. He dropped his hands and stuck out his chin. A sweet left hook from Peden cleaned him out of it.

Plenty of commentators have said I have a weak chin, but catch anyone square on the jaw and they are going to sleep. I have taken plenty of clean shots, wobbled and then pulled myself together. That's what the gym is all about. I have always known I am a better tactical boxer and Freddie taught me about learning when to load up the power shots even when a brawl was inevitable. When you see my frame in comparison to 90 per cent of my opponents, I should never be mixing it. But sometimes you have to test yourself.

6. Ten Rounds

I had tunnel vision about making my professional debut. It came against Rodrigo Ortiz at the Feather Falls Casino in Oroville, California on 19 December 2001. Ortiz had three defeats from three professional bouts. I wasn't long busting his nose open. He stayed on his stool at the start of the third round. It was all a bit ridiculous but I didn't care.

Tinley paid me $3,000 and promptly went broke. I was a professional boxer with legal issues, stuck in LA on a shoestring budget as America Presents tried to sell on the contracts of their fighters. Until they filed for bankruptcy I couldn't even start looking for another promoter.

I had no money coming in. This was worse than Sydney as there was no end in sight. I felt cursed. The Olympic failure, the brain problems and now broke in West Hollywood. The crazies on the corner had more money than me.

I was training every day but I was going off my rocker.

Wayne McCullough tried to help out by getting me on the undercard of his fight against Alvin Brown at Cox's Pavilion in Las Vegas but a suitable opponent couldn't be found. There were plenty of false dawns like this.

My second professional fight was eight months in the making.

Christian Cabrera made his debut on 2 August 2002 at Foxwoods Resort in Mashantucket, Connecticut. It was hardly the MGM Grand but it was the night I met Sugar Ray Leonard. He was a promoter now and I was fighting at his event.

Sugar Ray Leonard Promotions was set up in 2001. It lasted three years. For a change I was in the right place at the right time.

I knew Cabrera was a huge opportunity because the American cable-TV sports network ESPN were showing it live, I was a free agent and Leonard was ringside. I was, literally, coming off the breadline. I was also pissed off with not being able to show people what I was capable of.

Freddie was away so the Wildcard's conditioning coach Justin Fortune acted as my chief second. In fairness, I was his rookie and he had a pack of world champions to watch over. Brian Peters was also in my corner together with a cut man. Kevin McBride was towering over the ring from the elevated third row. The Monaghan heavyweight had been fighting in America since 1994 and was enthusiastic about supporting a young Dubliner. They will call him a journeyman but it was Kevin McBride who climbed into the ring against Mike Tyson in June 2005 and Kevin McBride who won the fight. Nobody can take that away from him.

Pamela had arrived over by this stage so life in America had improved significantly.

Leonard was there to watch the twenty-year-old Cabrera attempt to make the transition from the amateurs. Physically, he looked the part, but they made a huge mistake putting him in against the skinny Irish kid. After thirty seconds I caught him a cracking right hook. It shocked the life out of him, his legs were gone, and it should have been stopped there and then. He was way out of his depth. He made it to round two but never fought professionally again.

Sugar Ray got a good look at me. Afterwards he climbed through the ropes, smiling. 'Wow! We'll have to talk later.'

'Yeah sure, Ray.' I didn't have time to pinch myself.

Later that night we all went for dinner in a private room in Foxwoods: myself, Peters, Justin, Ray, his business partner Bjorn Rebney, the matchmaker Ron Katz and the operations manager Steve Riveria. They wanted to sign me up. They said a contract would be drawn up in a few weeks.

For all the complications and politics associated with the fight game, sometimes it can be that simple. For the first time since I arrived in America I relaxed and enjoyed my dinner.

It was September 2002 when I signed with Sugar Ray Leonard Promotions. I remember because my brother Eddie and his missus Debbie were staying with us in Santa Monica.

The negotiations had already been taken care of, so when Ray and

Bjorn arrived at our door with a five-year contract all I had to do was sign my name. I remember all the neighbours getting excited when he walked into the complex. *It's Sugar Ray!* The man is a megastar in America. He had the talent and the personality. He just walked straight up to my door. Everyone was down soon after for autographs and when he left they wanted to know what he was like. People in the apartment block took an interest in my progress after that. Sugar Ray opens doors.

I'm sitting at the kitchen table reading the contract, about to sign for SRL Promotions, when I feel Eddie's shadow hanging over my shoulder with his windy old camera, flash and all, as he tries to capture the moment for posterity.

'Eddie!'

'Hang on, Bernard – Howya, Sugar Ray. Just a little closer there . . .'

'*Eddie!*'

'Yeah, Bernard?'

'What are you doing?'

In fairness, I like looking at those pictures now.

I foolishly started to believe that I had made it. Las Vegas would be next. A world title shot in two years. Tops. A ticker-tape parade for the homecoming down O'Connell Street. The world is ours. Unfortunately, I was still dreaming.

A month later my third professional fight was due to be shown live across America. It never happened. Everything fell apart again. I was due to fight the Mexican Tony Espinosa on the undercard of heavyweight Baby Joe Mesi against David Izon, which guaranteed a 17,000 full house at the HSBC Arena in Mesi's home town of Buffalo.

The *Sunday Times* boxing writer Brian Doogan was doing a fly-on-the-wall type piece with me. He struck gold. I was already a decent story: young Dubliner coming good in America under the wing of Sugar Ray Leonard. Doogan was going to bring my story back home. Fine by me.

The fact that I was Irish, and white, opened up so many doors. It was a racial thing. My weight division was dominated by Hispanics and blacks. Then I roll in, knock out two opponents on live television and the commentators see another contender to hype up. The Irish brand sells in the US.

More recently, John Duddy is a prime example of the same phenomenon. John is an exceptional boxer but he is no KO puncher, yet he is white and he loves going toe to toe. Blood sells.

However, there is nothing Americans love more than a scandal. When the news of my condition broke in the States the local headlines screamed, 'Brain Tumor', and 'Possible Death', which can be very difficult stigmas to shake off.

Doogan, in fairness, was decent to me at the time but afterwards he phoned non-stop to the apartment trying to get information about what was going on, what tests I'd had and how I was feeling. He said he was phoning as a friend, not as a reporter, and that might have been true, but he was still trying to write his piece. I understand he was just doing his job but this was my life. That bugged me. My career, and my dream, was falling to pieces. Again.

Largely oblivious to the fuss, Dunne sat in a corner of the room, signing forms for the doctor who would conduct his own medical, wrote Doogan, describing the scene at the pre-fight weigh-in after matchmaker Ron Katz had been informed by New York State Athletic Commission medical advisor Barry Jordan that my pre-fight MRI scan had revealed 'white matter' on my brain.

Oblivious? Fuck. I knew well what was going on. I was playing dumb. I might have appeared calm but my mind was racing. *This is it. I've been found out.* Found out for what, though? *There is nothing wrong with me! I feel fine. If only Professor Phillips was here to sort this out.*

Due to this 'white matter' more tests were required and I wouldn't be fighting Espinosa.

Fight cancelled.

By now, Dunne was aware of the confusion. He walked over to join the discussion, believing the problem related to his opponent, Tony Espinosa, a Mexican who fights out of Denver.

I remember Hugo Spindola of the New York State Athletic Commission walking over to me.

'I want to see this kid when he's 80 years old and he has children and grandchildren,' Spindola said, looking straight at Dunne. *'When you have any*

potential risk with the brain, amongst the things that can happen are paralysis, permanent seizures and in the worst case you could be killed. We must not allow that.'

But there was nothing wrong with my brain! Ron Katz had already yelled down the phone at Barry Jordan but the heavy-handed approach yielded no results. For New York State Athletic Commission see BBBC. Neither was willing to bend.

This was new territory for me: utterly alone in a room full of people – in the middle of America – trying to hold off the waves of panic. I couldn't even box my way out of this one. I had to stay calm.

Dunne stood stoically as he absorbed this brutal blow.

I even climbed onto the scales. Numb. I remember thinking, *This is a nightmare. I am in Buffalo with a sports journalist that I barely know who is going to plaster this all over the* Sunday Times. *I won't even be able to go home and fight again.* My stomach was doing somersaults.

It was carried in the *Sunday Times* as a colour piece and the rest of the Irish media picked up the brain problem as a news line, but its severity was kept quiet. We were clever in managing that. No one joined the dots to uncover why I was in America in the first place.

I never actually provided a full explanation to anybody and no one pressurized me to provide one; they all just accepted that there was a glitch in the scan that would be clarified when I had it redone.

Doogan again: *Wayne McCullough is another who knows what it is to have your health questioned and your right to fight taken from you. The thirty-two-year-old Irishman was told by the British Boxing Board of Control two years ago that one more punch could kill him, the frightening consequence of a cyst lodged inside his skull which had been discovered in an MRI scan. Those results were subsequently overturned and last month he made a successful return to the British ring.*

I spoke to Wayne a few days later and he told me to relax – just go to UCLA and let them take care of it.

Doogan's piece also refers to something I mentioned to him the next day. That night I was out wandering the streets, running everything over again in my brain – my perfectly functioning brain – when a white Ford Royale drove by me on Delaware Avenue, did a U-turn and came back past me, turned and went by again. The driver shouted something I couldn't catch. I wondered what the fuck was going on. He was creeping by each time. Getting a good look. The street was deserted and I was alone, probably seemed easy prey, but I was thinking this would be a bad night for any stupid fucker to try and mug me. Jesus, I wouldn't stop hitting him. I would have lost control. After the third or fourth drive-by he took off. He would have needed a gun. He may have had one. I really didn't care.

There was a gang coming over from Dublin for the fight. Dad was with them and he was the only one to know the full extent of the problem besides Peters and Harry. I told the rest of them it was a mishap on the scan. They were trying to perk me up but it was a holiday for the lads. It should have been my fight, as Brian Doogan well knew:

By Friday evening the Irish were in town. Brendan Dunne stood beside his son in the HSBC Arena and sighed: 'What a pity. It would have been great to fight in an atmosphere like this.'

The mood was defiant and upbeat when Dunne was accompanied by Peters and a party of 12 from back home as they settled in the Anchor Bar for dinner. Before long, the Irish table was in full song and the toast was of fighting another day.

Dunne has never closed his mind to the risks inherent in the hardest game. Last Wednesday he declared that his ambition was to be remembered as Ireland's greatest fighter, 'better than Wayne, better than Steve Collins, better than Barry McGuigan but God knows what could happen with injuries'.

He had gone to Los Angeles last year to train under the renowned trainer Freddie Roach. He had travelled to the town of Big Bear last month to spar with stablemates Johnny Tapia and Willie Jorrin. He had handled himself well.

When he arrived in Buffalo last week he had good reason to feel on top of his game. He was looking for a fight. As he left yesterday, he was still looking.

In fairness to Doogan, it was a positive and accurate article. It was just hard being caught in the middle of something like that.

Baby Joe went on to extend his unbeaten record as a heavyweight to twenty-four fights by knocking out Izon. He last fought in 2007, when his record was 36 and 0. I can't remember anything about the Izon fight. I was lost in my own world again.

The whole situation was hardly a surprise to me and I was always confident of retaining my licence to box in America. I had to be. They were allowing me to redo the tests in UCLA and there was a reference point now. Professor Phillips was able to point out that there was no difference between the latest scan and the one he'd made two years earlier, and I had been boxing in the gym the whole time. The cyst on the brain was the same size.

Training continued as if I was preparing for a fight but there was nothing on the horizon. I was four months out of the ring. The American doctors told me not to train. Freddie just smiled and I went to work on his mitts. Obviously he knew about the whole brain situation by this stage but Freddie was cool and, just like Harry, he was only concerned about his fighters' well-being. Freddie Roach knows better than most when someone has taken enough punishment.

'It will be okay, kid.'

He already seemed delighted with me. He liked that I never complained, even through this tough period; no problems, just kept showing up in the gym. Kept sparring, which was for the benefit of others, but it was great for me to keep working. To keep learning. That said, I felt useless and even my supremely high confidence levels were slipping. Eventually, I took a break and came home. Freddie told me to come straight back when it was sorted out. I had to wait for Dr Barry Jordan, the neurologist with my career now in the palm of his hand, to alter his initial findings.

It was the week before Christmas, the middle of the afternoon, and I was in the Liffey Valley cinema with Pamela watching *The Lord of the Rings – The Two Towers* when Brian Peters's name lights up my vibrating phone. I was expecting to hear from him any time soon because Jordan had been supplied with evidence either to give me back my new life or to take it away altogether. If I was banned by New York I would be banned worldwide. It would be the same as being banned by the BBBC. We'd told him we would do brain scans every six months to monitor the situation, which was something we were doing anyway.

Jesus, I was nervous.

When I answer the phone a few heads behind me in the cinema start moaning. *Sorry, folks, this is my life on the line here.*

'Hello,' I try to whisper.

More groans.

Fuck Frodo.

Peters gives me the good news.

I leap up in the air.

Sit the fuck down, you fucking muppet!

I turn on the fella but only smile. Now there will be other fights to attend to.

It was time to get moving.

Not many boxers stage a comeback in only their third professional fight. Mine was against Simon Ramirez in the Thunderbird Wild West Casino in Norman, Oklahoma, on 3 January 2003. It was to be shown live on ESPN. No Christmas piss-up, then. Straight back into training.

Please let this be the start of my career.

I am back on a SRL Promotions undercard. Ramirez is a biker with tattoos all over his body. There are loads of them in the crowd. On the way to the ring one of them steps into my path and tells me I am going down. Finger in my face.

'Yep, see you later, son.'

This shouldn't take too long. I am wearing my tricolour shorts as I always do in the States. I have been a pro boxer fourteen months, even though this is only my third fight. Some fool tells me I am going down? Big mistake. When I knock out his friend after sixty-nine seconds, with a cracking left hook to the ribs, I turn back to the biker and point at him. In fairness, they applaud rather than taking out their shotguns and blowing me away.

Finally, I am up and running.

Eric Trujillo is my first fight in Las Vegas. (Okay, it is also my last fight in Vegas.) Still not on the main strip, we settled for Sam's Town

Hotel. A gang of Irish Americans from California led by the Conlon family, who had pretty much adopted me, make the trip over from Orange County. Wayne and Cheryl McCullough are ringside as well.

There are a couple from Clondalkin there on honeymoon who recorded the fight. They don't use much film.

I walk towards Trujillo and start hitting him. Freddie misses the first knockdown because he isn't even down the steps from the corner. I land some good shots but he is tough and refuses to stay down, so I have to settle for a TKO in the first. One left hook should have decapitated him. He is hard but limited. Bjorn Rebney and Sugar Ray are in the ring back-slapping me afterwards.

I rattle off six more fights in 2003. Oscar Villa takes me four rounds but I learn a few lessons. I also meet Arnold Schwarzenegger as the fight is held at his charity event in the Marconi Automotive Museum in Tustin, California.

Seven weeks later the curse of Mick Roche's elbow returns. It is my right hand that stops Oscar Rosales at the Thunderbird Wild West Casino in Oklahoma. Moments before I head to the ring I am told that my purse has been reduced as my bout is no longer on television. That was the whole reason I let myself be convinced to take a fight so quickly after Villa. Also, it is no longer six rounds, it is now just four. We'll see about that. The fight lasts 1 minute 49 seconds. I clatter him early but shock waves are sent rushing up to my right shoulder blade. I know my hand has gone again. Thankfully Rosales crumbles. He gets up and I jump on him, landing enough punches to force the referee to come between us. I will carry my right hand for the next two years. Even now it is not fully healed and never will be. A decent coach would always spot the weakness.

Fighting Terrell Hargrove was supposed to be a gamble. The man was huge for 130 pounds. I went up to 128 for this super featherweight bout. It was the first fight my dad got over to see so I wasn't going to be messing about. It was June 2003 and my seventh professional bout. Dad is a worrier before, during and after my fights. He can't help it. But he was pleased to be finally watching me. I knocked Hargrove out, despite his muscles, in the first. He shit himself as soon as I attacked him, which was right from the bell. He had gone the distance with bigger men but I sensed he wanted out so I helped him along. He was looking to his corner from the first blow. The doctor called it.

The Neilstown Avenue football team was in full voice. The Kellys and Paddy Jennings amongst others were enjoying the night out at the Mohegan Sun Casino in Connecticut. Freddie's family and my cousin Paul Magee were up from Boston. Paul was a regular at ringside when I was in the States.

I didn't notice any of them. Just Freddie and Justin. Like Dad and Peter Perry. I could hear Dad that night when he couldn't help himself. Just the little things that really matter. Afterwards I gave the boys the money shot: flexing my bulging biceps. They went nuts sending abuse back into the ring.

Now a fixture on SRL undercards, television was spreading my name around the boxing world. I was described as a choir boy at one stage.

They liked my aggression, as the *ShoBox* TV commentators stated:

'He is seven and o with six knockouts. What's behind those numbers, Steve?'

'Bernard Dunne is green indeed. In six pro bouts he has done a total of just twelve rounds. He is green all right, and not just because he is Irish. Not Dunne yet.'

Then they flash to my young mug and a soundbite:

'I want to be the champion. I wanna be the best. You know, I didn't leave home to come out here, to live alone for no reason. I've made sacrifices and I'm gonna try to stop everybody who gets in my way.'

Mario Lacey had fought up at light welterweight and had only one defeat from ten bouts but it only took 1 minute 51 seconds to get a clean KO. Just before the fight I sent Bjorn and Ray into convulsions of laughter. They were towering over me as I was about to charge out of the corner.

'Bjorn, is that a phone in your pocket or are you happy to see me?'

'What?'

Ding!

My first visit to the canvas for real – the gym stuff is forgotten the next day – came in my tenth professional bout against Alejandro Cruz in November 2003. It was my first six-rounder that went the distance. Early in the first I let my right hand go and it exploded in pain. I was minding it in the second, using it as a decoy to the body with the intention of coming back with a left hook. My chin was just sitting there in the wind. Cruz clipped me as I was spinning to finish the combination. I went down, rolled and jumped back up. I finished the round strong, even shaking him before the bell. I was cautious in the third but picked him off in the fourth, fifth and sixth to get out with a unanimous decision. Tucson, Arizona was never going to be the venue of my first defeat. No, I was saving that for a much bigger occasion.

The damage to my hand meant I missed the chance to perform in Madison Square Garden the following month. Regrets? I have few, but missing out on a really big American card is one – yeah, the Garden or the MGM would have been amazing. Nothing like topping the bill down by the River Liffey, but I probably would have found my way into the hallowed grounds of American boxing if I'd stuck around long enough in America.

I couldn't climb into a ring for three months so I went off and got married instead. Despite the hand giving me pain, we still invited Mick Roche.

I returned to see off Evangelio Perez up in northern California, again over six rounds, and afterwards we began suggesting the possibility of heading home. It had been two and a half years.

We kept the rhythm going. My first eight-rounder followed two weeks later as I won every round against Angelo Luis Torres. My opponents were getting more durable. He was a survivor. Still, it should have been stopped. I remember his cornermen approached me afterwards, they seemed delighted he went the distance, but they were wondering if I could get Bjorn Rebney to cash their fight cheque. 'Not my problem, pal. This is my problem,' I said, showing them my ballooned right hand as I went off in search of some ice and a large bucket.

Another three months followed nursing those three little bones.

A few days later Ray Leonard signed up for NBC's *The Contender*

television series with Sylvester Stallone. This was boxing's response
to the reality television craze that has swept the world. By the summer
of 2004 it was obvious that SRL Promotions was falling apart and that
Leonard and Rebney were no longer in a functional working relationship. They ended up in court.

Sylvester Stallone and *The Contender*'s English producer Mark
Burnett arrived in the Wildcard with a gang of corporate types to
watch me train. They got lucky as this was not your average sparring
session – it was one of the Nate Campbell sessions, and they knew who
Campbell was.

They offered me a chance to be on the show there and then. It wasn't
what I wanted to do. It seemed more like Hollywood than boxing and,
anyway, they eventually went with middleweights.

I used to call Harry Hawkins every month to give him a blow-by-
blow account of each fight. When I rang him that night he agreed with
me about *The Contender*, but wisely told me to let it all play out.

Pamela had gone home in May 2003 for a holiday and I followed after
beating Mario Lacey in July. I had told my family what I was going
to do. I got Derek Maher – my sister's fella – to pull a little stroke
before I came home. He told Pamela that he wanted to pick out an
engagement ring for Deborah and would she help him. We are a closely
knit clan so it seemed like a normal enough suggestion.

When they got to the jewellers Mahersy simply asked her, 'What
would you choose, Pamela?' She picked her favourite.

It was the perfect plan. Pamela didn't have a clue. When I arrived
home we went out for dinner in the Victoria Chinese restaurant in
Clondalkin village. I was going to slip down on one knee there and
then but I bottled it. Too many people. I'm twenty-three years old.
Nah, not here. The fight plan was altered slightly so I had to do some
quick explaining when I got back to my corner as the Dunne family
were all in on the sting at this stage and were waiting to celebrate.

'Get out of the kitchen,' I hissed. They scattered.

Jesus, I'd be less nervous for a world title fight. I knew she would
almost certainly say yes but I couldn't relax. We were drinking tea and
Pamela was sitting at the top of the table. I knew the rest of them were

pressed against the living-room door trying to earwig. Pamela really didn't have a clue.

'Close your eyes for a second.'

This wouldn't be unusual as I might produce flowers or something. I am an old romantic, you see. I took out the ring and got down on my knee.

'Right, open them. Will you marry me?'

She burst into floods of tears. Sobbing at the thought of having to marry Bernard Dunne.

'Well, are you going to or not? Answer the question!'

'Yeah.'

The eejits burst through the door. That was that. Pamela stayed home to organize the wedding. I went back to the Wildcard to prepare for Julio Cesar Oyuela that October and then Alejandro Cruz in November.

After fighting Cruz, with just my left hand, in November 2003 I returned home. It was an important stage in my development but Freddie gave me time off for good behaviour. He has never been married but he understood how important family was to me.

It happened on 10 January 2004 at the Church of the Immaculate Conception in Clondalkin. Pamela Rooney from Ballyfermot became Pamela Dunne. I was fighting Evangelio Perez in March so I didn't have much time to plan a honeymoon. This was when Martin Donnelly saved my skin. I had one job – sort out the honeymoon. Martin, along with a few others, had helped me through the tough times in America when America Presents collapsed. Peters passed the hat round. Five Irish businessmen helped me to stay afloat – Tommy Egan, Seamus Maguire and Co., solicitors, Frank Dunlop, Martin Donnelly and Des Kelly.

Martin first came into contact with Brian Peters through a man from the Liberties district of Dublin named Frank Cahill. He showed Martin my early fights on DVD in the States.

I was at a charity do on New Year's Eve and Martin was on my table. We got chatting, and drinking, away. When Peters dropped us both home we were still swapping stories. Life, boxing and all his various other interests.

Martin is one of a rare breed who acts as a genuine patron of Irish sports and sportspeople. He is an Irishman in the truest sense of the word. He has piled a serious amount of his own money into the GAA, particularly the now-shelved Interprovincial Championships.

'Where are you going on your honeymoon, Bernard?'

'I haven't booked anything yet, Martin.'

That simple, and his brain clicked into gear. Two days later his PA called and offered us the keys to his place in Marbella as a wedding present. He took care of everything. And this from a man I'd met only once. I know I'm a good drinking companion but I'm not that charismatic.

There were ten apartments in our complex in Santa Monica. Good people. A young Polish family lived above us. The husband was a university professor but his wife and daughter spoke very little English. Their little girl wanted to see 'Ben' whenever she got upset. Down she would come for a bickie or to play in the living room. Also upstairs was a band, FLO – For Love Only – that eventually became the Nick Johnson Band. I would sit in on rehearsals and went to a few of their gigs in bars around LA. They were from Boston but came to California to try and make the big breakthrough. They weren't bad and they are still plugging away as far as I know. Dan the Man was the bass player and Nick's roommate.

It's funny how people can come into your life when you are at a low point or simply in need of some support. The O'Driscoll family was there for me in Sydney. The Conlons from Orange County quickly became our surrogate family in America. They were Belfast people. Pat and Marie Conlon with their kids Tracy, Lisa and Pat Jr. Marie's brother, Eddie Shaw, was Barry McGuigan's trainer. Eddie lived for years behind the Holy Trinity club. Harry let the Conlons know I was on my own in Santa Monica so Pat called me first, then Pat Jr, before his son-in-law Jimmy – Tracy's husband and a self-confessed boxing nut – landed at our door. This became a regular event. He would drive out from Orange County, pick us up and take us to a BBQ in their place up near Disneyland. It was hot. It was a three-hour round trip so they always insisted we stay for the weekend. They kept in touch throughout the three years and still do to this day. Pat, Pat Jr and a couple of his workmates – he is a teacher – had just happened to book flights to come to Dublin around the time of the Cordoba fight in March 2009. It was nice to get them good tickets to see me fight for the world title. The least I could do was put on a decent show for them. It was special to look into the crowd afterwards and see them.

I didn't make many other local contacts as LA is a very fake place. We surrounded ourselves with Irish people. The Conlons and Freddie were the people we socialized with. We didn't go out much. One day on the bus a Cork girl called Máire asked about the tricolour on my bag. She worked in a clothes shop on the Santa Monica promenade. The upshot was that Pamela had herself a three-days-a-week job with other Irish girls. She is still friends with one of them, Anna. That helped her settle quickly enough. I had the gym as an outlet. It must have been difficult for her. The sacrifice was not mine alone.

Me and Pam supported each other, really. We are a married couple but we are also good friends. Always have been. She bought into what I was about and what I wanted to do. I needed her to do that. If Pamela hadn't been with me, my parents would probably have split up! Seriously though, Dad would certainly have come over and stayed with me. We probably would have ended up doing pads in the kitchen.

After dropping Dad out to the airport following one of his visits, me and Pamela grabbed a taxi home. The taximan presumed we had bags so he opened his boot. Being the helpful lad that I am, I went to close it for him only to slam it down on his hand. The only way to open it again was from a switch inside the car. While he was screaming in agony, we frantically tried to find the release button. He should have gone straight to hospital but he wanted his fare. The forty-minute drive back to Santa Monica passed in uncomfortable silence. We were like scolded children in the back seat, trying not to laugh.

We would tune into the talk shows on Dublin's FM104 on the internet so it felt a little like home, and shell out eleven bucks for *OK!* or *Heat* magazines for Pamela. Barry's tea bags in the post. Little things like that matter.

We didn't go out drinking much; not, that is, until Paddy Jennings came over. We'd be down on the beach body surfing – breaking our necks like typical tourists. It built up a thirst. He came with me to the Wildcard every morning but it didn't look like I was going to be in the ring any time soon because of my brain scan. One night Paddy went around chatting up literally every bird (two of them were sisters) in a packed bar. The man has no shame. He ended up bagging himself an auld one. Gave her a chocolate sweet and she gave him a kiss. That was normal enough behaviour from Paddy Jennings at the time. He is a reformed character these days, happily settled and raising a family.

I got up every morning, I trained and I went back to Pamela. I ran the Santa Monica beach as the sun was setting each evening. Not a bad life.

I eventually got a Jeep Cherokee for the last year. I needed to get off the bleedin' bus. This allowed us to investigate Malibu, which was a cracking place to hang out. Pamela, like most people at that time, was mad into *Friends*. One day Matthew Perry walked past. She chased after him to get a picture.

Adrian Valdez was my last fight in the States. It was on the 19th of August 2004 in the Aldrich Arena in Saint Paul, Minnesota. Live on *ShoBox* across America.

Early in the first round came a sound that changed the night. *Thump!* It was a nasty head collision – bone on bone. I got cut, though the blood was rolling straight down my forehead so at least I could still see, but the experience made sparring with world champions a redundant exercise. You can train with the best and be a technically supreme boxer but if you have a bad night there is nobody to save you. If your shots are not coming off there is no respite.

When Valdez saw the blood he grew about two inches. It brought him on – it always does. He came at me for ten rounds. I had only ever gone eight rounds so this was breaking new ground against a really hungry fighter.

This was to be my last lesson in America.

Before we headed out to the ring Freddie put on a big leprechaun hat.

'Freddie, what the fuck?'

'I know – great, isn't it? I'm Irish.'

'Irish? Jesus!'

'I'm in your corner, aren't I?'

'Let's go.'

My initial plan of feeling Valdez out and just staying out of range for the first round got binned as soon as I got cut. Got to get back to the corner and get this seen to.

Freddie's no cut man by trade but he should have been paid double for this shift. It ended up needing six stitches.

My combinations were refusing to click into any rhythm. I got to a stage midway through the second where I said, 'Right, let's slug it out.' I genuinely had no choice. Southpaws were never a concern to me but he was connecting with a lot of counter-right jabs.

This quickly became my toughest fight. I was the co-main event although the middleweight Matt Vanda, another local, was the crowd puller. The audience was neutral. They also saw my blood. That put some of them immediately with Valdez. (Vanda knocked out Armando Velardez. Five years later he went the distance but lost unanimously to John Duddy in Madison Square Garden.)

I started trying to walk Valdez down, get on top of him. I was back being the aggressor by round four. I whacked a right hook to the body and came back with my left but his counter kept picking me off.

When this happens in a fight you must relax. It quickly became apparent that it was going to be a long night. I was due a fight like this in America. Dig in for the long haul and find a way to win ugly. It's boxing; the counterpunch is going to catch the aggressor. His corner was screaming for uppercuts.

To Valdez, I was a huge opportunity. The blood pouring from my head made it all seem possible to him. He had a simple game plan. The counterpunch. He grew visibly in the early rounds. He sniffed a chance of a better life. He was only on television because he was fighting a white Irishman. Most of the Mexican guys I came up against were never given anything easy in life. They are brought up tough. He was no mug with fourteen wins, two defeats and three draws and he was unbeaten in three years. Many of the guys I fought and beat in America were either pups or old guys hanging on for pay days.

Whoever won that night would get springboarded into the top fifty.

I knew I was heading home after this fight and to have a blemish on my record would be disastrous. I was 13 and 0. Nobody wants to lose an unbeaten record.

I began thinking my way through this durable Mexican's armour. He had the frame of a welterweight but I had to keep walking into his shots. Wear him down. On this night, it was the only way.

He was moaning to referee Denny Nelson about a head collision. Bad move, Adrian. There is nothing I hate more in boxing than bitching. Especially since it was him who smacked me with his head.

I remember I sparred with Martin Castillo – his nickname was The Peacock – and he hit me a three-punch combination in the nuts. Bang-bang-bang. But this annoyed me more. I have never had a problem with someone hitting me low or a headbutt or an elbow because I will do it myself if circumstances dictate, but if you are going to whine about it that's a different story.

I jump in and try to take his head off when he turns sideways. Defend yourself at all times. It's the golden rule. Stand there and look for sympathy and I will treat you with contempt. It was going past your normal Marquess of Queensberry Rules. I hit him like I would some lad who had threatened me as a teenager in Dublin. I catch Valdez a cracking right hand to the eye socket.

Steady. Back thinking my way through it again.

Pamela was there sitting ringside next to the promoter Tommy Egan and she was getting worried. Everyone could see I was under pressure and that it wasn't going as smoothly as previous fights. She would be reacting to the crowd but Tommy was reassuring her all the time. Telling her I was figuring him out. Well, I was trying to.

Back to the corner and Freddie was as much working the cut as talking me through our now-shredded fight plan. We were on the same page at least. He wasn't balling me out over it, just seeing the good things I was doing and the bad things Valdez was doing and trying to drum into me the angles I could pursue.

The bell rings.

Obviously Valdez couldn't understand my Dublin dialect and I don't speak Spanish, but we were getting our respective points across. We exchange words.

Cracking right hand again. At this stage I was trying to draw his left hand out, slip it and come back with my right. Pain was irrelevant. My right was an important weapon if I was going to beat a southpaw. He was trying to do the opposite – wait and counterpunch. We were both evolving. I was throwing in some feints, trying to get out in time so he would release and I could counter his counter.

This is boxing.

Nelson breaks between us but Valdez catches me one anyway.

I smile . . .

The alter ego has completely taken over now. Bernard Dunne is off down one of the long corridors of this boxing mind. My personality is completely different at this point than, say, if I was relaxing at home. There are things I am capable of in the ring that I would be appalled by in real life. Because this is not real life. We don't feel the blows any more. It becomes primal. I stand back, lock his eyes and welcome him in. Let's rock and roll, son.

Back in the corner, Freddie is in my ear while simultaneously stemming the flow of blood from my forehead. Round five and we are dead even. 'Combinations, Ben!'

That was just a reminder in case I decided to throw a few punches in succession like we had practised every day in the Wildcard for three years.

'Move around to his right . . .'

Move to my left. Which is what you do with a southpaw. Stay on the outside, away from his big left hand. I continue to close him down. No combinations.

But Freddie knows what can happen in a fight. He knows what differentiates boxing from any other sport. You have an off day in a soccer game or, say, a round of golf – that's okay; just come back tomorrow, work on what you did wrong and it can be turned around pretty quickly. Especially if you have acquired the habit of winning. A blemish can improve your progress in other sports, but not in boxing.

In pro boxing a bad night can put you out of the reckoning for two or three years. There is so much pressure on each fight. No margin for error. Even in the amateurs, get beaten and there is always another tournament around the corner. In pro boxing even the narrowest defeat can send you shuttling down the ladder.

I'm still trying to get my combinations off but his style is cancelling out mine. I need to try another key to open the door. I bide my time. Round seven. Okay, I'm going to move around. I feel fresh – let's see what he has in the tank. Let him come on to me. There are some fights when you can't take a break, can't find a breath. You just have to fight until someone drops. Mostly, though, you need to take time to figure him out again.

Everything is happening instinctively. You don't have to think about unleashing a right hand. It just comes. It will get to the stage where you are surviving purely off instinct. At the same time I am analysing every reflexive move he makes. Every twitch. My actions don't require conscious thought any more.

I keep shoving my left hand into his face. Next time he takes the bait I'm going to throw my right. I am waiting, always waiting, for that reaction. Eventually he comes in wildly, out of frustration, and I deliver a crisp counter. There is no sweeter feeling. I had been waiting for seven and a half fucking rounds.

Some things work. I am still trying to walk Valdez into the dirt. Get close. Throw shots. No early night tonight. Right hand is stinging again. I'm losing confidence in it against a southpaw. I caught him a right hook earlier – the pain is always the same. Shooting up your arm. It hurt him but not as much as it did me. My head had already opened him up and an elbow let him know what was going on. But I was pulling back on the right-hand deliveries now and he knew it.

Dublin accents in the crowd.

Bernard Dunne, Bernard Dunne, Bernard Dunne.

My cousins John Dunne and Paul Magee are here.

I hear them but then I hear nothing. That Valdez has noticed my weakness makes me angry. I keep on walking in and I get tagged by his counters.

Freddie is talking.

'Double jab, son. The single is giving him time to counter you. Don't give him that time. And don't be loading up on your shots. Let them go. Nice fast hands. Like we talked about.'

Before Freddie I was a one, two, three step and wait for the power shot. The one that ruins your opponent's night. Freddie was trying to train me into breaking guys down more. Hitting them and then stepping out and then jumping back in on them. Shane Mosley had said it to me as well.

This is the reason why.

Deep breath.

'Stop going backwards in straight lines. Double jab and then slip off at angles and eventually let the right go.'

You can't turn around in the corner and say, 'Well, Freddie, I agree but my right hand is rather sore this evening.'

Going backwards in straight lines meant he could step in on me and throw shots. Move at an angle and he wouldn't find me.

Another frustrating round follows. My hand speed is laboured. I don't know what is wrong with me. I'm not even throwing right hands at this stage. He is holding me a lot now. I can feel his weight.

I am disgusted when I go back to Freddie. It isn't as if I'm raw. I'm just feeling dead. Okay, I'm in deep water, but Justin has me well conditioned, yet nothing I've been told to do is happening. I haven't been ignoring them like I sometimes did Peter Perry and Dad as an amateur. It's just not coming out of me. Any genuine sportsman can relate to those nights when it just isn't there.

You just have to find another way.

The television commentators have turned on their 'great white hope'.

The story of this fight: Ben Dunne – aggressive but very often walking into left hands. Valdez has been countering with long left hands. Power shots. Ben Dunne is getting hit by those shots. Valdez is under control; allowing Dunne to come to him.

There is nothing wrong with my chin tonight as Valdez pops my head skywards with an uppercut.

Freddie: 'You got to be first to this guy, okay? Be first. That is all that matters now.'

Two more rounds. Forget Sugar Ray and *The Contender*. Forget about going home. Forget about my dreams because if they are dreams they will never come true. Just be first. Land my right before he lands his left. Two rounds. These must be my six minutes. Take his shots and land more. I will be criticized but it doesn't matter. Just be first.

We knew this would be a step up for Ben Dunne. We didn't know how big a step up.

I was a big body puncher during my time in the States. The left hook was my weapon of choice. My KO machine. They called me the white Mexican. That is all on the line now. Valdez is visibly tiring. Sucking air. His cornermen are screaming at him – '*You are strong, Adrian! You are winning the fight! Keep your feet planted. Body shots.*'

But he is covering up and waiting to throw left hands.

I am wrecked as well but I am going for a big finish. My right hand is coming over his guard now. The pain forgotten. Valdez comes back strong. I slip. I'm back up stalking him again. He catches me flush with a left. Still my round.

Freddie: 'You need this one now, Bernard. Hook and roll.'

Olé, olé, olé, goes the crowd. The Irish *olé*.

I get up off the stool for the tenth and I feel fresh. I know it is the last round. My mind tells me it can be done. Be the aggressor. I give him a hug before our final three minutes. Complete respect. We just beat each other up for nine rounds – it's never personal. It's what we are paid to do. I love what I get paid to do.

I catch him with a right. He is tired. Another right. He counters. We are both running on adrenaline. There are more counterpunches coming over my right. Ignore them. Once I get inside I can bang away. Still no combinations, just keep plodding. No spark. This wasn't my night to shine. We stand in the middle of the ring and unload on each other for the last ten seconds. The bell parts us.

Freddie's words from a few months earlier still hold: *Just experience. When you're in complete control, then you can go for the power shots. Until then, if you go for the power shots too early, you're capable of being hit with a power shot back. You just don't want to get caught swinging with the guy and not following his shots. That's when you get knocked out. So, Bernard needs to settle down a little bit – use his boxing ability, break these guys down a little bit, take them into the later rounds, and take them out when they're ready to be taken out.*

I have experience. I am extremely frustrated but I know I have won. Ron Katz – the matchmaker – informs us with a wink that it is a unanimous decision. I closed out the fight well. Early on I applied all the pressure despite the crystal-clear shots he landed. Overall, my industry was enough. The scorecards. Mark Nelson went 96–95. Rex Walker had it 96–94 and Ed Kugler stretched it out to 97–93. Good man, Ed. I thought it was a close fight but at least one of them was looking at every round and not just the clean shots that I walked into.

Denny Nelson raises my hand.

The crowd give us a split decision. The commentators go with Valdez by a point. Both have been influenced by the blood and the counterpunches. It was a mixed reaction but at least I showed I wasn't a one-trick pony.

Valdez goes on to knock out two top-ten guys in quick succession – Cesar Soto in the first and Hector Javier Marquez in the third – only to get stopped by Robert Guerrero when challenging for the NABF featherweight title in early 2005.

They call Guerrero 'The Ghost'. We had previous in the Wildcard. Another war. In that same interview earlier in the year, Freddie had predicted the problems I could have with Valdez after seeing my sparring session with Guerrero: *Ben's a real talented kid, but he's another one flirting with danger too much by keeping his hands a little too low . . . for no reason. When you're fighting a southpaw, it changes the rules: it's hard to keep your left low to counter the guy's jab because that's his closest punch to you. You gotta keep the left hand up, especially when fighting a southpaw because, otherwise, he's gonna beat you to the punch every time. And that's what happened yesterday; Guerrero was beating Bernard to the punch with his jab.*

There was a local lad named Jason Litzau calling me out the whole time. He was ringside and came into the ring to stand toe to toe with me. But SRL Promotions was crumbling and I was already looking to reignite my career at home. I never saw Litzau again but I heard The Ghost's uppercut took him out in 2008 with the IBF featherweight world title at stake. Apparently he never saw it coming.

In September 2004 SRL Promotions officially folded. Rebney and Leonard were at war through their lawyers and the ESPN deal expired. I got out of my contract clean.

Ray Leonard showed me how to handle myself as a professional boxer. I never met a more media savvy man in my life. Very clever.

And I think how he deals with people rubbed off on me. I was around him a lot. He carries himself like a world champion should do. He gave me a chance. He told people I was an entertainer: 'Ben reminds me of myself when I was fighting,' he said. 'Not his style, not the way he boxes, but by the way he entertains the crowd. He's a performer. It's not just the boxing. That's important.

'He has also impressed me with his confidence. Sometimes he's over-confident. But I also believe that his work ethic is excellent. I like this kid's motivation. It shines through every time he steps into the ring. It's very important to have that. Sometimes fighters don't. It's embedded. It's there. It's part of the personality.'

Pamela and I wanted to start a family and we were only going to do that in Dublin. We had begun to love the LA lifestyle but we are home birds. Our kids were not going to be Americans! I couldn't handle that.

My apprenticeship with Freddie Roach was the Harvard of boxing. Freddie deserves all the plaudits that have come his way these past few years. You can set your watch by him as he moves through the weight classes each day, stopping to chew the fat between devilishly hard sessions. This is a man who lives and breathes boxing – it really does keep him healthy. Other Dublin lads, Dean Byrne and Jamie Kavanagh, have been out to California more recently, and the Wildcard is the best place for them. They will spar, like I did, with the best. The place tells you a lot about yourself. The environment teaches you to live like a world champion. I felt I had achieved that.

'We're always here for you – come back any time,' was the last thing Freddie said before I left. That meant a lot, but my future was back in Dublin. I said my goodbyes to Freddie, Macka and Peppa. I didn't even glance at the Vagabond as I came back onto Vine Street, but I did sneak in one last burrito from Taco Bell. I jumped in my Jeep Cherokee and waved goodbye to the solitary transvestite working the early shift. 'Fuck you, honey,' he/she responded.

We never did spark up much of a relationship.

No more blue bus line. No more training without a fight on the horizon. No more collapsed promoters. RTÉ Sport had been on to Peters. My future was in my own hands.

The sweat box that is the National Stadium was calling. I had to go back and reintroduce myself to my own town.

There was a void at home that I believed I could fill. I could have stayed in America and got another promoter but I wanted to give it at least two fights in Ireland. Just to see whether I could do what nobody had done for a very long time: breathe some life into pro boxing in Dublin.

Pamela agreed. We found a house on the internet. Number 37 Neilstown Avenue.

There was one priority. Getting Harry Hawkins back as my coach.

7. Harry Hawkins

Hood up, out of the front door, down the hill and onto the Glen Road, up the Andersonstown Road, down into the Falls and past Milltown cemetery (some days curiosity got the better of me and I would wander in for a look at the Republican grave sites). Around the Falls Park and back again. I could keep going until I reached the Holy Trinity Boxing Club but I was always very fussy about who I worked with and Harry Hawkins wasn't home until evening.

Looking at my career from the outside, it must seem like a three-man team was working in unison. That was rarely, if ever, the case. Brian Peters played a substantial role as my manager from the moment I turned professional and doubled up as my promoter from 2005, but it was never a cosy band of brothers. Never.

From the moment I came home from America it was just Harry Hawkins and Bernard Dunne.

Harry lives up off the Glen Road. His house is in the countryside but my run brings me into the heart of West Belfast before I can break sweat. Privacy with civilization just a stone's throw away. Not that they are throwing stones around these parts any more.

Harry and Michael Hawkins started up Holy Trinity in 1972 so the young boys of the Turf Lodge estate could have some form of normal social outlet in a world gone mad.

The curate in the parish at the time was the inspirational Fr Paddy McWilliams from Anahorish in south Derry. The place made famous by the Seamus Heaney poem of the same name. Fr Mac took one look at the lay of the land in Turf Lodge and came up with a visionary regeneration plan centred around boxing. Up in Turf Lodge that meant the Hawkins family. Fr Mac approached the clan leader to see if her two eldest sons would be interested in coaching. Harry was only eighteen and Michael twenty-one but they were already grown men – you grew up very quickly in Belfast during the early 1970s if you wanted to survive. Otherwise you got on the boat to England, and that brought its own dose of reality.

The brothers had previously boxed out of Holy Family in North Belfast, with Gerry Storey, but once 1969 arrived, and with it a constant stream of horrific sectarian violence, it became too dangerous to travel the few miles across the city on a daily basis. Bridie wasn't too happy with her boys risking their lives for their love of boxing. There was a decent chance they would eventually be dragged into the senseless and at times random brutality that was fast becoming part of everyone's daily lives. The odds were not good even if you sat tight.

Young fellas were in desperate need of something to keep them off the streets. Fr Mac had a plan.

Harry only boxed up to schoolboy level but he had the gift for coaching from a very early age, something that most boxers never develop. I don't even know if I have it myself. It is a completely separate art form. Mickey Hawkins had competed in the Irish youth championships. Then the rioting began. All they could do for a time was play football locally so they agreed to Fr Mac's suggestion without having any idea of the appetite bubbling just beneath the surface. Belfast has always been the capital of boxing on this island – especially professional boxing.

The wooden hut they used to train in had been burned down but Fr Mac somehow raised funds to build a youth centre in Norglen Gardens. It started with the most basic of facilities. Led by the boys' father Tommy Hawkins, Harry, Mickey and others got stuck into the groundwork alongside the young priest. Soon enough the local council building control arrived and tried to halt the process – this being a common enough occurrence when anybody tried to do something positive in West Belfast. The community was under siege but they had a secret weapon. Fr Mac would stop working, slip out the back door, put his collar on and come in the front asking if he could be of any assistance. The Catholic Church outranked the inspectors. They completed the job.

Kids began trickling into the gym. Word spread and it became a flood. No one could have imagined the Hawkins brothers and a few others would transform the boxing landscape into a centre of excellence – built with their own hands – that has produced thirty senior Irish champions and backboned several Olympic teams. (Mickey was an Irish coach at Seoul '88 and Atlanta '96.) Another brother, Thomas Hawkins, became the club secretary and took responsibility for ensuring write-ups for the newspapers. Thomas is now sports editor at the *Irish News*. There were ten kids in total.

Boxing, like everything else, suffered in the maelstrom of the Troubles. Harry remembers the Ulster finals in the early 1970s being held down the Lower Falls Road and he and his lads having to dodge their way through burning buses and lorries to get there. And back again. The people rioting on the streets didn't know who they were. But the club tracksuits gradually became their protective cloak.

Boxing went against the grain of those times. Holy Trinity is a mixed club. It may be situated in Turf Lodge, a predominantly Catholic area, but even at the height of the atrocities boxing stubbornly ignored the divide. The issues that divided people in the North over the years were never allowed through the doors. Anyone who went there was not seen as Protestant, Catholic or anything else. They were all simply aspiring boxers. You will still find all religions and nationalities training side by side in that gym today.

The Hawkins name was even respected on the other side of the divide. Harry would bring Holy Trinity to the Loyalist clubs. There was an Ireland versus Germany contest in the Shankill Leisure Centre at the very height of the Troubles. A Catholic was all but committing suicide by coming up the Shankill Road in those days but Harry Hawkins and his boxers were guaranteed safe passage.

All the Belfast clubs attended meetings together. No one ever got touched in boxing; that was just the way it was. The boxing people on the ground weren't influenced by events around them. Or religion. Or politics.

Maybe it is just an unexplained phenomenon in what was a deeply traumatic period, or maybe it was something else.

It takes patience and years of hard work to acquire the skills necessary to handle any opponent with just your fists and movement. It has nothing to do with sectarianism. Controlled violence transcends unchecked aggression. In some sections of society, boxing has long been condemned as a blood sport, but the discipline of a boxer contradicts this argument every time. It thrives in downtrodden places like the Mexican barrios, West Hollywood or even Neilstown.

Boxing can come into an area with a deep-rooted violent history and save young men from that violence. Boxing teaches you how to defend yourself by inflicting damage. With this knowledge, a physical confrontation can nearly always be avoided. A potentially violent situation outside the ring can be calmed with a look or a few simple words. Any trained fighter will understand this. Yeah, just a look can do it. The threat of what's coming next is usually enough. A complete fool might misunderstand this but most people quickly cop on.

Another of Harry's brothers – Gerry, or 'Diddler' to all in the gym – went to the Moscow Olympics in 1980 as a light flyweight. The first light fly to represent Ireland at the Olympics, of course, was Brendan Dunne four years previously. Gerry was beaten in his opening bout by the Bulgarian Ismail Mustafov, who went on to claim a bronze medal. He made it to Los Angeles in 1984 but, again, lost his first fight against an Italian named Salvatore Todisco, the eventual silver-medal winner. Still, two Olympic Games is a serious achievement. Diddler has since been inducted into the IABA Hall of Fame.

Holy Trinity has gradually become one of the premier clubs in Ireland. The knock-on effect was that a host of Irish amateur training camps were held up there. Hence, young boxers like me are given over to Harry. If the Wildcard was where I got my boxing PhD, then CIE and Peter Perry gave me my secondary-school education and Harry Hawkins and Holy Trinity taught me as an undergraduate, so it made sense to set up my boxing practice there!

It helped that they took me in as one of their own.

I came home from America in September 2004. I spoke to Dad about our original post-Olympics plan from four years ago. Not competing in Sydney and the subsequent brain scan had thrown all that out the window, but I was back on course and with a new set of skills – I was an American fighter now.

The CSP problem could recur if we took a fight in Britain, but we didn't require the major boxing hub across the water. Dublin was calling.

Brian Peters had the RTÉ deal in hand. There was going to be a fight in early 2005 to showcase my return to Ireland as a professional. If we were to do this right I needed someone who could replicate the quality of coaching I had become accustomed to in America.

Dad liked the idea of training up in Belfast and working with a practical man like Harry Hawkins.

I called Harry coming up to Christmas.

'Well, old man, I'm home to fight. I want to put something to you.'

'Fire away, Bernard.'

'I want you to train me.'

'Well, how is that going to work? I'm up in the Holy Trinity.'

'I'll come up to Belfast for training camp – like I used to. I would like to become the champion of the world, Harry. So, are you in?'

I enjoyed the training camps up in West Belfast but didn't want to rush Harry or take him away from his commitments to Brian Magee and the amateurs. On the other hand, I knew he wouldn't be able to resist.

'Think about it, Harry.'

'I will, Bernard.'

Harry hung up the phone and turned to his wife Noreen in the kitchen: 'That was Bernard there on the phone. He wants me to train him.'

'That's a great honour,' she said. 'What did you tell him?'

'He told me to think about it. He'll have to come up and live here for training camps?' Harry was checking. As an amateur I had always stayed in the Balmoral Hotel on the Blacks Road and trained at Holy Trinity, but this was different.

'Well, where else would Bernard stay!?' cries Noreen.

The Hawkins family wouldn't let just anyone into their home but Noreen always liked me for some reason. My West Belfast mother! They insisted that for the training camps I would move in with them Monday to Friday. They treated me like a son. An older brother to Terence, Clare and Kevin, who were four, five and six years younger than me. Harry calls that family planning!

Just like at the O'Driscolls in Sydney and the Conlons in Orange County, I was well looked after. Harry told me not long ago that some days they miss me still. That means a lot. Although he did stress 'some'.

'We have a big house here. Plenty of room, Bernard,' said Harry when he got back on later that same day. That was that sorted. It worked out really well but it was always about hard graft with Harry.

Harry knew how to handle my training, having prepared Jim Webb, David Lowry and Brian Magee – with whom he really began to pick up the nuances of the pro game, having been in his corner since Brian turned pro in 1999.

Harry's knowledge of the politics that constantly muddy boxing's waters has proved invaluable in my career. After each of my fourteen fights in the US I would tell him what Freddie and Sugar Ray were saying to me. Harry would listen and encourage me. We stayed close. He always supported the idea of my coming home and going the European title route. Harry saw *The Contender* developments and the demise of SRL Promotions as opportunities rather than setbacks.

The coaching styles of Freddie and Harry are very similar, despite the Irish media presuming I was taking a backward step by leaving the Wildcard. The pair did differ on one point, however – my career path. Harry never actually suggested I come home as he saw I was learning plenty in America. Freddie said if I stayed in America then after about thirty fights I would get a world title shot, but I would never achieve that opportunity at home. Harry felt America could have bottomed out for me. I was getting popular with the TV networks and that meant they were speeding me through the contender list. Each fight was getting progressively tougher. Considering I was without a promotional deal again but had developed a decent reputation I could have been thrown in against some seriously seasoned featherweights. I wasn't ready, yet I would have taken such a fight. It would have been a mistake. I had so much more still to learn and that only comes from making mistakes in the ring. Dublin was the place to do it.

Harry always felt I could be better minded at home, where we could tailor my route. Get a European shot and push on. He was right. We'll never know if Freddie was as well.

The way I see it is simple: a happy fighter is a good fighter. Dublin was home. Training camp was two hours up the road and that suited me perfectly. I took three months off and then got back down to serious preparation to fight a guy named Jim Betts.

When I first started travelling up to Belfast it was by train. Harry would pick me up at the station on Monday afternoon and drop me off again on Friday or Saturday. Martin Donnelly eventually sponsored me with some wheels, but initially, just like LA, I was back on public transport.

Harry went to work every morning. He runs his own plastering business. I would jog around the Falls Park and return to the house with nothing to do. Boredom is a curse that must be overcome. Daytime television was better in America. Sometimes it was tough being in Belfast as, again, I was isolated. I've an overactive brain and constantly need something to keep it ticking over. I got on with all the Hawkins children but they had their lives to lead. Noreen would be back at lunchtime because she did administration work for the local priest, Fr Matt.

I was let off the leash at around six every evening. Harry would come in the door and I would start getting excited. Unfortunately, he is no spring chicken, so he usually required a 'wee siesta' before we could get down to business. If there was sparring to be done we would go to the gym earlier because we didn't want anyone watching the sessions. The main problem with an audience is it gives the hired help an incentive to perform. Also, we don't need any stories of the old days as the here and now is what preparation is all about. We just wanted to work on dismantling the upcoming opponent's main weapons.

The reporters would disrupt this process as they always want in on the sparring sessions. I'm aware of their importance, and many great writers have been drawn to boxing because the human element of two men slugging it out is so appealing and dramatic. It was of no benefit for me to give them an eye-witness account for their prose. We would put on public sparring sessions before each fight but the day-to-day stuff was always behind closed doors.

When not in Belfast I would stay in shape at St Matthew's in Bally-fermot. Dad drifted away from CIE after I left but he would be wasted outside this game and was drawn back to work with the next wave in St Matthew's. These kids want to go to the Olympics so they want to be coached by an Olympian.

In time we settled into a weekly routine. I would do my road work Monday morning in Dublin and then travel north. Tuesday morning would be road work again and sometimes a weights session. That was the pattern. We would go to the gym Friday morning so I could go home. The boxing was a priority but I had a wife and eventually kids as well. Being around them whenever possible mattered. Caoimhe and Finnian were growing when I was in training camp. We came home to start a family but I had to go missing for large chunks of my kids' childhood.

By the late 1980s and early 1990s Holy Trinity was firmly established as a boxing centre of excellence so Harry's expertise had him travelling the globe with his fighters and national squads. At the same time his three children were growing up. He gives Noreen all the credit for rearing them. They remember him being absent for long stretches. That must have been hard but he was utilizing a rare gift: turning young men into champions. Noreen knew the way to go was education. Harry agreed. All three children got degrees and jobs. Without people like Harry Hawkins there would be no Bernard Dunne, but I was never sure that was the way I wanted to go with my little ones.

No one else coached me in Belfast. Just Harry. Alec Docherty did my body work in Holy Trinity. His son Connor boxed up there too. Alec was a martial arts expert and liked all the UFC stuff. He, like Justin before him, punished me. Alec would have me moving in the ring with my hands up and he would be hitting me with a ball as I moved so as to imitate body blows in a fight. Torture.

We would fly sparring partners in from all over the world depending on the opponent. Peters was paying most of the bills so Harry would give him a shopping list to arrange for about four weeks out from a fight. The idea was to get three weeks' solid sparring and then ease it all down for the last few days.

The first spar, before Betts, was James Gorman – a big light welterweight based in Belfast. Next they brought in John Simpson, a featherweight with fifteen wins and two losses, from Scotland. He went on to claim the Commonwealth title.

There was something similar about all these guys. They didn't move like I did. I was always good at this essential boxing skill but in America I had honed the art of slipping punches so they rolled off my constantly moving head. Only problem was I came home from America as more of a fighter than a boxer. They had encouraged me to brawl over there. It was encouraged in the Wildcard every day. The TV networks went crazy for it. Freddie was less enthusiastic, as any good coach would be when they have a natural technician at their fingertips.

Harry wanted me to become a slave to my jab but sparring was always about cutting loose. Harry was trying to get me to use the time in the ring to work into fight situations but, initially at least, I just wanted to send the lad out on his back.

'Box behind the jab, Bernard.'

'How about I just knock this featherweight out, Harry? Wouldn't that be easier for everyone involved?'

Simpson, or whoever it was, could hear this. Every boxer worth his salt loved the invitation to fight, especially from someone smaller than them, and this was me laying out the welcoming mat.

The Wildcard was guaranteed to give you a good spar simply because there were world champions in and around your weight class lacing up every morning. Harry has always had a web of connections around British and European gyms. Still, some guys come in to spar with their own agenda. That's the same everywhere. I have been as guilty as others. Some listen, some don't.

I might want to practise slipping straight rights and left hooks. If they are good and do what they are told we would keep them for the whole three weeks. They would get paid. Some guys can't resist, though, and they will tag you with left uppercuts and right crosses when you are focused on the opposite. Bang. Bang. What the fuck? I would go nuts and unload. Bloodbath, either mine or his.

The behaviour of Joseph 'King Kong' Agbeko was a case in point. Before I fought Sergio Carlos Santillan in April 2006, Harry was on to Roy Hilder, chief of the Peacock gym in London, to find me a decent spar. Roy said there was a kid from Ghana knocking everybody out. Harry regularly went to Hilder for sparring partners, describing him as a straight-talking crafty cockney who knew his stuff, so we welcomed Agbeko to Holy Trinity.

He was supposed to be brilliant for me. I needed someone to test me and was looking forward to the sessions, but it turned into a complete disaster. All I wanted from the guy was a good spar, but his ego wouldn't allow him to give me one. We weren't weighing him down with specific instructions, like the others. His fortunes had dipped since losing a split decision to the tough Hamburg-based Ukrainian Wladimir Sidorenko in 2004, and this was an opportunity for him, but he didn't want to spar the first day. He said he was tired. I was fucking tired too, but sparring has always been precious to me. I wasn't losing a session because Agbeko wanted a rest.

The second day he started whingeing again, saying I hit him a kidney shot. (It was a perfect left hook to the body.) He was doubled over on the canvas. I felt like unloading on him there and then but instead I turned to Harry and said, 'Get rid of this fucker, he is wasting our time. And you are not getting paid. "King Kong" me hole . . .'

Miracle cure. He got to his feet and we went to work.

Day three was the real deal. Three rounds. Right out the gate, he threw me a petulant slap. This made me happy. Here started the lesson. It got nice and nasty in there. I finally got my decent spar.

For CIE see the Wildcard. For the Wildcard see Holy Trinity. It is the same all over. You do the job you are asked to do or you get punished. I dropped him in the first and knocked him out in the third. We put him on a plane and sent him home. His manager was on the phone the next day, saying that his fighter had been treated poorly. We explained how our boxing club operates. We were helping him to work.

Agbeko ended up signing for Don King and going on to win the IBF bantamweight title in 2007 when the ringside doctor intervened to stop his fight with Luis Alberto Perez, so he obviously had talent. We never saw a world champion, though. Just a stroppy fucker.

The problem with sparring was that I was constantly risking damage to my right hand. But I needed the rounds.

Before my fight against the American David Martinez in 2006 we had the English lightweight Gareth Couch over. A tall, undefeated, tricky opponent, Couch was a quality sparring partner. I was determined to hurt him. I wrecked my hand in the last round on the last day of sparring as a result.

Couch was due to be driven to the airport. I wanted to lay him out in the back seat.

The last day of sparring was always my favourite. I wanted the intensity of a proper fight. No instructions. I wanted to push myself to the limit. It was mental fuel for me.

I caught him with an overhand right to the top of his head. His head was more durable than my hand.

Harry wanted to cancel the fight there and then. He lost his temper.

'You were trying to send him home in a box,' he accused.

'Yeah, so? This is the fight game we are in, Harry.'

'Well you will miss the fight now, and how do you plan to get a European title shot with a damaged hand?'

'I've beaten Americans with one hand before, Harry. I'm still fighting next week.'

After a few more West Belfast curse words were flung in my direction, he departed.

Thankfully, Noreen had given me a spare key.

It was a problem. We went to a doctor in Dunshaughlin for a painkiller injection. Another one-hand job. I had to drag it back all night or time the delivery so I was hitting with only a certain part of the hand. Really, I used it as a decoy all night long. It took eight rounds.

Harry never wanted to take away my flair and panache. He just wanted to add structure, perfecting what was already in place. We were constantly trying stuff and that's what made the sparring so important. We always kept it simple with our fight plan. I just needed to listen and carry out the instructions.

Harry was an old-school coach but he understood the need to market a fighter as well. He advocated slavery to my technique but he knew I had to pack out the National Stadium to progress. He only reeled in my showmanship when he felt it was threatening my undefeated record. He would admonish me in the corner when I was leaving myself open against a dangerous opponent.

Find me a Dubliner in his twenties who packs out the Point Depot and doesn't begin to start enjoying it a little.

Harry, like everyone else, saw that I could be knocked out at any turn but in the heat of battle he told me to do what came naturally. If I was forced into a corner he understood it was better to fight my way out. Otherwise, I would be back there before too long. Winning a boxing match is as much about convincing your opponent you will not be intimidated as it is about landing the shots. Even if he is on the offensive. Make him doubt he can knock you out or even hurt you and his mind will start to play tricks.

Harry played another crucial role in my career that has been kept hidden from public view all this time. In all but name, Harry Hawkins was my manager as soon as I returned from the States. He was the man assisting me to earn the money I felt I deserved.

My official manager was Brian Peters. My promoter was also Brian Peters.

There is a law in America that prohibits promoters doubling up as a manager. The reasons why are obvious. It is a manager's job to get his fighter the best deal possible. To get the best fights for the best money and at the right time. The promoter's priority is to sell the event and make as much money for himself as he can. The bottom line is all that matters to him. There's a massive conflict of interest.

That's where Harry came in. Harry provided a buffer, where possible, to allow me to stay focused on upcoming fights because the closer to the night the more problematic it tended to become. It very nearly damaged Harry's reputation and certainly hurt his other interests, but he still put his loyalty to me above everything else. Peters, as my manager, was supposed to be getting me the best deal possible but it seemed to me he always kept the promoter's hat on when it came to divvying up the spoils. For a long time I had to sit and take it as I was locked into contracts.

Harry kept a lot of stuff from me when a fight was looming. He had to.

The problems started as soon as I came home. The television deal was a major sticking point. Peters never disclosed the details so I didn't know how much to be asking him for. I was selling out the National

Stadium for €10,000 a fight. Two and a half thousand people and ten grand for me. So how do I negotiate a fee? Most boxers would ask their manager to sort it out with their promoter, but in my case the two were one and the same. That was the root of all our problems. I could never trust someone acting in this dual capacity.

As much as I disliked Peters, he deserves credit for certain aspects of my career. With the right headline attraction Peters can run a decent show. There are worse than him out there.

In truth I gave him too much power. When we signed I was just desperate to put all the cyst problems behind me and start boxing professionally, but letting him do both jobs meant that I suffered financially as a result.

Harry was trying to guide me to win a European and then world title, but he seemed to spend half of his time sorting out my promotion/managerial problems. It was a constant concern, but Hawkins kept them at arm's length. He was nothing short of heroic in this regard.

Every time myself and Harry negotiated with Peters we would go back to one simple point: Peters would have a hard job selling a boxing match without Bernard Dunne as the headline. He had the RTÉ deal, which was invaluable in transforming a fighter into a household name, but nothing else.

Once negotiations broke down between Harry and Peters – and they usually did – there would have to be a meeting with all three of us regardless of what stage in preparation for a fight I was at. When that failed to produce an agreement Peters brought in Martin Donnelly to arbitrate because everyone trusted him. Martin is the most honest man I have ever met. He played an important role and he was very good at it. Why did he do it? Because he was asked to, nothing more.

I believe the fates of Harry Hawkins and Bernard Dunne have always been intertwined and this period was a test to see if I had the mental fortitude to succeed. The easy option would have been to drop Harry, as Peters eventually wanted, but the easy option does not deliver world titles. Harry Hawkins was staying in my corner. I believe things happen for a reason and there was a reason why Peter Perry sent me up north as a teenager and why I went to America and why Harry was waiting at the other end when I came home.

'Believe me, this is going to be a tough fight,' said Peter Perry a few days before I took on Ricardo Cordoba for the world title. 'But it is a fight that Bernard can win if his head is right and I am sure it will be because he has an excellent team around him. Harry Hawkins is sure to have him right on the night. He is an excellent trainer and he has worked wonders with Bernard.'

Peter Perry knew what he was doing all those years ago.

So, yes, Harry was my manager all right, just not in name and certainly not when it came to handing out the cheques. I would have been screwed over several times if it hadn't been for him. Hopefully I can repay the favour further down the line.

What makes him a great coach is his calmness. When I danced into the ring to 'The Irish Rover', dipping under the ropes, the adrenaline would be flowing but he would get in front of me and remind me why we were there. The mantra of the past nine weeks' training would be repeated.

'You have done all the work. Remember the basics. Never forget the basics.'

And then he would remind me of them. It seeped into my thick skull – most of the time.

So, I stuck with Harry Hawkins and at the defining moment of my career he saved me. I had no idea where I was. I thought I was dreaming. I was on my knees. I tried to put my right hand down to steady myself. I missed the floor. 'What just happened?' At the other end of a dark tunnel I heard his thick Belfast accent.

'Get up on your fuckin' feet, Bernard. Get up! Get up now!'

I must be in the ring. I must be on the canvas. I must be all right. If I was hurt he wouldn't be telling me to get up. He would be silent and the towel would be in his hand.

It wasn't a dream. It was the fifth round. I was all alone. But I heard Harry's voice when surrounded by those black lights.

'Get up.'

I couldn't hear the referee counting '. . . three, four, five . . .'

I got up because Harry Hawkins told me to. I survived.

No, we survived, because this journey is as much about him as it is me.

8. Homecoming

In early 2004 a letter dropped into Glen Killane's cubby hole out in Montrose.

Someone from Neilstown wrote it. They wanted to know why RTÉ were ignoring a young Irishman who had gone undefeated twelve times in the United States.

The Head of RTÉ Sport had my name on his desk. That was the start of it.

A boxing story. Glen wandered down the corridor to find Jimmy Magee. My old verbal sparring partner quickly filled him in on the Sydney debacle that denied me the profile Andy Lee was about to receive as an Olympian, but he also provided a glowing report of my progress since the amateurs.

Jimmy was always a believer. He was one of the few people I remained in touch with during my time in America. Darragh Moloney threw in another reference, as did Mick Dowling.

The timing was perfect. Niall Cogley had joined Setanta Sports and Killane had just succeeded him as chief of sport on RTÉ television. Glen sought to make an immediate impact in the role. One of his pitches in the interview process for the job was the potential ratings puller the return of pro boxing could have for terrestrial television.

Sitting in front of the RTÉ board, he referenced boxing's glory days of the 1980s when Barry McGuigan had the nation glued to their television screens late into the night. This was before the soccer epidemic that was Euro '88.

The sight of the 'Clones Cyclone' taking on all comers was the first real sporting occasion, on a worldwide scale, that RTÉ packaged and presented to the public. The pitch was simple – this type of drama sells itself. Everyone old enough remembers that Loftus Road night in June 1985 when McGuigan stalked the Panamanian Eusebio Pedroza over fifteen rounds to capture the WBA world featherweight title.

I was only five but already a boxer and I knew something was going on downstairs to do with my sport! There is a picture of me perched on McGuigan's lap at home. Like most Irish sports stars he was in touching distance.

Just twelve months later the reality of professional boxing came crashing down around us all and it was gone. Nobody can forget the doomed decision to have McGuigan defend and ultimately lose his title against Steve Cruz in Las Vegas's Caesars Palace car park at high noon.

The courageous manner in which he both won and, in particular, lost his crown seemed almost like a dream. It was such a fleeting moment that will never be forgotten by the hundreds of thousands who tuned into RTÉ.

The national broadcaster made Barry McGuigan a household name.

Killane admits he didn't know anything about me. He always liked his boxing – mainly because he grew up watching Muhammad Ali with his father and then saw how McGuigan became a heroic figure for the whole island of Ireland. Another Ronnie Delany. An Eamonn Coghlan for the ring. Cyclists Stephen Roche and Sean Kelly followed. Then Sonia O'Sullivan back on the track. All world beaters that the people could embrace and take personal pride in.

Glen identified a gap in the market. He just needed the means to exploit it.

He opened the letter. Honestly, to this day, I have no idea who sent it. Paddy Jennings can barely spell, never mind write, so it couldn't have been him. Any number of people, and not necessarily a friend or family member, could be responsible. Glen has lost the original, so we may never know. Either way, it was the first domino to fall.

The letter asked 'Mr Killane' why a former national amateur champion at every age grade and with three senior titles was not being tracked in America, especially when the sports channel ESPN had been televising his fights live across the States.

Glen liked what he was hearing from all quarters, yet he is no fool. He hoped Bernard Dunne wasn't another dud but the trust in boxing had plummeted in media circles since Steve Collins and Wayne McCullough, while neither world champion had been presented to the Irish public by RTÉ. Sure, they are household names, but that only really happened after their careers had peaked. Terrestrial television is the key to making any individual sportsperson known on the way up.

Glen knew that boxing had enough pedigree in Ireland and, if packaged correctly, it would sell. The Athens Olympics enhanced his view, with Andy Lee attracting decent audience figures for his bouts. He wanted to continue that momentum.

RTÉ were flush – Jaysus, wasn't everyone – probably for the first time in their history and sport was a guaranteed crowd puller. The RTÉ board went with Glen's recommendation for an outside broadcast unit to set up shop in the National Stadium as a trial run was organized.

All roads led Killane to Brian Peters. He made the call.

The timing really couldn't have been better, considering I had just lost my American promoter. Peters knew how big an opportunity this was to have RTÉ involved, having been part of a brief boxing revival in the mid-1990s. Understandably, he milked the situation and maximized profits for both myself and his fledgling promotional company.

Just as SRL Promotions went belly-up, RTÉ brought me and my 14–0 record back home. Fate smiled kindly on me for a change.

All I had to do now was repay the favour. This was the right move as I still needed to take small steps. I didn't make much from the deal initially but I was not too concerned as we all knew it was a trial run. Boxing as a sport was on trial and I was the guinea pig.

The initial RTÉ arrangement was for one, maybe two fights, depending on the viewing figures. Later on the agreement went fight to fight again as the finances began to tighten in Montrose just like everywhere else. But Killane gave his full support and stayed the pace.

The first fight in the Stadium against Jim Betts drew a peak viewing figure of 219,000. This was the key figure for RTÉ as a live boxing programme might be over an hour long but not all of it is action; this particular fight only lasted seventeen minutes, including the breaks between rounds.

The boxing media gave me a fair bit of stick for coming home. They suggested it was a backward step to leave Freddie Roach. There had not been a decent professional card run in Dublin for years so they were understandably sceptical. They didn't bank on my stubborn nature.

Peters and Killane struck up a working relationship and began to craft the fairytale story of my return. I also hit it off with Glen and I knew Jimmy and Darragh Moloney well, so it was great to be back working with them. Jimmy is nothing short of a legend while Moloney is a true pro.

All I had to do was keep on winning.

There were others showing an interest. Liberty Films wanted to do a fly-on-the-wall documentary. It was to be a record of my career during these two years. Maria Horgan – a sister of Leinster and Ireland rugby player Shane Horgan – was the brains behind it. The final product was excellently produced and proved very revealing. It shines an interesting light on Peters:

Synthesizers and me working the mitts with my auld lad. The voice of Brian Peters:

In the last twenty-five years we have had Barry McGuigan, Steve Collins and Wayne McCullough. I believe Bernard Dunne could go on to certainly be as good as them if not better . . . As far as Ireland is concerned there are not too many people who can put on a show as good as myself, he adds modestly.

Flash to Peters leading me into the National Stadium.

It is show business and you have to entertain.

And then me: *Fighting is what I do best. People ask me if I am nervous. I say, no, I'm not. I know exactly what I am able to do.*

Peters again: *Myself and Bernard, we are going to rule the world together, really.*

The programme is called *Big Time – The Bernard Dunne Documentary.* It goes back to my time in America briefly before jumping forward to the Burlington Hotel and the announcement of my return home.

Peters: *Today I'm announcing a new era for Irish boxing. I want to give the sport a profile it has lacked for too long.* He is flanked by myself and Francie Barrett. Francie was still a name to be put up in lights and he was on the undercard. *Boxing, I believe, is going to become very fashionable in Dublin this year.*

Switch to a wet February night outside the National Stadium and a young fella with a shiner looking suspiciously into the camera.

Anyone looking for a spare ticket?

A very young Brendan Dunne receiving the first ever Irish light flyweight title in 1974, from Billy Wright, Irish lightweight and welterweight champion in the 1920s

With my brothers Eddie (*left*) and Willie (*right*), and a python. They let me follow them everywhere. Not that they had much choice.

Ready for anything

Signing with Sugar Ray Leonard and Bjorn Rebney in my Santa Monica apartment

Wildcard crew: Macca Foley is at the back with Peppa Roach second from right.

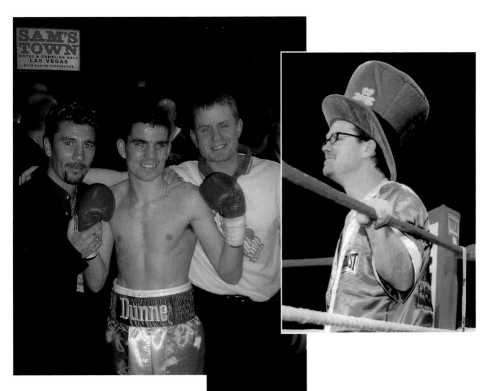

(*top left*) All smiles with Wayne McCullough and Brian Peters after I took out Eric Trujillo in the first round at Sam's Town Hotel in Las Vegas, February 2003

(*top right*) Freddie Roach in full Irish mode before my brawl with Adrian Valdez – which turned out to be my last fight in America. Freddie soon discarded the leprechaun hat, as he doubled up as a cut man

(*right*) With the pro career up and running, I asked Pamela to marry me – in my mam's kitchen. We tied the knot on 10 January 2004 at the Church of the Immaculate Conception in Clondalkin

Tuning in to Harry Hawkins: moments before my debut in the Point Depot, fighting for the vacant European title against Esham Pickering

Breaking Pickering's nose in the early going opened the road for my best ever performance to that point. Winning that EBU belt was my first taste of the big time

Kiko Martinez reels away after eighty-six seconds as I'm left staring into the black lights . . .

My head might be carved open, but I plead with Harry to let Benny work the cut against Cristian Faccio during my detour to Castlebar

At the end of the fifth round against Ricardo Cordoba, I nearly catch referee Hubert Earle.

This is the Cordoba fight summed up perfectly by Dave Maher in one iconic shot. It was a relentless war . . .

. . . that I eventually won

Dad grabs hold of me in the ring moments after my victory over Cordoba

I gave Poonsawat my best shots . . .

. . . and then he gave me some of his. I've never been hit harder

My turn next! Caoimhe looks on as Pamela and I swing Finnian

Is there many people up there watching? asks a younger version of myself from the back of a taxi. Excitement obvious in my voice. Harry sitting calmly beside me.

Jammed, says my driver.

This makes me happy.

I am 14 and 0. Unbeaten. My first pro fight at home was on 19 February 2005. Between Brian and Harry they came up with Jim Betts. We needed a guy with a decent record – he had eighteen wins and three defeats – and an Englishman would help ticket sales. They wanted to avoid someone trying to make a name for themselves but he had to be a respectable opponent. Training camp in Belfast began on 17 January.

Smoke-filled corridor. 'The Irish Rover' starts up, hood down, arms raised.

'Come on!' I yelp.

I remember coming out of the dressing room and seeing a massive sign that read: 'Bernard Dunne – a Neilstown Hero'. That was a great moment. It filled me up with pride.

The rest of the place wanted to see what I had learned these past few years. They had heard all the stories about Sugar Ray and Freddie so now they wanted some proof. *Sure, he wasn't even in the Olympics.*

The travelling Clondalkin crew was front and centre.

I slip early on. Then I stalk him. I am back in the National Stadium. Back where I made my name. So many positive memories come flooding back. My combinations are solid. In round five I catch him a left hook to the body. He bowls over in pain. Winded. Finished.

Jim Betts ended up marrying one of the girls who worked on the promotion for Peters so he did get something out of it. I was invited to the wedding but I was off chasing another opponent. It was a successful night but, of course, it got inflated out of all proportion. When was I getting a title shot?

Nicky Cook was the European featherweight champion. Harry had seen Nicky in the flesh on several occasions when he featured on the same card as Brian Magee. He was struck by his size in comparison to me.

Harry noticed that I was making the weight fairly easily. He felt my future was one division lower at super bantamweight, not feather-weight.

Yuri Voronin made that decision for us. He was noticeably wider around the shoulders. Same weight but bigger man. I boxed the ears off him for nine and a half rounds. Aside from a cut from a clash of heads, he couldn't touch me.

'I don't want to see that showboating business. Get behind your jab!' Hawkins was not happy as we chatted between rounds. I had started playing to the natives. Harry knew I would do this but he had a bad feeling in his gut about this one. He had foreseen the problems with Voronin and had asked Peters to get a few more English lads before this guy. Peters liked the sound of the Ukrainian name and was trying to keep RTÉ happy. Movement up the rankings was also important.

The power to stop a decent featherweight was not coming out.

I began to tire entering the last three rounds. It was the weight of Voronin's upper body in the clinches that was wearing me down. He was solid. Well made.

Halfway through the tenth and final round he is backing me up to the ropes but I am punching away. I throw a straight right but, before I come across with a left hook, he catches me as clean a left as you will ever see. I don't even see it. I am out cold on my feet.

I come back to reality but my legs are halfway down the South Circular Road. Oh, no. I'm going down in just my second fight back home. It's all over. Luckily I bounce off the ropes because I'd be still falling otherwise.

Dad was off his feet. 'Hold on to him, Bernard! HOLD ON TO HIM!'

Peters was yelling the same. Everyone was.

I'm fucking trying to. I couldn't find him to grab him. When I did he leaned on me and I went down two or three times. Jesus, he felt heavy. No count from referee David Irving. I was looking for any excuse to take a break. I was in bits and he was desperately trying to finish me off. I began moving and feinting and barely avoiding his big swinging shots. He should have relaxed and just walked me down but he was running out of time and we both knew it.

'Twenty seconds,' Peters roared.

My instincts saved me. I hit him a straight left that kept him off for the last few seconds. Thankfully, he was shattered as well. It was the only round he won, I felt. David Irving gave it to me on a 96–94 score.

The knives were out. Voronin proved himself a decent opponent the following February when he took Nicky Cook the distance in a European title fight.

Maria Horgan's hand-held camera shows the haunted expression on my face as I am slumped on a chair in the dressing room.

That'll stand to me, anyway. I was staring into the abyss. It felt like a defeat. I certainly hadn't made the impression I'd been trying for. Everyone would quickly forget the first nine rounds when I'd been on top.

Jimmy Magee was constantly promising the public that I would have a title shot sooner or later but we had to stop and reassess now. The trick was to make me look like a decent but beatable opponent to the Englishmen who were swapping the European title during this period. Cook seemed the likely man I would have to face and he was not shy in appearing at a few of my weigh-ins just to keep it all interesting. But he disappeared up to super featherweight as I went in the opposite direction.

The RTÉ powers that be were not put off by my tenth-round showing. It was high drama, but that's entertainment. They could market that, but I'm sure Glen's heart skipped a beat or two. And Peters's. I know my dad's stopped for a few seconds. But once I survived they could use it to their advantage. It would have been a disaster if I'd lost but it began to build that vulnerable image around me.

That drew people to the stadium and their television sets who had not watched boxing since McGuigan or, in the younger people's case, ever.

The peak viewing figure increased to 251,800; no great leap but an improvement. Justification. The momentum was building.

Irish people do get behind you and the support I have received from all over the country has been a humbling experience, but the story of the lobster pots sticks in my memory. A fisherman is on the pier unloading his pots. Two elderly American tourists are there. It has been a good day and every pot is full; lobsters are overflowing from all of them bar one.

'Excuse me, but how come that pot down the end is full to brim yet no lobsters are climbing out?'

The fisherman smiles. 'That lot are all Irish lobsters. Whenever one of them gets to the top the rest drag him back in. Keeps the others warm, they don't want anyone getting out and having a better life in the ocean.'

Dunne might get a beating tonight. He is shite. Let's watch it.

By the time of my European title fight against Esham Pickering in November 2006 the peak viewing figure was just shy of half a million. In 2009 the average viewing figure was nearing half a million for both my fights and well over 600,000 were tuning in for the main event. Killane had delivered on the massive return he had promised the RTÉ board. He has since been promoted to Managing Director of Television.

The general perception seemed to be that I was talented but tiny, fragile even, so I could be knocked out at any moment. I was about to get smaller still. Harry and myself sat down and had a good yarn about it one night. He said, 'Look, super bantamweight is eight stone ten. There is only four pounds the difference. You are making the weight easy, but you are fighting bigger and stronger guys at featherweight. Let's give it a go.'

We had initial doubts about the drop in weight but we got away with it five months after Voronin when I fought Sean Hughes, and by the time David Martinez came to Dublin in June 2006 I had dropped another two pounds. Against Pickering I was making 121lb easy. The media said I looked gaunt. I felt fine. I only went up to featherweight because of my Olympic aspirations. Making the lower weight was never a problem, as it can be for so many other boxers and jockeys, but it did require a lifestyle change. Noreen Hawkins became my personal chef, working off the advice of a dietitian named Sharon Madigan, who had worked with Commonwealth Games athletes based up in Belfast.

'Cut out them Coke cans there, for starters.' Harry would take a half-full can out of my hand. 'You are eating crap and it has to stop.' Simple advice about diet and my general conditioning was something I had never been properly given.

Killane was understandably pushing for a few tune-ups and then straight into the Point Depot for the real deal – a challenge for the European title. So was I, but the boxing game is never that simple. Peters and Harry were both thinking another twelve months, citing the change of plan as being caused by the drop in weight class – Harry felt I needed more rounds and Peters knew we could milk the situation some more. Our initial plan overran by nearly a year, but boxing is always a slow burn. Managers and promoters want to squeeze every last drop out of it on the premise that just one defeat can prove so damaging.

Peters convinced Killane to hold the course and Glen convinced his boss Noel Curran. The OB funding kept coming but RTÉ wanted to see results. At that time RTÉ were able to remain patient, but it would not have been possible today. In 2005 and 2006 the sun was still shining on our little Celtic Tiger economy.

There were one or two bouts that were filling a gap because the venue was booked and the scene had been set. Killane understood how it worked by now and let Peters get away with a few stunts.

Sean Hughes came in with four days' notice as a replacement for Noel Wilders (who had pulled out at short notice and was contemplating retirement). The vacant International Boxing Council world super bantamweight title was on offer. It was an absolutely meaningless belt but Peters wanted me up to twelve rounds, which was a good idea in theory. The super bantamweight European champion Michael Hunter had knocked this guy out seven months beforehand. We might have convinced the public of genuine progress if Hughes hadn't lost his nerve on the way to the ring. He went white as a ghost and told me afterwards his legs were shaking.

'So, it probably didn't help, Sean, when I started throwing punches?'

By that stage a trickle of local celebrities like Boyzone's Keith Duffy, a few knowledgeable sports stars like Shane Horgan and, of course, many of the Dublin criminal element had become regular faces in the crowd. They had become a pack of vocal Dublin Rottweilers. Hughes had just fought Peter Buckley at the Light Waves Leisure Centre in Yorkshire. This was a different and very hostile venue. He didn't like it.

Early in the second I feinted to the body and landed a right hook square on his chin. Hughes's legs weren't shaking any more. They buckled. A left, then a right, and referee Paul Thomas was between us.

'Easy, easy, easy,' went up the chants.

The lessons of Voronin had been learned. I had more power as a super bantamweight.

My next three fights were put in place to keep busy and improve my European ranking, but they were not without incident. Two of them were on the road as Peters told RTÉ he would bring me around Europe at some stage. This was also a cost cutter as I became just another fighter on someone else's bill.

Marian Leondraliu was a last-minute replacement for an African guy named Daniel Kodjo Sassou from Togo who Peters had sourced. Kodjo's record was all over the shop and Harry smelt a rat. We had only done four weeks' training and his video didn't arrive until five days before the Saturday bout in Leipzig. Paul McCloskey, the future light welterweight European champion, had been in as a sparring partner the week previous. Paul is a disaster to hit with the way he hunches down below opponents. No harm practising on an awkward fella like Paul.

Harry had relented on the decision to fight Voronin, against his better judgement, and felt my lack of stamina as a featherweight had cost us. He said it was bad planning. He vetoed Kodjo after he saw the video – which was an unofficial fight as well. Harry didn't even show it to me. He just got on to Peters and told him to find another opponent. Africans were dangerous as their records tend to omit the twenty or so knockouts they inflicted deep in the Congo during those long gaps on their official rap sheet.

Kodjo had won just one of his first sixteen fights but Harry said he was too dangerous and I wasn't fighting him. It would have been different if the fight had been in Dublin but it was an away gig for us as well. It was a lose–lose situation with zero potential benefit to my European ranking. Almost certainly a long night with no reward at the end of it. Peters cancelled Kodjo's flights and had to throw him a few quid as compensation.

Peters and Harry had regular spats over prospective opponents but after letting Voronin slide Harry was not prepared to make the same mistake twice. Certainly not so soon after. His attitude was always to err on the side of caution. The European title shot was our only goal; there were guys we had to fight to get that opportunity and there are others we didn't need to test ourselves against until the time was right. There are plenty of hustlers like Kodjo out there. You think you know what you are up against until the bell goes and then you realize it is something completely different.

As Harry said, 'The whole reason we have you home is to control your progress.'

I agreed.

Leondraliu was found on the day. He had been due to fight the following week anyway, so he was in decent shape, but he was a light-weight at best. He came in nine pounds over the weight we had agreed on.

'Get the weight off or you aren't getting paid,' was Harry's stance. By lunchtime they were back in and seven pounds had been shed. Grand. Fight back on.

Harry told me I was good enough to beat whoever was put in front of me and that our preparation was excellent. Just go out and dominate. This is a common occurrence when you are down the card. You suck it up and get to work.

We were so relaxed on the night that when the live TV camera crew crept around our dressing room door the two of us were caught embroiled in an epic game of Don. Instead of the intimidating sight of Bernard Dunne shadow boxing or working up a sweat we were playing cards! It wasn't arrogance, we had trained hard and we were ready. I destroyed Hawkins and then headed to the ring.

It was just a chance to get out. Keep busy. Get a fight in as I'd got very little from Hughes two months previous. A left hook to the body brought matters to a conclusion in the sixth. I boxed clever. Went out and did my job. Not having the pressure of fighting in Dublin seemed to help.

'America is definitely calling us back,' I said afterwards. That was still an option. If an offer came in, I wanted to fight in Las Vegas on a big card.

Noel Wilders changed his mind about retiring and so we rescheduled the bout for January 2006. He had been the EBU champion in 2003 so at least there was pedigree, but really he was out of shape and past his best. Wilders took a sound beating off me over six rounds, and promptly retired for good.

We laugh about Sergio Carlos Santillan now. But not then. The fight that April brought us to Rivarolo Canavese in Piedmont, which is about sixty miles north of Turin. It had been a damp March and everyone in the Hawkins house was laid low with flu the week of the fight. Harry wanted to postpone but that is not how I do business. I refused. I was in bits sitting in the dressing room about two hours before the fight. Harry turned to me and said, 'Are you all right?'

I was hangin'.

'Yeah, I'm grand, Harry.'

He taped me up and said, 'All right, then. I'm off to check this venue out and find out what time we are on. Just try to relax a bit.'

He could see I was pale.

I remember closing my eyes and leaning back against the cold wall. I was trying to slip into fight mode and then I started thinking about nothing at all. Yeah, I'll just relax a bit . . .

Harry came back twenty minutes later to find his contender curled up on the bench, fast asleep.

'Bernard, do you want to wake up there?'

'Jesus, fuck.'

Harry looked concerned. I began dripping sweat.

Santillan had his Argentina football jersey on so I got the local team's strip and wore it into the ring. It was a tiny arena. A handful of people. A few of the hardcore element from west Dublin, naturally.

It was the first fight that RTÉ showed live online.

I saw Tommy McQuillan, a singer who is a friend of Peters, getting into the ring so I presumed he was going to come out with the national anthem. Instead, he started yodelling. I think we were near the Alps, but come on.

If I wasn't about to get into a fight with some chap I knew very little about, in some Italian fuckin' hall, feeling like death warmed up, I might have seen the humour in such a ridiculous situation.

I looked at Harry. 'These Italians must think we are crackers.' Harry noticed they had taken the blue corner. He sent them packing to the red corner as previously agreed. 'Get you over there, boys.' In Belfast they take the corner they are given very seriously.

I dropped the thirty-two-year-old Santillan with a short right – the first shot I landed – but he got back to his feet. We clashed heads. I got cut in the corner of my right eye. A real stinger. There was no brawling on this night. Sergio got a pass. Of course, he would have to be an awkward little bastard. You could hit him with a hammer all day and he would keep coming. He was small and annoying. I couldn't find him. A weak and sluggish eight rounds of boxing. Get the decision, hug my opponent and raise his arm. Visit the red corner, take my pats on the head and out the gate we go.

I was shocked that I could fall asleep before the fight like that. The adrenaline is supposed to be flowing and there I was sleeping like a baby. Lesson learned. Sometimes the body betrays the mind and vice versa.

Two months on, the David Martinez night would be my last visit to the National Stadium for a while, but it will not be remembered for the main event. No, an unscheduled altercation overshadowed what was my most competent showing as a professional up to that juncture.

I only heard about Steve Collins and the Albanian bouncer when Peters told me in the changing room after the fight. Steve had gone outside between the earlier bouts and on re-entry through the VIP door, he was stopped by the security guard, a guy named Adrialik Voda. Steve didn't have his accreditation with him, but explained he was working for television. No accreditation, no entry, came the reply. The guy didn't recognize him. How can you not know who Steve Collins is while working security at a professional fight in Dublin? It was ridiculous. This was a boxing show. Your man may have put his hand on Stephen, who knows? Whatever happened, Steve gave him a dig and that was the end of the argument. It ruined Voda's mouth, though not before his teeth had lacerated the former super middleweight world champion's hand. Dr Joe McKeever dispatched Steve to James Connolly Hospital in Blanchardstown for stitches and a tetanus injection.

It meant Michael Carruth was forced to step up from radio to the television panel and probably ruined Steve's chances of doing any future work with RTÉ. (Collins was charged with assault, but the jury failed to reached a verdict. A retrial was scheduled for November 2010.)

That got rid of one of the two ambulances stationed at the Stadium. The other had to stay in case an injured boxer needed treatment, so a problem arose when an uninvited punter opted against shelling out €50 for a ticket and broke both his legs while trying to scale the back wall. It was that type of night. Crazies everywhere!

Martinez was American and he had that typical American persona, all talk and brashness, at the weigh-in at the Plaza Hotel in Tallaght. He was going to do this and that. I remember Pamela was pregnant at the time with Caoimhe and he said something like he would hate to ruin the birth of my first child by beating me. Plonker.

After the fight, though, he turned out to be a nice guy – he went over to Pam and spoke some kind words.

They call Martinez 'El Finito' and in seventeen professional fights only Tomas Villa had got the better of him – a technical knockout in the tenth round the previous July after a cut opened by a headbutt – so I was prepared for my toughest opponent yet. He, on the other hand, wasn't.

He took too many shots off me. His right eye was closing by the middle rounds. I was hitting him at will. At one stage I was walking back to the corner and I said to referee David Irving, 'How much longer you going to let this go on?' The guy was a punch bag. Considering the state of my right hand, Harry was delighted.

I put on a show. Dropping my arms and sticking out my chin but always ghosting away and landing counterpunches. Harry looked set to burst me.

The end of the one-sided bout came in the eighth when Martinez's trainer Sergio Chavez threw in the towel. The place was heaving that night. The support had gone up another notch. We were in full flow. We needed a bigger arena.

The States was my apprenticeship. I went there wanting to establish myself. I felt I had achieved that now. The idea had been to come home and give it a few fights, then go back to America if it didn't take off. But that was officially shelved by this, my seventh performance since Betts.

Top promoters in England like Frank Maloney were starting to peek in on us. They knew we had the RTÉ deal and that a bit of a stir was building around my progress in Ireland. The promoters all have that same sixth sense: they can smell the money from miles away.

The Martinez exhibition convinced us that now was the time to go for the European crown. Harry looked at me as if to say, 'You see? Work the jab and let the body shots flow.' *Break an opponent's nose and then his ribs*. That was how I put it into my own head. I felt ready.

Harry agreed. Peters agreed. And so did the European Boxing Union.

The next challenge was to transfer the carnival atmosphere of the National Stadium onto a bigger stage. The European champion Michael Hunter had the Borough Hall in Hartlepool doing something similar. But a little pea-sized cyst inside my skull meant I couldn't box in Britain and Hunter wasn't keen on leaving his own backyard to risk everything against an undefeated twenty-six-year-old Dubliner, especially when the IBF world champion Steve Molitor was willing to travel over from Canada.

Hunter went for broke, giving up his European title for a shot at the world crown. The floor was open for purse bids to host a fight for the vacant EBU title between Bernard Dunne and Esham Pickering. The gap had opened for Peters to deliver what we had promised RTÉ.

The Point Depot had been a dormant volcano for ten years. The venue was booked for 11 November. None of us could have imagined the eruption that was to follow.

9. Waiting for Bernard

He's on his way.

Martin Donnelly

The left jab is never for show. It got me through two years in America when I was nursing my right hand. It opened up everything against Esham Pickering. I believed it was my pathway to the world title. I had so much control.

In reality, I was miles off where I needed to be. I had no idea. But I could always box. That became apparent to a wider audience in 2006.

The Point Depot had petered out as a boxing venue. The last big show was in August 1996 when WBO featherweight champion Prince Naseem Hamed forced the corner of a bloodied Manuel Medina to stop him going out for the twelfth round.

I was ringside when Wayne McCullough showed up the previous March to defend his super bantamweight title against José Luis Bueno. My dad brought me to see WBO super middleweight champion Steve Collins fight Cornelius Carr in November 1995 and I was there when Lennox Lewis dismantled my future conditioning coach Justin Fortune earlier that summer. (This was the only non-world-title fight, but Lewis was already on the road to recovering his WBC heavyweight belt from Oliver McCall.)

In just over a year the Point Depot had hosted four major boxing events but they all failed to capture the public's imagination and the trail went cold after Prince Naseem. This was surprising when you consider Collins is a Dub while McCullough's Olympic heroics in Barcelona occurred only three years beforehand.

I was still only a contender. Why would my headlining of the venue be any different? Boxing is a slow burn and we had been stoking the embers for twenty months.

Still, I never, even in my wildest dreams, imagined cramming 7,000 into the old train station for my fight against Pickering. But we did it. We created something special. Not once during all those years chasing my dad's achievements did I ever believe I'd get such an amazing response from the Irish public.

I was twenty-six, unbeaten still and cocksure, but this humbled me. Even the media were wondering, 'How the hell is he doing this?' The boxing fraternity as one were pinching themselves. It was further proof that the country had changed dramatically since the mid-1990s. People had more money in their pockets and they were getting used to being entertained.

Also, we had built up enough momentum to create this madhouse but there was another clever ploy that Brian Peters and RTÉ can take credit for: instead of avoiding other major national sporting events, they made sure a Bernard Dunne show coincided with them. On Saturday 11 November 2006 Ireland beat South Africa 32–15 at Lansdowne Road. Over half the country was already in the pub or melted into their couches from early afternoon. RTÉ merely told everyone to sit tight as there was more sport on the way: Bernard Dunne is fighting in a few hours.

People get very excited about the possibilities of blood being spilt. Once the rugby chatter ran its course, already high on sport, the conversation shifted. People began talking about boxing again.

When the bar-stool experts start lecturing it means the public are hooked.

So, who is this Esham Pickering fella?

Brendan Ingle looks after him.

Oh yeah, he trained Prince Naseem Hamed.

Ingle is from Ringsend.

What ever happened to Naseem?

After years of sticking his chin in people's faces, hands down by his side and relying on lightning reflexes, he was eventually caught out by a hard Mexican lad named Marco Antonio Barrera.

Knocked out?

No, worse. Barrera beat the stuffing out of him for twelve rounds at the MGM Grand in Las Vegas.

Oh dear, a US prime-time humiliation – slapped that puss off his face?

Yeah, at one stage Barrera whipped him into a half-nelson and drove his head into the corner buckle. Shut him up for good.

That was the end of him?

Pretty much. He was jailed earlier this year for dangerous driving. He just got out.

Naz. What a wanker.

Ingle and Naz broke ties before all the problems.

Remember when he fought McCullough?

Yeah, where is McCullough now?

Las Vegas, I think.

What weight was that?

Featherweight.

What is Dunne?

Super bantamweight – one division down.

Is Dunne any good?

Don't know but if you shut up we might find out.

Michael Hunter had gone after Steve Molitor's IBF world title at the Borough Hall in Hartlepool the night before our show at the Point. The Borough Hall was where Hunter took the EBU and Commonwealth belts off Esham Pickering back in October 2005 after a controversial split decision. Hunter was the British champion at the time so it was a mini-unifier; a real English grudge match.

Pickering possibly reached for the stars a little early in his career, bringing the Panamanian WBO bantamweight world champion Mauricio Martinez to Sheffield in December 2000. He was knocked down twice in the first and never made it back to his corner.

Three years later he recovered to capture the European title with a tenth-round stoppage of the Italian Vicenzo Gigliotti in January 2004, defending it twice before Hunter presented him with another chance to reach boxing's elite tier.

Pickering went for broke early, putting Hunter on the floor twice in the opening rounds, but the local man recovered, even doing some damage before the end of the second. Hunter broke Pickering's nose. Harry Hawkins made me sit and watch Pickering walk stubbornly into Hunter's jab for twelve rounds.

'You see? This is how you can become European champion.'

In a split decision two of the judges gave it to Hunter – 114–113 and 115–112 – while the third called it a draw. 'I still feel I won that fight and it's held up my career. I wanted a rematch but Hunter's gone in another direction. Now I've a chance to get back to where I want to be by beating Bernard,' said Pickering.

Losing to Hunter was his own fault. He should have finished him off in the early rounds when he had a chance. He would try the same with me.

Harry rated Pickering higher than Hunter. Physically, Esham is bigger and I knew he was coming to rough me up. It was crucial I avoid letting him work on the inside.

Peters came into his own with the scheduling of the fight by ensuring it was on twenty-four hours after Molitor and Hunter. Twinning the event with the rugby grabbed the floating sports fan in Ireland; putting it in the shadow of Molitor and Hunter made it look like the winner was next in line for the IBF belt. The wily old Dubliner Brendan Ingle, having spent years mentoring kids at St Thomas's gym in Sheffield, including Naseem Hamed and Herol Graham, wasn't long catching on. 'This fight is going to sort out everything. Whoever wins takes a step forward. Whoever loses takes a step back. It's going to be a cracking fight. It's fifty-fifty. It's a world-title eliminator. Don't blink.'

I sat with Harry in the hotel room to watch Hunter and Molitor go at it the night before we were in action. The weigh-in was behind us so I was munching away on something, building up my energy reserves. It was not my immediate concern but if Hunter won we could get him over to Dublin, as the Borough Hall only holds around eight hundred people. But he bottled it. Molitor is a world-class southpaw. Hunter's main strength is his engine. He is a fighter. He sacrificed his aggression by trying to out box the slick action of Molitor. It was a suicidal tactic. The Canadian caught Hunter flush on the chin in the fourth round. By the end of the fifth, Hunter signalled to his corner he'd had enough when gasping for air on his knees as the referee counted for a second time. There was a nasty gash below his right eye. He quit on his knees.

Molitor attempted to unify his IBF title with the WBA in November

2008 but Celestino Caballero had other ideas. Despite fighting on his home patch in Ontario, Molitor seemed to freeze on the night. It can happen to anyone at any time in their career if they are not mentally tuned in. What goes around comes around in this game. Molitor regained the IBF belt in March 2010 by beating Takalani Ndlovu, but how that came about is another story. Caballero remains his only defeat as a professional.

None of this concerned me. I was primed to showcase my own ability on the European stage.

There was an unhealthy build-up to the fight, which I always enjoy. Esham was eleven months out of the ring but looked in decent shape. Either way, there was an arrogance about him and he clearly didn't rate me.

'I can look him in the eye and say I'm going to knock him out. I did it at the weigh-in and he couldn't say it back to me.' He leans over and looks at me. 'I'm going to knock you out.'

My temper stars to boil but I swallow it. For once, I had no interest in pre-fight posturing. This was too important. 'I will do my talking in the boxing ring,' I reply with as much calmness as I can muster. I wasn't going to get dragged into this. All my life I have accepted the challenge to exchange blows; now was the time to get smart. I'll fight, but I'll box first. I didn't think he had the power to knock me out so if it did become a scrap, well and good.

Lord knows there would be unavoidable wars in the pipeline. The con was also fairly obvious. Pickering was thirty and didn't have a heavy punch but he was a tough customer and had made a career of going toe to toe.

This was my first big chance at realizing a long-stated ambition. No thanks, Esham. I'm going to box.

My life outside the ring had changed dramatically leading up to this massive moment in my career. Caoimhe Dunne arrived into the world on 1 July 2006. She was two weeks late but we forgave her. It quickly became apparent that I would forgive this little girl anything. She has realized that by now as well. I had to leave Pamela and our baby daughter to prepare for the fight. Pam couldn't have been more supportive.

That allowed me to focus. Thankfully, there were two other mothers down the road in Neilstown and Ballyfermot, both with unbeaten records over long careers, to lend a hand.

After a month working in St Matthew's alongside Dad, and Harry coming down on weekends, I legged it up to Belfast to avoid all the nappy-changing. Six weeks of Noreen's cooking as well. It was great food but there was not much of it. Sharon Madigan's diet ensured I weighed in at a scrawny 121 pounds – the lightest I have ever been. I felt in great shape though.

'I just need to be up here,' I told Maria Horgan's hand-held camera as we drove to the Holy Trinity. 'I need to be focused on what I am doing. I'm on the phone to Pamela quite a bit. She lets me know how her nights go. I let her know that I had a good sleep. That's the only unfair part. Pamela has to do everything at the moment. That's not really fair on her, but it's important to both of us that I achieve my goal and win a European title. I've trained all my life now for this. It is a couple of small sacrifices you make now that will pay off later in life. This is what I want to do.'

We had Andrew Wallace back in for most of the sparring. Andrew is an English featherweight based in Belfast who does what he is asked. He can take a dig too. On the first week of training I gave him a cut above his eye. We bandaged it up, gave him the weekend off, but back he came on Monday, eager as ever. Andrew was rewarded with fights on my previous undercards in the Stadium and he got to perform at the Point, beating Nikita Lukin over eight rounds. He deserved it for going ten rounds every day, without complaining, with a busted eye.

On 21 October we did a public training session in the National Stadium. Sugar Ray Leonard and Barry McGuigan were in town to keep the media happy.

Back up in Belfast we brought in Martin Lindsay due to his similarities to Pickering. Andrew was back, along with Damaen Kelly, a former world champion at flyweight under the watchful eye of Mickey Hawkins. We used Damaen for his speed. They were a decent mix of styles each day. I was happy with the quality of each spar.

My hands were delicately double wrapped and religiously iced each night.

We came down to Dublin on the Wednesday. I stopped in with Pam and Caoimhe for a night, before setting up camp in the Burlington on the Thursday. The city was tuned in and up for the fight. I could feel it everywhere I went.

The morning of the weigh-in Harry got a little feel for the buzz around the city. I sensed it immediately. We came out of the Burlington for a stroll in towards St Stephen's Green when a few winos stopped me. Harry walked on but had to come back as a crowd of people on their lunch break had gathered around for a chat. That felt good.

We had been selling my name for almost two years to the public. It helped that I was undefeated. Now there was a title fight in town and people began climbing onto the bandwagon. We had room for everyone. They wanted to believe. I just had to give them a reason.

When we get to the Point on Saturday night the place is already buzzing. Everyone I see on the way in seems excited. Always a good sign.

Peters has a few tricks up his sleeve to unsettle our lippy English friend. Esham Pickering comes into the ring at 10.40 p.m. I haven't even laced up my gloves. There is a thirteen-minute delay between entrances.

The crowd go a little over the top, with someone throwing a coin at Esham on his way to the ring. He didn't deserve that.

Pickering is going nuts waiting. 'Jesus, this is long,' he says. His cornermen go over to Martin Donnelly: 'Where is he? Is he coming out or wha'?'

'He's on his way,' Donnelly, towering over them, replies politely.

Back in the changing room everything is calm, although we decide not to play cards and I manage to stay awake.

Simple stuff from Harry: 'This is your time. All the work is done. Go and get it now, kid.'

'Bernard Dunne – champion of Europe. I like the sound of that,' I reply.

'Right, let's go,' Harry is always calm but I can see he is excited. His confidence helps me.

I appear up on the balcony overlooking the ring. Hood up. The crowd go bananas.

It is a hoax. I'm backstage listening to the madness. It was actually the 1992 Olympian Paul Griffin in disguise. We are the same shape.

Pickering is bouncing off the walls.

The uilleann pipes of Seán Óg Potts start up next.

The smoke machines are switched on. 'O Fortuna', the theme tune from *The Omen*, takes over. The curtain drops and there I am for real as 'The Irish Rover' cranks up. A wave of noise washes over me. Jesus, the place is heaving. This is a new experience. We ain't in Albuquerque, New Mexico or Norman, Oklahoma any more. The natives are restless. Mostly Dubliners. All in party mood.

It is an amazing walk to the ring. Paul 'Pillar' Caffrey and some of the Dublin footballers are in my path. I have gotten to know Jason Sherlock well over the years. The team presented me with a signed jersey earlier in the week. That meant a lot.

I can see Pickering pacing in the ring. Everyone in the place feels they are in on riling him up. Dubs love to mess with your head. I take my time. Don't you know boxing is a slow burn? No point getting too excited now.

Esham tries to get in my face as I duck under the ropes but the Clare man mountain moves between the skinny fighters. Martin Donnelly is more than just a sponsor.

'You're in my town now, son.' I meet his aggression with some of my own.

He was all mouth and I let him know it. Brendan Ingle gets into his fighter's ear.

Harry cuts across my eyeline.

'Box clever. Nice and sharp. See the shots coming. Hands up. Okay?'

Okay. I can't take my eyes off Pickering.

The Celtic Tenors belt out 'Amhrán na bhFiann'.

Just before the bell I look into the crowd. No crimes in Dublin when I am boxing. The crooks, the cops, politicians, boy-band singers, reality-television celebs, sportsmen and soap stars populate the first five rows.

Forget all that. This is about me and Esham. Everything I had done, all my life's work, has been building up to this moment. I relax. Nerves are no use here. Nerves will stop my jab from working. This opportunity might not come around again. Not on my terms, anyway.

I am going to enjoy myself. So much has changed since the Adrian Valdez fight two years ago. I feel comfortable. On that night in Saint Paul there were half a dozen Dubs chanting behind Pamela and Tommy Egan when they saw I was in trouble. Tonight, 7,000 lunatics have escaped from the asylum.

Usually the crowd has no impact on me but, on this night, their energy surges through my body. Something special is happening.

I know most of Neilstown is in the building. My family are decked out in Team Dunne colours – black and gold specially designed T-shirts. Even Ma and Pamela.

Finches is packed. Clondalkin is a ghost town. Everyone crammed into the pubs to see the home-town boy try and take the big step.

The National Stadium is empty. The lights are out, doors locked.

I start perfectly. Good right hands send Pickering against the ropes. The crowd gets the opening three minutes they desire. They respond with an avalanche of noise. We are of Dublin.

Harry pulls me onto the stool.

'Focus, Bernard.'

Back to the game plan. Benny King, my Scottish cut man, leans in for a look. Benny will be needed later. He always is with me.

The left jab ruins Italian referee Massimo Barrovecchio's shirt early in the second round when I break Pickering's nose with a cracking combination.

He is worrying about the jab now. This allows me to start unloading double right hands. He isn't ready for them. It is a new string to my bow. A special gift for Pickering. Straight right hands one after the other.

Esham is all about angles and trickery. Switch hitting. This is when he switches feet and brings his hands across at the same time. He always seems off balance, which means I can pick him off. He is physically stronger but the power behind the blows is nothing to worry about.

There is no love lost. He has been promising to do all sorts to me. I clock his head back with a jab. Straight right. Another straight right. I'll do my talking in the ring, you gobshite.

I box like never before. I go up to the level I have hinted at these past two years. Controlled, clean shots. No brawling, just combinations. When he eventually starts covering the jab and countering the double rights I unload with a left hook to the body.

Back to Harry.

'Pick the shot. Everything off the left jab. Keep your distance.'

His voice was full of enthusiasm. I could also hear Dad in the front row.

Hands up, Bernard.

That's it!

Keep boxing, Bernard. Keep boxing!

I can always hear my dad. He has gone silent. As usual, that is a good sign or a really bad sign. I know it is a good sign. The crowd gets louder but, by now, they are just a slight din in my ears.

I keep seeing Esham's left hand coming so I punch over it with my right. My timing is excellent tonight. The blood is flowing out of his nose.

Ingle is trying to get him to force the pace but the busted nose is probably affecting his breathing. Four rounds all to me. Back in the corner Harry is animated. He is doing an impression of what he wants.

'One, two step. Bang. Keep working that.'

He wants a straight one-two combination, sway off Pickering's counter and then counter his left with a straight right. It is all working. We had talked about this a lot in the previous week. The closer you get to a fight the more tactical it gets.

Ingle is screaming: 'He is tiring, he is tiring.' I wasn't. Five rounds all to me. They are trying to pick him up. My corner has become a mantra. Harry on the fight plan. I like that. It is calming.

I am moving a lot. I am slipping his best digs. He is clever enough to recognize the damage that could be done by getting inside and leaning on me. It begins to sap my energy. I have never gone twelve rounds but Pickering has only done it twice himself – against Hunter and when he lost on a split decision to Alejandro Monzon in the Canary Islands. So many fighters would have been great if not for those twelve three minutes. They can crush your spirit. Most guys need to get the job done quickly.

He has a good go in the eighth. I am tiring now. The ninth is harder

still so I stay away. He can have these two rounds because I know my
second wind will bring me home. I am supremely confident. What a night.

He hits me after the bell at the end of the ninth. I try to retaliate as
there is no way I am letting him away with that. The place explodes
in anger. Ringside security earn their night's pay. Massimo pushes me
to the canvas as he separates us. Harry is in the middle of the ring just
in case. So is Ingle.

Harry Hawkins and Brendan Ingle – well-travelled ships brush past
each other between the ninth and tenth rounds. Just in the eyes. Howya,
old man. Howya, kid. Two of the same breed. Words are not required.

Pickering comes hard in the twelfth round. He needs a knockout.

Keep moving and he cannot hurt me. Caution, but my energy levels
are unreal as we enter the last minute. I break my golden rule and let
them in. The crowd's volume gets turned up. Their collective voice is
carrying me home.

I hear Peters yell, 'Thirty seconds!'

I'm going to be European champion in twenty-nine seconds. Ring
the fucking bell. He lunges and connects but I easily dodge the full brunt
of it. He comes again. I time my counter-right to perfection over his
straight left. Then I stand there, raise my right arm and attempt a bolo
punch. It doesn't really come off but I finish with a flourish. It is over.

We celebrate. Everyone is in the ring. My family and Martin
Donnelly. Friends of Martin – Dave Cribbons and Declan Crowe – are
hugging me.

Ring announcer Mike Goodall takes over:

'Jean-Louis Legland, 111 to 117.'

'Freddy Christensen, 111 to 117.'

'Kurt Stroer, 113 to 115.'

I get a little shock. The ringside judge from Germany must have
been checking out the ring girls for half the fight. One round fucking
swing!

Is something horrible about to happen? Boxing is littered with inex-
plicable yet official scorecards.

'By unanimous decision, all three are in favour of the winner and
new super bantamweight champion of Europe . . .'

Everybody starts celebrating. The crowd, my dad, my ma, Harry punches the air, Donnelly and Pamela are jumping up and down. They all forget it was a vacant title – either of us could be the new champion. I don't move a muscle. Neither does Peters.

'. . . Bernard Dunne.'

I sink to my knees. Jesus, this feels good.

I am the seventh Irishman to win a European title.

They bang on the 'Put em under pressure' tune that leads into choruses of *Olé, olé-olé-olé*. The place somehow finds another decibel level.

This is my first real taste of big-time success. It is what I have always wanted.

Peters follows me wherever the camera goes. He loves his face on television. Perched on my shoulder.

Several columnists had got a day's work out of me by criticizing RTÉ's loyalty and patience. Many people had been drumming their fingers for over a year. They didn't understand the boxing game. They may have learned something new tonight. They probably got another column out of it as well. I understand how it all works, but this was the whole reason I came home.

There is always the loser's tale and Esham Pickering's eventually took him to the city of Donetsk in Ukraine.

The defeat at the Point wasn't his last chance. A boxer can always rationalize going one more time. He won his next three fights in England but somehow lost on points to Sean Hughes twelve months later. Yes, Sean Hughes who was intimidated by the National Stadium crowd. He quickly got a rematch and stopped Hughes in the ninth, though the horse appeared to have bolted on Esham. But two defeats and one win later, in September 2009 Pickering was given a crack at the EBU featherweight champion Oleg Yefimovych. Dropped twice in the second, but saved by the bell, he was knocked out early in the third by an overhand right. All the way to Ukraine to be a pay-day opponent.

I promised myself I would never become that kind of fighter.

There is a party back in the Burlington. I am stiff but I go in for a few minutes. My hands are aching. We try to slip in the side door but get spotted and I'm carried in on top of people's shoulders. I do ten minutes of pictures and chatting before disappearing upstairs. I am European champion now so someone brings the ice buckets up to the room. I don't have to go searching like that time against Angelo Luis Torres in the Marconi Automotive museum in California. No one is asking me to cash cheques for them either. I must be moving up in the world.

Yeah, this is one of the more enjoyable sleepless nights. I think back to my time in the Vagabond Inn. The sounds down below are similar. People cutting loose. Tonight they are drinking to Bernard Dunne's European title. They can make all the noise they like.

I am a confident man but I understand the folly of arrogance. Yet, I still want so much more. I know I'm capable of it. Pamela has dozed off beside me. Caoimhe is at home with her grandmother Olive. I remove my hand from the bucket. It burns. This is the life. Swollen head. Broken hands. I don't get carried away.

Fuck this. I deserve to get paid but forget about me for a second. Time to start showing this little family of mine the fruits of my labour. The two girls in my life deserve more for all this sacrifice. I am European champion now. I am packing out the Point Depot. Live on RTÉ television. All this money being made off my swollen head and broken hands while I have yet to secure Pamela and Caoimhe's future. I dip the metacarpals back into the ice bucket and munch on a sandwich for the first time in weeks. I missed bread. And ketchup. And onion rings. And mayonnaise. Sweet, sweet mayonnaise.

It is a couple of small sacrifices you make now that will pay off later in life.

It *is* later in life. Yeah, time to start looking after my family.

The end-of-year awards circuit followed a few weeks later and I was in demand. I was back in the Burlington for the Texaco Sports Awards. I went home early. Harry and Peters got talking about the next move. Harry did some sums out loud. A packed-out Point Depot is 7,000 seats, right? Peters was already talking about booking Croke Park for a world-title fight.

Harry told Peters I should be paid what I was entitled to straight away.

I got €80,000 for winning the European title. Myself and Peters had a big whopper of a fight not long after when he offered me just €100,000 for my first defence. It was 2006. Things were still on the up and up.

'Are you for real? Is that all you can offer me?' I shouted. 'We are packing the Point. You have the RTÉ deal hidden away in your back pocket. How much is that worth?'

He would never tell me, of course.

I'd delivered my end of the bargain and all he could come up with was a hundred grand? The cheapest ticket was sixty euros. It was €250 for a ringside seat. I might have been punched in the head a lot but I wasn't stupid.

I let it go for a while but my resentment was simmering beneath the surface and it was only a matter of time before I blew a gasket.

There was another serious row about the lack of marketing of me outside the ring now I was European champion. I thought Peters was dragging his feet. He told Rosie in his office to do it. I'm sure she did her best but she is an administrator. Marketing a European champion was hardly her area of expertise.

I told Peters I'd do it myself and suddenly he had sponsors for me. Hunky Dory Crisps were there and Ladbrokes the bookmakers were involved.

A few days after beating Pickering I was asked to parade the European belt on the pitch for the last soccer match at the old Lansdowne Road: Ireland's World Cup qualifier against San Marino. I was shocked when I noticed Peters coming out beside me. The impression he gave was that we were blood brothers. Best of mates. A fella called Brian Whitehead intervened and said to let me go out on my own.

I was in the Irish dressing room afterwards. John O'Shea of Manchester United gave me his jersey. It was hard to accept it from a Manc but John is a real gentleman. All my mates enjoyed his company when we crossed paths for a few pints.

Whether you like it or not, things change when you become European champion.

The day after the fight we all went to the Silver Granite pub in Palmerstown and eventually headed into town. I was famous all of a sudden. This means people want to approach you. Especially young people full up on drink. They are not intimidated. They want to stand beside you with a clenched fist. The invention of camera phones must be every celebrity's worst nightmare! You can't be rude, but Caoimhe would get scared when teenagers started surrounding us in a supermarket. I would politely ask for some space. Nothing is more important than family.

I kept my feet on the ground as I was well aware of the potential pitfalls that come with notoriety. Life in California was an eye-opener in this regard. You start rubbing shoulders with all types. Watching Ray Leonard certainly helped. Generally, though, you can tell if someone is just being a fair-weather friend.

I met most of the so-called famous people of this little, big city. I even went out on the town with one or two of them. But I got bored of all that very quickly and was soon back training.

Yersin Jailauov from Kazakhstan was eventually pencilled in for 25 March 2007, back in the Point. It was a Sunday, which was a risk, but Peters knew his business. We had a classy Mongolian featherweight, Choijiljavyn 'Choi' Tseveenpürev, in for sparring. He was a great opponent and keen to mix it up. People would have paid to see us spar.

I couldn't concentrate properly, though. I was still seething about Peters. It was a Tuesday at the end of February when I finally lost it. I was sitting in my room back in Harry's after a good session in the gym when I discovered the ticket prices for my first defence as European champion had been hiked up.

Something clicked in my brain. I went through another sleepless night thinking about the big picture. The next morning I told Harry I was going home.

'You can't just up and leave training camp. What the fuck are you doing?'

I explained it all to Harry. 'I'm not fighting unless I get paid what I am due. Peters thinks I am going to keep taking what *he* thinks I am worth. Well, I'm not.'

Harry tried to convince me to stay for another good day of sparring but I refused. I wanted to drive to Dunshaughlin and have it out with Peters. I was in a dangerous mood. Harry convinced me to drive to Dublin instead, and he would set up a meeting.

We had to send Choi home early. That was a waste of a great spar. But something had to give. All I could think about was the need to start looking after my family's future.

Harry arranged a meeting for the Sunday at the County Club. I brought it forward to Friday night in my house in Palmerstown, where we had moved the previous summer in preparation for the new addition to the family we were expecting in December. My territory this time. The meeting took place in my front room.

I had barely calmed down when the meeting started and wasn't long getting my point across. I felt like I was being robbed and I said as much.

Brian Peters always sold us as a team. He portrayed himself as my friend and my mentor to the media.

He spoke of the massive expenses he was incurring.

At midnight the meeting was adjourned until the morning. At 11 a.m. Brian returned with a list of expenses that, according to him, meant he was running shows at a loss.

I told him what I was worth. From his initial offer of €100,000 we eventually got up to €225,000, but only after I threatened not to fight. I know it was just business but the manner he went about it disgusted me. True, Peters always delivered the fight dates, but I believe that was as much down to RTÉ being loyal to their commitments.

We went back to work and I presumed all the problems were sorted. I was unaware that Harry was now shielding me entirely from Peters, who was constantly complaining about money at this point. Matthew Macklin and Neil Sinclair were dropped off the bill due to my increase in pay.

I went on the *Late Late Show* a few days later. It was a great opportunity to publicize the fight but there was no sign of Brian Peters. He could have sold out the Point on prime-time television. A week before the fight he wanted another meeting, with Martin Donnelly to mediate, but Harry stated it would ruin my focus. I only heard about it afterwards.

I fought Jailauov the day after the Republic of Ireland's 1–0 defeat of Wales at Croke Park. The first soccer international in GAA headquarters.

Again, I was given the honour of walking out to salute the crowd with my belt. Stephen Ireland scored the winner.

Despite most of the 8,000 punters having to show up for work on the Monday morning, they came to see Jailauov get destroyed. I appreciated that and told the crowd as much afterwards. It also seemed to be a promotional success.

Jailauov's record was nineteen wins and four defeats but he was a handy voluntary defence. I was enjoying myself.

He was a boxer who never learned how to keep his hands up. My jab was rocking his head backwards within seconds. He was smaller than me, which was rare, and he wasn't throwing many punches so I finished it in the third.

The undefeated Kiko Martinez was being mentioned at regular intervals as a challenger for my European title, but I liked the idea of facing Reidar Walstad again. The Norwegian had outclassed me as an eighteen-year-old, when he was twenty, in the European amateurs. It was my second major international event. I was inexperienced back then. Now I was the European champion, it would be different. Reidar is a decent chap but he was saying I was the same type of fighter and predicted a similar result to what had happened in Belarus nine years earlier.

Apart from the fact that Harry Hawkins was still manning my corner, everything had changed since then. Still, it was in the back of my head that he had beaten me. He had a decent record as a professional with only one defeat. He was strong but I had been grappling with Rocky Dean and two hungry Venezuelans in preparation. They were small, explosive and just tried to walk on in and pound me.

A fortnight before the fight Peters landed in camp crying about money again.

Another meeting was scheduled for the County Club with Martin acting as mediator. Peters claimed to have made only €2,000 profit from the Jailauov full house. He couldn't afford my fight fee. He asked me to take a drop in pay.

I refused to bend. You don't have long in this game. Harry had always insisted I keep my cool during meetings with Peters no matter what was said. Also, we never made a decision on the spot. We would go away and discuss it. Give him no read. A week before the fight he was back at Harry's door and eventually I relented and agreed to a drop in pay. I should have had tunnel vision on the fight but Peters was distracting me with money issues. Hardly ideal preparation for my second defence.

I went on Miriam O'Callaghan's chat show with Michael Carruth and Barry McGuigan a week before the fight. Again, this was a chance at free publicity to flog tickets but Peters was nowhere to be found. We presumed he was sulking.

Harry was unhappy about the decision to fight Walstad. He didn't see the need to have such a dangerous opponent as a voluntary. Harry was always looking at the big picture. Small steps before any big leap. Peters set it up because he knew he could market the amateur defeat. We all knew the Point Depot was closing at the end of August so the mandatory defence would need to be squeezed in before then to ensure maximum return. It was planned that I'd be fighting Kiko Martinez in a couple of months, so Harry wanted me to have an easy night. Avoid a twelve-rounder. Let's just knock some guy out and get out of there. He was more worried about my right hand than I was.

I was not concerned by Walstad or Kiko or anyone else for that matter. I really believed I could handle whatever came my way.

Reidar Walstad comes out, hands held high, dips his shoulder and flings a big right that grazes my chin. He should have saved it up. It could have knocked me out but he gets too trigger happy with the right hand. It would have hurt me but now I know where it is coming from. I begin to time and slip it before delivering some nice left hooks.

I hit him with a counter-right at the end of the first round that shakes him. That's the end of my right hand. Shock waves up to my shoulder. It is throbbing. Back to America. Fighting with one good hand.

The left jab needs to dominate Walstad. It shatters his face. He keeps trying to bang over the top. I mix it up and down. Slip off at angles. Some really cracking left uppercuts straight up the middle.

It is a right hook that ruins his plan of walking in hands up and trying to trade shots – this is his only option: bully his way in and do some damage, but now he is cut over the left eye.

I move, keep a distance between us with the jab and punish him with the hook. Slow it all down. My belt, my pace.

Inevitably, the heads, elbows and low blows start flying. I am European champion. Any challenger will do whatever it takes.

He practically runs over to meet me in my corner at the start of every round. I hurt him again with my right hand but instantly regret it. More shock waves up the arm. Jesus, I'm not doing that any more. Left jabs for the rest of the night.

In the fifth round we trade shots. He catches me some decent digs and raises his hands in the air. I am cut. It is not a new one. I smile. I step back. Jab. Raise my right hand in the air and throw out the left. He marches in. Bang. Pot shot. Left hook.

Walstad is dangerous when he gets inside but the cut above his eye is getting nasty. I go to work on it for the rest of the night. At the start of the seventh we clash heads and the wound starts spurting blood. It is deep. He motions as if it is my fault. I catch him there again. The doctor looks at it twice.

It is more ripped flesh than burst blood vessels so it doesn't bleed that heavily. He is desperately trying to knock me out, knowing they could stop the fight at any time. Every round starts at a rapid pace. It should be stopped. It is the worst cut I have ever seen. It reminds me of the one I sustained in Sydney.

In fairness, Reidar has genuine heart. He keeps coming. I am taller with a better reach so, again, I keep him off until the temptation to mix it becomes overwhelming. I finish the twelfth by pinning him against the ropes and delivering a little flurry that the crowd enjoys. It felt like a comfortable night but the Spanish judge José Vilas Muller manages to score it 115–113 despite the two men sitting beside him seeing a completely different exchange of blows. Richard Davies of England marks it as 118–111 and Heinrich Muehmert of Germany scores it 116–112. It is scary how wrong some of these guys can get it.

Kiko Martinez was at home in Spain watching how low I kept my left hand. He saw how Walstad tried to finish me early. He felt he could do better. Kiko is five foot five inches, just a half inch taller than Walstad. There was a chance to explode over my guard. In the ring after Walstad,

Peters confirmed the little Spaniard mandatory challenger was coming to the closing-down party at the Point Depot on 25 August.

My boxing technique had delivered a European title and I firmly believed I was reaching my full potential. I was wrong. I was maturing as a man – fatherhood will do that to you – but I lacked the power to go any further. I struggled in the featherweight division so we dropped to super bantamweight. That was a short-term solution.

There were storm clouds on the horizon. It was the summer of 2007. The economic good times were at an end and my climb up the boxing ranks was about to hit a hard dose of reality.

I should have realized nothing was ever going to run smoothly in this boxing career of mine.

10. Kiko

Everyone underestimated Kiko Martinez. Everyone except Harry. I was supposed to use the same tactics as against Reidar Walstad.

'It is crucial, Bernard, that you keep him on the end of your jab for the first four rounds. After that you will punch holes in him.'

So Harry visibly gasps when I stand tall and fire off a combination about ten seconds into the fight.

I was confident I could handle whatever Kiko had to offer. I was unaware of my limitations. I was caught cold. I could make excuses all day but it wouldn't change the fact that I got knocked out. It happens in boxing. I had done it to fourteen other guys.

Ask Ali. Ask Barry McGuigan. Ask Sugar Ray. What goes around eventually comes around in this sport and when it does you know all about it. Actually, that's not true: when it comes, you know nothing about it. That is the killer. Everything you are certain of is stripped away. That's why most boxers can't come back from it.

The build-up was all a little rushed, with constant distractions over money. I went twelve rounds with Walstad on 23 June and Kiko followed on 25 August. I had to restart serious training less than a fortnight after defending my EBU title, but I have no complaints. I felt in perfect physical condition.

And yet, the back story to my third defence of that title is a perfect case study of just how ridiculous professional boxing can be.

On 11 May 2007 Pat Magee, the manager and sometime promoter of Harry's other professional fighter Brian Magee, had called Harry Hawkins to cancel their weekly round of golf. Pat was in Alicante. He has just signed up the promising young Spaniard Kiko Martinez. He had been trying to get involved with my career for a while now, and this was his chance. Since I'd returned from America, Pat couldn't but notice the full houses at the National Stadium, the exposure on RTÉ and my general marketability.

As Brian Magee's representative, Pat was a regular visitor up in Turf Lodge. I knew him well from being around the gym. He had brokered my initial deal with Panos and Frank Maloney after the Sydney fiasco and probably would have ended up directly involved in my career if my brain problems had not sent me to America. Having been in at the ground floor, he felt entitled to a piece of the action now we were filling the Point Depot. Now he'd signed up Martinez, the mandatory challenger in line for my title.

Harry was shocked and annoyed by this latest development and told Pat as much but he said nothing to anybody else, me included. He was already fuming over Walstad being thrown in as a voluntary defence with Kiko in the pipeline. This new piece of information would prove irrelevant if I failed to put the Norwegian away. He also had a cheque for €300,000 burning a hole in his pocket.

Unbeknownst to me, around the time of the meeting with Peters in my Palmerstown front room, Pat Magee had made a move for my signature. Pat presented Harry with a cheque for €300,000 to give to me. Harry had put it to one side. Now wasn't the time, he thought. Let's deal with one promoter/manager at a time.

Unlike most people, Harry can shoulder heavy burdens while staying focused on the job at hand, but he had just entered nightmare territory. He was trying to balance my training, and that of Brian Magee, while keeping the next wave of Holy Trinity boxers streaming through. Now he was stuck between two promoters, and promoters are all the same. Thankfully, Harry was immune to their powers. He would never compromise his fighters' careers in exchange for what they could offer. Heroically, he held them off. He was under immense strain that was only going to get worse, but he never once showed signs of buckling under.

Pat Magee may have been an old friend and golfing buddy but he was a businessman first.

Harry and Noreen's twenty-fifth wedding anniversary was on 28 May. He convinced Noreen to come down to Dublin for the weekend so he could train me at Dad's boxing gym, St Matthew's in Ballyfermot.

Peters was on to him, moaning about ticket sales for the Walstad fight. Harry explained how he was thanking his wife for twenty-five years of loyalty. In the heat of constant bickering, the two men could only laugh. Peters was back on a few minutes later.

'Harry, forget your plans. You and Noreen are staying in the Merrion Hotel and there is a table booked in Patrick Guilbaud's restaurant. Enjoy.' Five star, all expenses paid. Again, that is Peters. Out of nowhere he will bring you to a cash-and-carry and tell you to fill up the car. He could be generous like that, but all I ever wanted from him was what I deserved. I wanted the money so I could buy my own food.

That was only a brief truce, as once Peters found out about Pat Magee he became openly hostile towards Harry.

The next summit meeting took place a week after Walstad, on Thursday 28 June at the County Club in Dunshaughlin. Harry, Peters, myself and Martin Donnelly to mediate. Money was the problem once again. Peters was concerned that the Kiko Martinez show wouldn't be a success. Harry encouraged him to work with Pat Magee as it was clear Pat wasn't afraid to throw money at the promotion up front.

Peters and Magee did little to disguise their contempt for each other. But Peters had left the gate open for a fight with Kiko. Ever since I'd beaten Esham Pickering, Kiko had been on the horizon.

In addition to his business partner John Rooney, Pat Magee had drafted in Denis Hobson, who was promoter for Ricky Hatton at the time and had contacts at Setanta Sports – who ended up with rights to replay the fight. They thought they could sell the fight to Setanta.

It looked as though they planned to muscle in on Brian Peters Promotions. Pat threatened at one point to outbid Peters at the purse bids and take the fight to Spain.

Stuck squarely in the middle of all this, Harry pushed for a co-promotion.

I wasn't privy to the meetings between Hobson, Magee, Rooney ('Team Magee') and Peters, but everyone admits it was a struggle to reach an agreement.

I felt nothing but hatred for Peters by this stage, as he never seemed to be acting in my best interests, but Harry kept reminding me of the problems countless other boxers had faced with other promoters and managers in Britain. They were always having dates cancelled, he told me. And, to be fair, when Peters and RTÉ said they were putting on a show, they always did. Their record was impeccable.

On 12 July, for the Orangemen's Day bank holiday up North, Harry took Noreen for what he intended would be a nice, peaceful drive around the Vale of Avoca in County Wicklow. At this point there was the very real threat that Peters and Magee would put aside their personal differences and carve up the spoils by making a minimum-purse joint bid (this sort of collusion is common in boxing). Since my pay was 55 per cent of the purse, that would be a disaster for me. Harry spent most of his bank-holiday drive juggling phone calls between me, Peters and Pat Magee. After several hours Noreen turned to Harry as his phone rang yet again while they were overlooking some scenic mountain: 'Let's just drive back home, shall we?'

The three-way call with Magee and Peters lasted the entire journey from Wicklow to Belfast. Not many women would put up with that. Noreen Hawkins is a saint.

A deal was struck that ensured my best ever pay day, but that was not the end of the bitter rivalry between Magee and Peters.

Two days later the American-based Derry middleweight John Duddy fought Alessio Furlan at the National Stadium. Duddy stopped him in the tenth and last round. I was there and so was Kiko. We climbed into the ring together as my mandatory title defence against him was officially confirmed for 25 August at the Point. Harry regrets not insisting on more time to prepare, but the Point was soon to close down for a complete refurbishment and that deadline dictated everything.

Training started straight away in St Matthew's. Harry stayed in Dublin for a week and then we both travelled up to Belfast for a five-week camp. Rocky Dean was back in for sparring with Stevie Foster Jr stretching the rounds out. Peters also drafted in the undefeated Spaniard Sergio Blanco and a Mexican guy named Jorge Perez.

I began trying to develop my usual tunnel vision, but it didn't last long.

Peters landed into Holy Trinity about a fortnight before the fight. Ticket sales were a disaster, he said. He wanted me to take another cut. I was just finished three rounds with Blanco.

The latest problems stemmed from it being a co-promotional event. Peters was put out about sharing the event with Magee and, from where I was standing, he was not flogging tickets in the same enthusiastic manner as his one-man shows. The recession was looming and belts were tightening, but I felt he had not done enough. I told him to stop sulking and promote the show like he had the previous cards.

Around this time, Harry landed at my door with the cheque for €300,000 to sign with Pat Magee.

'This I have to give to you,' he said.

There were no strings attached. 'It is your decision what you do with it. Your career.'

I turned down the offer. Trying to get out of my contract with Peters would have meant a messy court case and I wasn't going to put my career on hold again.

My fight fee from Team Magee, as the promoters, was €300,000. When Peters got wind of this he suddenly became my manager again. He wanted his 25 per cent. 'If you want to be my manager, I'll need a new promoter,' I told him. It was eventually sorted out some time after the fight, when Martin Donnelly was drafted in to bang heads together, as he described it, and we agreed on 12.5 per cent. That was fair enough with me – I still got my pay day. Peters got his €37,500.

We kept the tension out of the public eye but Maria Horgan was able to capture it: *In terms of boxing, Brian wouldn't have any influence over my boxing. Brian's never boxed in his life. But he knows how to organize things and how to run a business and that kind of stuff*, I said frankly to camera.

I've been really boxing non-stop this year. Been away from the family non-stop.

Cut to the gym and Harry overseeing my workout: *You're into your last minute. Push it.*

Back to me: *And with Pamela being pregnant again, it is really not fair on her for me to be away for so long.*

Back to the gym and Harry giving instructions: *And the last one. Side to side. You'll have to do plenty of them for Martinez.*

It's been tough, I have to say, I tell her, *but it has been a good year for me. An enjoyable year. It really has been. It's been the biggest year for me yet.*

And so it had, but my confidence was masking deep-rooted problems.

It was the most impressive bill I had ever headlined. Brian Magee was on the undercard, so we were training together. Brian is one of the most dedicated trainers in the business. We went running together most mornings. Brian was fighting for the British light heavyweight title against Tony Oakey. This was the first time a British title had been contested outside the jurisdiction of the BBBC. They sold it as a historic moment. Nobody really cared. But it was a good opportunity for Brian as he was coming back from the only knockout of his career. A year previous, Carl Froch had stopped him in the eleventh to retain the British and Commonwealth super middleweight titles. Brian had won all three of his fights since then and was now ready for another title shot.

Pat Magee wanted his other fighter on the bill regardless of the mounting costs. It meant Harry had two corners to run. He had always insisted this would never happen, but he was already doing enough fire-fighting in other areas as my unofficial manager. Of course, a tit-for-tat situation then developed, with Peters putting his boy Matthew Macklin on as well. Then another of his fighters, Andy Lee, comes in from America.

The result of the Oakey fight hardly helped Harry either. Judges Terry O'Connor and John Lewis scored it as a draw while Mickey Vann gave it to Brian, 116–113. Oakey retained his title as it went down as a majority draw.

'A disgusting decision,' was how Harry described it, but he refocused as soon as he entered my changing room.

The great boxing trainer Emanuel Steward – of the Kronk gym in Detroit that produced Tommy 'The Hitman' Hearns – was back in the Point for the first time since Lennox Lewis's fight against Justin Fortune in 1995 as his prodigy Andy Lee had little problem taking care of Ciaran Healy in four rounds. Ricky Hatton worked Matthew Macklin's corner as he knocked out Darren Rhodes, also in the fourth. So there was an entertaining build-up to the main event.

Peters explains to the camera how things are developing: *I think Pat just realized – he says, 'So we are going to take a bath' – it means we are going to lose money on tonight's show. Someone comes in and they see the place and it's packed – they think, sure, Peters is getting a fortune.*

He might be getting a fortune but he is giving out two fortunes. That's the fucking problem.

How many seats are we down? Monetary-wise we are down about a hundred and sixty. Thousand. I don't think there is 4,200 seats sold. So, that wouldn't pay for a lot now.

Whenever I negotiated fees with Peters he could never remember how much he made on the shows. Yet he was able to list off his losses immediately.

None of this was of particular concern to me. My mind was on the job in hand. I knew Kiko was a puncher. Harry had studied him in detail. He kept insisting I stay out of his way in the early going. This is not Esham Pickering.

Peters backstage at the Point: *This is going to be a career-defining moment for Bernard Dunne. Extremely tough fight, you know, this kid is twenty-one, full of piss and vinegar. Never been beaten. Sixteen and 0, thirteen knockouts. Never beaten as an amateur. This is a serious one.*

Our preparation was good. The gruelling twelve rounds against Walstad eight weeks previously should have conditioned me. Instead, it probably filled me with false belief. Both Walstad and Martinez were small. Both would try to come inside and do damage. But I'd taken Reidar's best combinations. Well, I'd seen them coming a mile away so I could move and pick him off. Why should Kiko be any different?

★

On the morning of the fight I feel ready. The build-up is fine. My entrance on the night sends the usual jolt of electricity coursing through my veins.

The Clare hurlers Davy Fitzgerald and Tony Griffin are alongside my main sponsor and their fellow countyman Martin Donnelly on my path to the ring. I give them a nod. Into the ring I go. Harry repeats our simple fight plan: 'Survive the early rounds and he is yours.'

Survive the early rounds and the world is yours, I am thinking.

The bell rings.

Eighty-six seconds later I am still looking forward to the fight. *Why am I on my stool?*

Jesus, no. I have to be told it is over. The Point empties. That is the difference between boxing and any other sport; the majority of people present are floating supporters. They vanish. The bar-stool boys are back to their local:

Told you Dunne is shite.

Yeah, suppose you are right. When did you say he was shite again?

Many of them never come back. Well, not until the bandwagon is up and rolling again. I still manage to deliver prophetic words for Marty Morrissey: 'It's moments like this that will show whether I am the fighter I think I am. If I can recover from this and work my way back . . .'

I take it like a man. I keep it all inside. That is how I was brought up. A real boxer can handle defeat. I walk away with my head up.

Moments later the water is beating down on me. I am on the floor of the shower room crying. I am lost. I have to dry off and piss in a cup. Title fight; mandatory drug testing. It doesn't take long: I wasn't in the ring long enough to be dehydrated. At the press conference I refuse to offer up any excuses: 'Disappointed. Disgusted with myself. I let myself down. Let my team down. I let the people down. But . . . that's boxing.'

Peters: 'We will take a bit of time now. We'll take a rest, sit down and think about it.'

Back on my couch, a few days later, I try to put some sense on it for the documentary but I struggle: *I didn't see the punch. That's what done me. After that . . . the rest was immaterial. I was done after the first shot. Maybe if it went a bit longer. Five rounds, ten rounds, twelve rounds, then we could analyse it, but what the hell can you take from eighty-six seconds?*

Nothing gained, everything lost. This should be humiliating but I am not concerned with the inevitable backlash. I am just disappointed in myself.

I should have listened to Harry. He has never given me bad advice. Why the fuck didn't I listen to Harry?

In the ring, immediately afterwards, Kiko's corner confirmed that family and friends had gathered up €10,000 and laid it on their man to stop me in the first. They got 66/1 with William Hill. That night, while a small pocket of Spaniards celebrate somewhere in Dublin city, I replay it all in my head a thousand times. Had we done enough in training? I thought we had. Where do I go now? I have no idea. The longest of long nights follows. I have no answers.

The next day I rise and life carries me along for a while. A gang of us are going to the All-Ireland semi-final in Croke Park between Dublin and Kerry. I would have to have died in that ring to halt this session. The lads don't have to drag me out to see the Dubs.

Pamela's mam, Olive, is minding the kids in our house, where we're all going to meet up before the game. A couple of the lads beat me there. Big Mark and my cousin Stephen.

'How is he?' Olive asks.

'Ah, he's grand, but Martin's after taking the car off him.'

'He did not?'

'Yeah, that's it. Once he got beaten Martin said he is no longer sponsoring him.'

'He never did.'

'Yeah, all the sponsors are gone. This place won't last much longer either,' they say, looking around the living room with sombre faces. 'They'll have to sell it now.'

I come in the front door and the lads are sniggering in the corner. Next thing, Martin shows up with a mini-van to take us all to Croker. Olive glares at him.

'Don't mind them, Olive,' I say. 'Look, the car is in the driveway.'

Martin is off the hook.

My brother-in-law Alan comes in next. 'Jaysus, Bernard, it's good to see you standing on your own two feet again.'

It quickly stops being about me. There is no way I am going to hide away. Myself, Martin, Alan, Stephen, Mark, Declan and Finnian. Seven of us in the van. We pick up Ricky Hatton and Matthew Macklin at the Burlo. Ricky is a sound man. No airs or graces about him. It is well publicized that he enjoys life between fights. Today is between fights for all of us. We are in the Ard Chomhairle section again. Lower Hogan stand on the halfway line.

I am easy prey for the rest of the day.

'I take it you are not walking out on the pitch at half-time?'

'His trousers would only fall off him in front of the Hill.'

'He has no belt.'

'How are the legs? A bit shaky?'

Donnelly is smirking away. 'Some friends you have, Bernard.'

Outsiders show genuine concern. Countless Dublin and Kerry people come over to see if I am okay. 'Great to see you out, Bernard.'

Dublin lose narrowly. That night I meet up with some of the Dublin players. They'd really thought it was their time as well. They'd come so close. We drown our sorrows together. It is good to be around my own tribe.

Opinions of those I respected were sought after my first defeat.

'From the very first time I met and worked with Bernard Dunne, I saw incredible potential,' Ray Leonard told American sports writer George Kimball. 'But I've always felt what I knew back then – that he has the potential. Bernard has to do what is quite difficult for all fighters, including yours truly, to do: He needs to ask himself: "Is this (my boxing career) a priority?"

'It depends on his health, mind-set, and desire – which nobody knows but Bernard himself. What he needs to do now is answer that tough, but honest, question himself . . . "Do I still have what it takes to succeed?"'

Freddie Roach told Kimball: 'I honestly don't know if it was psychological or a matter of conditioning. If you could figure out exactly *why* it happened, you might know how to address it, but other than getting him to warm up better – or maybe sending him out into the alley to box a couple of rounds before he goes into the ring? I'm not sure what you'd do, because otherwise Ben is a very talented fighter with a lot of tools.'

There were some cheap column inches to be got from the fireman story. I was going to join the Brigade before I turned professional in 2001. It looked like a good career option as I knew boxing wasn't going to last for ever. Also, it was a bankable job that would have suited perfectly if I stayed amateur for the Athens Olympics.

I have never actually worked properly in my life. Never had a day job or anything part-time. I worked full-time in the CIE gym. I dipped my toe into university life but boxing always got in the way of further education. I was learning enough.

When I went to America in 2001 the Fire Brigade exams were shelved, although I finally sat them between the Jailauov and Walstad fights.

Some people interpreted my application as showing a lack of ambition on my part, but I was already European champion and was showing no signs of standing still. Chances were I'd be retired within five years. I just wanted a back-up plan for my young family. I wanted control over my future. I had no intention of waking up in my thirties with no options.

I got some funny looks when I turned up for the aptitude tests. I had to sign a few autographs and pose for some pictures. After the written exams you watch a video tape of three smoke-filled rooms. The video ends. You are asked questions. In room three, what colour were the bags? How many of them were there? How many people in room two? What kitchen utensils were on the counter in room one?

It is about observation under pressure. From several thousand applications only the top 160 make it onto the panel. I aced the exams and was accepted. I have yet to take up the opportunity but my links with the Brigade remain solid today. I would be proud to serve.

Harry will still argue that my mind wasn't right leading up to the Martinez fight owing to the constant arguments over money. He's wrong. It bothered me, yes, but that had nothing to do with getting knocked out. Kiko's overhand right cannot be blamed on Brian Peters or Pat Magee or anyone else. I was the one put on the canvas three times.

Team Magee tried to put Kiko in against Wayne McCullough on 1 December at the King's Hall in Belfast, to be televised on Setanta Sports. It didn't get past the weigh-in.

It was a non-title fight but McCullough jumped at the chance to re-establish himself at home. He was thirty-seven years old and had not fought since July 2005, when Oscar Larios knocked him out at the MGM Grand with the WBC super bantamweight title on the line. It was the second time in five months that Larios had beaten him. All Wayne had to do was outbox Martinez and maybe then I would fight him. That would mean a decent pay day for everybody.

The agreed weight was 8 stone 12 lb. On 31 November McCullough weighed in at 8 stone 9 lb. Coming in under the weight was strange in itself, but when a pudgy-looking Kiko was almost two pounds over matters began to unravel. Kiko was given a few hours to shed the excess baggage. He didn't shed an ounce. Wayne was furious: 'I couldn't believe it. He comes in over the weight and then after being asked to take it off he just sits there and does nothing. I just can't believe what has happened. I was ready to fight and ready to win and he comes in that much over the weight.'

Attempts were made to resolve the dispute but the day ended with accusations flying back and forth. The fight, along with the entire undercard that included Brian Magee, was cancelled. Harry was right.

I would have loved a rematch with Kiko but Peters flat refused to do business with Pat Magee, Hobson or Rooney.

I am still disgusted with myself. I gave the European title to Kiko. I made him king for a day, because that's about how long it lasted.

The English bin man Rendall Munroe stayed away from his pile-drivers six months later to strip him of the title on his first defence. Munroe kept his hands up. Split decision. One round swing. It was in Nottingham. Kiko expends a lot of energy trying to knock you out. After that, he is controllable. I would beat Munroe in my sleep. I've always been able to handle technical fighters. It's the ones who are trying to take my head off that cause me problems.

After losing to Munroe, Pat Magee sent Kiko around the houses.

They had him out in Tallaght next, at the National Basketball Arena, to fight a novice named Lante Addy. He weighed in almost six pounds heavier than our bout. It went the full eight rounds, Kiko winning on points. Then it was back to Spain for a first-round TKO against Silviu Lupu, a guy with a 0 and 7 record, then to Dublin City University to fight Gheorghe Ghiompirica, a Romanian who is 8 and 43. It went the distance.

He got a rematch against Munroe in February 2009. This time the unanimous decision wasn't even close. Harry was in the crowd and agreed I could take Munroe with something to spare.

Next he was given an IBF title eliminator against Takalani Ndlovu in Johannesburg – 6,000 feet above sea level. To handle the adjustment to altitude a fighter is recommended to arrive several weeks in advance. Kiko is from the Spanish sea port of Alicante but he only landed in South Africa a few days before the fight. A left uppercut dropped Ndlovu in the first round. He got up and stayed behind his jab. Kiko finally slowed in the seventh. It was another unanimous decision with one judge scoring it 115–113 but the other two had it more clearly in Ndlovu's favour (Steve Molitor beat Ndlovu to win back his IBF title in March 2010). Kiko is not finished, but he remains a contender to be a contender on the world stage. He will get another crack at the EBU title and world champions will probably fight him too.

Peters went missing after I lost to Kiko.

I had a bad feeling about it on the night, he told the camera. *I said to Harry after thirty seconds that it was all over. Things have changed dramatically, like, the landscape is completely different now.*

Switch to Tara Towers Hotel in Dublin . . . still Peters talking: *You see, the whole thing was getting too driven towards 'Bernard Dunne is Irish boxing'.*

Brian Peters Promotions in association with Irish Ropes presents another fantastic night: John Duddy on his march towards a world title . . .

Duddy was back beating Prince Arron at the Stadium in October and then up to the King's Hall to slug out, as Duddy does best, a points decision over an aging Howard Eastman in December.

Peters (driving in his car): *He was my Mona Lisa, you know what I mean? Picasso, you know what I mean? Everyone has their masterpiece. Bernard Dunne was my masterpiece.*

I can only cringe. I was his 'Picasso'? His 'Mona Lisa'? I was his cash cow. And he presumed I was all out of milk.

The gas thing is, he was involved in the editing process of the documentary.

He was riding as high as you possibly could. Probably two fights away from a world-title fight. Boxing is a bit like snakes and ladders. Boom. Here he is down the bottom of the ladder again.

And that's where he wanted to keep me. Under his fucking thumb. I didn't want it to break in public that we had difficulties. I didn't want it to become the same old story of the naive boxer and the clever promoter falling out over money. I didn't want to end up in court, delaying my career again by another six months or a year trying to get rid of him.

I get knocked out and his new approach is, 'Irish boxing is not all about Bernard Dunne. There are other boxers.' I can accept that, but the manner he went about it all left me with a feeling of disgust. Again.

I had a missed call from Brian Peters on my phone the morning after the fight and then I didn't hear from him for over two months. He didn't return calls or messages. Silence. He was trying to teach me a lesson. *You need me more than I need you.* He knew we wanted to go again as soon as possible yet he refused to respond.

Then, out of the blue, a phone call.

'How are things, Bernard?'

'I have been trying to contact you non-stop.'

'Let's meet up.'

We gathered in the Shebeen in Dunshaughlin. We sit down around a big open-hearted fire that's burning away. It was November. Peters, myself and Martin Donnelly. Harry Hawkins was banned. Peters wanted him gone. He believed I needed a fresh voice in my corner. He said the Kiko defeat was Harry's fault, but I'd told Harry straight: 'There is no way you are taking the fall for this. It is my fault. You told me to stay off him for three or four rounds and I didn't do that. I got tagged.' Harry had offered to step down but I said no. Peters told me to get rid of him. I refused.

Peters said he had been hurting since that defeat. That he took it badly.

How do you think I felt? Where have you been for the past few months? I believe he was trying to see whether Brian Peters Promotions could move on without Bernard Dunne. It hadn't so far.

He blamed Harry for the Pat Magee situation.

Harry had nothing to do with Pat signing up Martinez, but because Pat was his friend he was tarred with the same brush by Peters. Harry told me he would understand if I took that stance as well. He said he would take responsibility for the Kiko Martinez defeat. I could have looked after my own vested interest – Harry would have understood – but this was a matter of integrity. I was fucked if I was going to cut my ties with Harry Hawkins.

Micky Ward was down the country somewhere and Peters had appointed him as my new trainer. 'Irish' Micky Ward is a former light welterweight from Lowell, Massachusetts. Everyone in boxing has seen or at least heard of his epic trilogy with Arturo Gatti in 2002–3. He has had a colourful life to the extent that Mark Wahlberg is playing him in the movie *The Fighter*. Christian Bale plays his half brother Dickie Eklund, who fought Sugar Ray. The actors used the Wildcard for their preparations.

His life story should make a good film, but Ward hadn't trained anyone that I was aware of and he always fought with his face. What was he going to do for me?

The Peters plan was that I drop Harry and go back to the old-style training routines of chopping down trees and running up mountains or some shite like that. This was the Brian Peters boxing theory. Shortened robes. Old school. Fairytale stuff. There was talk of going back to America. Harry might have been absent but I remembered his words: *Stay calm. Make no definitive decision at a meeting.*

Peters gave me an ultimatum. Him or me.

Fuck staying calm. I make a definitive decision: I'm not getting rid of Harry. I refuse to take up with Micky Ward or comply with any other bullshit idea Peters might come up with. Peters is a shrewd promoter and understands the boxing game but he knows fuck-all about training fighters at any level. My fear was that I'd be fighting seriously tough opponents for minuscule purses.

I had very little to say to Peters after that. Harry conducted the meetings on my behalf through January and February 2008. On Sunday 10 February they appeared to have reached an agreement in principle but twenty-four hours later Peters was back on to Harry with a three-way call that included his solicitor and everything had changed again.

There were other options. Promoters Tommy Egan and Frank Maloney were out there while Pat Magee offered to cover my legal fees if I attempted to break my ties with Brian Peters Promotions. That was all well and good, but Pat had no television deal.

I needed legal advice before signing my name to anything. I was put in touch with John Hogan, a partner in Leman solicitors of Dublin, as another three months of negotiation followed. Peters was trying to make me believe I needed Brian Peters Promotions more than he needed Bernard Dunne top of his bill.

John Hogan is the type of guy you want in your corner if you ever get badly cut during a legal disagreement.

The other concern was the cyst. What was to stop a pissed-off Peters blabbing about it to anyone who would listen? Also, a switch to Pat Magee would eventually have me over in British jurisdiction, and that was not an option. I was determined that the legal ramifications of trying to break ties with Peters wouldn't result in another period of inactivity. The collapse of America Presents and the brain scan problems in the States had sentenced me to enough time in boxing purgatory.

John's partner Larry Fenelon had warned me that a court case could cost up to €50,000. The contract I'd signed as a young kid desperate to box pro made Peters my manager for five years, with a two-year extension if I got into the top ten, a two-year extension if I won a European title and another two years if I won a world title. So he had me pretty well sewn up.

The decisive meeting began at 4 p.m. on 14 February 2008 in the Temple Bar offices of Carley & Connellan, solicitors. Peters was represented by John Connellan. It was six months since I had last fought.

Harry and I met John Hogan in Bloom's Hotel an hour earlier. John told me I had to be willing to stand up and walk out if the other side did not meet our demands. I had to accept the fact that going to court was a possibility and not let that threat dissuade me from standing my ground. I agreed. It came close twice. We stood up to leave and they asked us to sit back down. A while later and Peters was packing his bag as we sat calmly in our seats. He never got up out of his.

Hogan insisted beforehand we had to sort it out that night one way or the other – either sign a new deal or get ready to go in front of a judge. I trust John Hogan's judgement. This was a definitive moment in my career. It was vital I got back in the ring. I was desperate to get some structure back, return to training camp in Belfast.

The meeting is a long one. Several wives' Valentine's Day plans are scrapped. Finally, we establish that Harry Hawkins is going nowhere.

We sign a four-fight promotional contract. Peters is still my manager but only for the fights he isn't promoting. The money I will receive for the next three fights is agreed.

This was great. No more arguments leading up to fights. No more meetings. It was all put to bed. I was thrilled as I walked out into Temple Bar at 11.30 that night.

I gave Pamela her Valentine's Day roses at the stroke of midnight, together with a card and a new four-fight contract. Climbing into bed I thought of poor Harry driving up the road to Belfast. I texted to let him know how comfortable I was. He finally landed home in the early hours to a pizza and a bottle of beer, left out by Noreen. Happy Valentine's!

Peters went away to figure out a new slow-burning plan. This is what he is good at. I have given him a heavy going over on these pages but I know there are worse out there in the boxing game. I negotiated deals with Peters for almost nine years and every time I went into an argument with him I always came out with what I wanted. Better the devil you know.

Some fighters crumble when they lose their unbeaten record. Naseem Hamed. Mike Tyson. It never once crossed my mind not to box again after my first professional defeat but Harry still needed to be sure. He drove down to my house in Palmerstown. He wanted to see for himself whether I had the stomach to continue. I did. No doubts.

'If this fight showed us anything it's that we need to increase your strength to keep guys off you. We have to look at ways of doing that. Whether that means bringing someone else in or . . .' This is what I needed to hear. Harry was looking to the future. He knew we had to evolve as a team.

You find out very quickly who really cares. Carruth, Collins and McCullough were all quickly on with words of encouragement.

I am of strong mind. I didn't need to discuss my inner demons with anyone. I just needed to get back into the ring. Dad kept it simple. European champion is an awful big achievement. If you wanna box, keep going.

Philip Phelan had done some weight training with me in Dublin before but in comparison to Kiko I had no muscle definition. I started using Alec Docherty more in the gym to coach the more physical stuff. A lot of wrestling and grappling.

There are all these theories about holding on to your opponent after receiving a big shot. I'd tried to grab Kiko. It didn't work. When you are dazed and your equilibrium is gone it is all well and good to say from the other side of the ropes that you should have done this, you should have done that. But when you are in that situation it is hard to remember what your name is, never mind what you should be doing. Instinct takes over every time.

We needed something special to bring me on.

Harry and myself discussed this at length. We came up with a provisional solution. An Australian strength and conditioning coach named Phil Moreland was working at the University of Ulster in Jordanstown. Phil gave me a weights plan.

It was Shane Horgan who first told me about Mike McGurn. Shane had been into boxing since he was young and had followed my career since I'd come home in 2005. I also knew his brother Mark, who is a producer of the sports show *Off The Ball* on Newstalk FM. The highly respected masseur Martin 'Mocky' Regan was another to recommend McGurn. I'd been talking to both of them about trying to improve my core strength and they each passed on the same mobile number. 'Call this guy.' Interesting.

My first defeat, my first time being knocked out, defined me as a boxer. I still believed I was good enough to win a world title. I still wanted to go up to Belfast for training camp. I still had the buzz when the bell went at the start of the first round.

Thanks to Leman solicitors my career could finally move on. Life had not stopped either. Finnian arrived on 14 December 2007. My son.

Peters is right. Boxing is like snakes and ladders. I had just encountered a slippery snake. I was back on a ladder. We took the show on the road. Breaffy House in Castlebar was the surreal venue for my comeback fight.

11. Squats, Cluster-chins and Detours

Mikey McGurn revolutionized the strength and conditioning with the Irish national rugby team as head of fitness. Starting from a position where Ireland could not compete physically with the top nations, Mikey through his programmes and motivation developed Ireland into one of the best-conditioned outfits in world rugby. It is no coincidence during his time with Ireland that we won three Triple Crowns, which set the basis for a Grand Slam.

Shane Horgan, Leinster and Ireland rugby player

Halfway through our first session, I turned to Mikey and said, 'I can't do this any more.' I was heaving.

'You can, Bernard. You need to push yourself. This is how it will feel in the twelfth round of a world title fight.'

His response was clever as it gave me no way out. Mikey McGurn has a natural gift when it comes to motivating his subjects. I had told him the first time we met that I wanted to be champion of the world. This was my chance to prove it. I somehow finished the near-impossible assault course he had laid out for me.

I will never know what the twelfth round of a world title fight is like and Mikey can take plenty of credit for that.

Some of the stuff he made me do was inhumane. It got to the stage where I'd finish one of his evil sessions and I would be standing there, hands on knees, thinking, 'How did I do that?' After two minutes recovering Mikey would shout, 'Let's go again.' Ten minutes later my whole body would be aching. I'd be dry retching, my legs and arms shaking and about to buckle under the strain. Running across a room carrying a barbell weighing 60 kilos will do that to you.

I drop it and sprint back to pull these big chains with steel balls on the end of them. Other people working out in Liffey Valley Fitness or up the Devenish gym in West Belfast look on in shock. I would give Kiko Martinez a free dig to put a stop to this torture. Oh wait, that's why I am going through this torture.

What is going on here? Jesus, my arms are going to fall off.

'Where is the break, Mikey?' the words are spat out.

'Keep going, Bernard!'

My heart is pounding. When you finish a Mike McGurn session you realize you can do anything. I learn more about my body in those punishing ten minutes than a lifetime taking blows in a boxing ring. Forget the fitness element; it is the psychological boost that makes the difference.

Although he'd been recommended to me, we first met by chance. I was working in the Devenish gym in March 2008, about two weeks before my first fight since Kiko Martinez.

Most people assumed I had already fought the fight that would come to symbolize my whole career. I was in unknown territory – coming off my first defeat as a professional. Harry still believed, but not many others. I was damaged goods.

I noticed some lad clocking me for a little longer than necessary. I was at fight weight so I looked gaunt. I had a skinhead and was wearing a Dublin hoodie. He stared. I stared back. Mikey thought I was a junkie. Then he saw people coming over to talk boxing.

Mikey being Mikey, he approached me.

'You Bernard Dunne?'

It clicked. 'Yeah, you're Mikey McGurn.'

'I am.'

'You come highly recommended.'

'Yeah, yeah. What are you doing?'

'I'm preparing to fight a former world champion named Felix Machado.'

We chatted. I liked what I was hearing straight away. I have not worked with many people when it comes to boxing. There has to be a very good reason for me to trust a new trainer after being blessed with such a select band of high-quality coaches throughout my life. My dad led me to Peter Perry who, in turn, sent me up to Harry Hawkins. Besides the three-year apprenticeship with Freddie Roach, that's it.

I had a good reason to broaden my horizons but it still had to be the right man. Shane Horgan's word was good enough for me.

Mikey was hesitant to get involved so close to my next fight and he had never worked with a boxer before. He gave me very basic instructions but I immediately felt we might be on to something. It felt right.

He insisted on meeting Harry. Mikey has worked with professional coaches in enough sports to understand the benefit of not stepping on toes. Otherwise, his presence would only create tension.

He was just finishing up seven seasons with the Irish national rugby union team under Eddie O'Sullivan and was poised to link up with the Ospreys rugby squad in Wales as their strength and conditioning expert. He was in demand, but he seemed genuinely interested in working with me.

Turns out he lives about 400 metres down the road from Harry. The three of us sat down that night over a pot of tea to discuss how his expertise could be transferred into a boxer's routine. Mikey dived straight into what was required to improve my strength and how we would go about it.

Harry wanted me to start bullying guys in the ring. Not let them lean on me and wear me down any more. I felt I needed more punch power. After a few hours in Mikey's company I realized I had no actual history of conditioning to speak of. We also realized he could accommodate both our requests.

I needed to do all this without increasing in size – I was picturing the size of the rugby lads. Mikey said this was a good thing. His philosophy applies to all sports: every exercise was based around improving speed and power. Zero body fat is the target.

'There is no point in me getting involved before Machado as it would only disrupt your preparation. So, see you after,' said McGurn.

It seemed like a really progressive step to begin working with someone who had helped so many elite professional sportsmen. Mikey wasn't name-dropping when he spoke of the improvements in power of guys like Horgan, Brian O'Driscoll and Paul O'Connell under his supervision. Well, okay, he was name-dropping, but these men were backing him up.

Mikey was a decent athlete himself, so a mutual respect was easy to develop. He was an Irish cross-country and 5,000-metre champion in a former life. He is from Fermanagh, deep in GAA country, so the move into rugby should have been alien to him, never mind the switch to boxing. Even stranger still, his name only came to the attention of Irish rugby after a phenomenally successful period with English rugby league club St Helens. Former Leinster rugby coach Matt Williams tried to hire him in 2002 but Eddie O'Sullivan also liked what he saw and took McGurn straight into the Irish camp. He helped condition the Irish forwards into one of the most fearsome packs in the world. I don't know much about rugby but I have seen those men in action and they are enforcers.

We switched our focus back to boxing and the visit of the Venezuelan Felix Machado on 12 April. The training with Harry was largely the same. We knew it was no time to panic. Gone in eighty-six seconds or not, I was the same boxer. I worked hard in Holy Trinity every evening for six weeks.

When all the contract stuff was sorted I suggested a rematch against Kiko but he had already lost the EBU title to Munroe and going to England simply wasn't an option. And Peters flatly refused to deal with Pat Magee or John Rooney, so Kiko was off the menu.

It meant a new road map had to be drawn up. My advice to anyone is to avoid the cross-country trek from Belfast to Castlebar. It takes ages.

The Breaffy House project seems like a dying kick of the Celtic Tiger. It is an International Events Arena designed to draw in top sporting teams for training or a boxer who has recently lost his undefeated record after being knocked out in the first round.

Everything starts again when you are beaten. I had to climb back up to my old prime-time slot. It was a process of rehabilitation.

The hotel had hired rugby's Keith Wood and ex-soccer international Paul McGrath, amongst others, as sporting ambassadors. The capacity of 2,000 was something similar to the National Stadium, but with better ventilation.

Peters did a deal and brought us 'into the West'. At least I was in Ireland and headlining a bill again and, more importantly, it was still on live terrestrial television.

RTÉ could have dropped me after the Point Depot disaster. Who could have blamed them if they'd gathered up their chips and moved on? But in Glen Killane's eyes professional boxing in Ireland hadn't bottomed out and neither had I. They had invested over a year in my progress and saw my defeat as no more than a setback. Killane knew the ratings would dip, and he knew it would be difficult to sell this fight to the public. He was also working with a smaller budget than he'd been given in 2005. And yet he sent an outside broadcast unit down to County Mayo. RTÉ had agreed to go another year to see where it took us. Such loyalty is rare.

Harry and Peters were taking no chances with my first fight back. Still, they needed someone with pedigree to repay RTÉ's loyalty so they got a name, albeit an aging one.

Machado had been IBF super flyweight champion from 2000 to 2003 but he was now thirty-six years old. We brought him up ten pounds for this featherweight bout. He was a rangy five foot seven and a decent technical puncher who hadn't knocked anyone out for eight years. A southpaw, he was made for me. The complete opposite of Kiko, really. Hand picked. No excuses.

McGrath and Wood were joined in the crowd by Tyrone football manager Mickey Harte, John Maughan from Mayo and the legendary former Meath manager Seán Boylan.

At the National Stadium they would introduce well-known faces in the crowd. The boy band types would get hammered but Keith Duffy showed he wasn't just a fair-weather fan. He made the journey. I have worked with Keith on charity gigs and he is a good fella but Paul McGrath was the only one to unfailingly command respect even from the most raucous Dublin crowds.

This was not Dublin. We were down the country. It was a different type of boxing crowd. I made the same entrance to the same music. Peters out first, of course, then big Al Gannon and myself with Harry trailing.

On arrival in the ring we realized I had no gumshield. Brian Magee, who was working my corner having had numerous fights cancelled in the previous few months, legged it back to the changing room. He returned just before Luan Parle finished the national anthem and you can see on camera as Brian slips the gumshield into Harry's hand. Oops. It was that type of nervy evening. To be honest, it was a weird atmosphere. Everyone seemed on edge. The crowd didn't know whether to cheer or stay quiet.

It felt like my pro debut in Feather Falls Casino seven years earlier, except that then I was way more relaxed. I was the same weight as well, 125lb.

This was all about getting back on the horse. Take the first punch and see how it felt. Get into the second round for a change! We'd tried to simulate fights in sparring with Alvaro Perez, and I had a cut over my nose to prove it, but I desperately needed this after eight months dealing with a loss on my record.

My right hand was sore beforehand and it was about to get worse. I let it go in the first round and it hit his elbow. The familiar pain rushed up my arm. I welcomed it for a change as it always focused me. Better make the right hands count because they are going to hurt. Not a great start but I was happy to be back in the ring.

'Jab, jab, left hook and step to the side,' Harry had my full attention. What he was really saying was, *Soften this guy up and let's get the hell out of here.* We were both leading with jabs and uppercuts so there were several head clashes. From the back of my right ear to the front of my forehead was completely swollen by the fourth round.

My timing is my best weapon but against southpaws you need a big right hand and mine was killing me. His corner was complaining about low blows but his shorts were up around his neck. 'Focus on the left hook.' Harry knew my hand was gone again. I had rope burns across my chest that looked worse than they were.

I got through all ten rounds but my frustration became apparent down the stretch. I was miles ahead but I didn't think I was making the impression that I needed to after being knocked out. I began to force it a little, but stopping such a wily old veteran like Machado was proving difficult. Felix is a survivor and he gave me four stitches above my eye for my exuberance.

Referee Emile Tiedt gave me every round.

The problems exposed by Kiko – like anyone else on the planet, I can be knocked out – weren't of great concern. There was another, more pressing worry. Harry had noticed it before we fought Yuri Voronin in 2005. Freddie Roach identified it early in the Wildcard gym. Even though my boxing ability was always steadily improving, I lacked the power to become world champion. Reidar Walstad, the previous June, had become a gruelling twelve-rounder because I'd been unable to stop him clean in his tracks. I had enough about me to stall his progress but I couldn't put him down. And the manner in which he was able to occasionally make those kamikaze raids under my guard meant a clash of some sort was inevitable. I should have knocked him out in the early going, or at least hurt him enough to dissuade those wild, swinging haymakers.

It wasn't that I lacked the killer punch (I knew I was never a big puncher). It wasn't that I got too embroiled in brawls (that was essential sometimes). It was my physical make-up. Walstad, Voronin and Valdez before that caused me the most problems when they leaned on me. I needed more than my left jab, body shots and technical ability to be considered world-class material. I needed to build up the physique to make an impact in the grappling department instead of letting them wear me down; denying me the opportunity to become a twelve-round championship performer.

I took two weeks off before getting down to the most gruelling experience of my life. It was the end of April and Mikey was over with the Ospreys so he set me up with Fergus Connolly. Mikey operates by getting in your face and challenging you while Fergus has more of a sports-science approach. He put me on numerous machines to test my endurance levels and determine a benchmark. Fergus ended up working with the Welsh national rugby team.

I didn't know if I could get my career back on track at this stage but between Fergus and Mikey I suddenly had an excellent team of conditioners. It felt like the start of something.

When Mikey's season finished he took a hands-on approach. That meant all I focused on was training and resting. He always insisted on coming to me, saying this was important as he didn't want me expending energy before or after as he was going to drain it all out of me anyway. No excuses, basically.

When I was at home he would travel down to Palmerstown and we would work in the field across from the house or in Liffey Valley. When up in Belfast we would go to the Devenish or a local Gaelic pitch that Harry's living room overlooked.

After a session with Mike McGurn you need to be in the right environment to recover. He wanted me to get home, eat well and rest because he'd be coming for me in forty-eight hours. Just as the pain subsided he would be at my door again.

He cut out my long, early-morning runs – which are the heartbeat of a boxer's training routine since the dawn of time. He felt they blunted progress. It took a while to convince me of that. He said it would only make me slower in the ring.

'Bernard, you never run ten miles in a fight. Seven metres is the only distance you need to cover.' Short, sharp stuff became the order of the day. Get in the gym, train aggressively for thirty minutes, be explosive and then leave. Go and refuel with the correct diet.

For our first session I was squatting 40 kilograms. In our last session before I fought Ricardo Cordoba I was squatting 115 kilos. My first dead lift was 50 kilos. Before fighting Cordoba it was up to 130.

I developed a new vocabulary when it came to power sessions. Squats: 5x5 reps, followed by two minutes' recovery and then 3x10 reps with one minute's recovery. Speed bench press: 4x8, as fast as you can, with 45 seconds' recovery. Cluster-chins (you don't want to know) followed by single arm jammer (you really don't want to know): 5x8 with one minute's recovery. And on it went.

Mikey climbs inside your brain. The idea was to make training so hard that taking blows would become almost easy. It worked. The sessions were not nice. Lord knows what could have been achieved if he'd got hold of me as a teenager. I would be the welterweight champion of the world by now! He was teaching a twenty-eight-year-old how to dead lift and squat for the first time.

What shocked Mikey was that I had got so far on such limited support. It was just me and Harry. He called my physical training 'prehistoric'.

Soon I began to love the sight of Harry returning from work in the evenings as it meant a respite from McGurn's torture and I got to go to the gym to do some boxing training.

Harry was pleased with my progress while he was off running his plastering business. I became noticeably stronger very quickly. I am naturally fit, having been training away since childhood, but this was a completely new methodology. Mikey had never trained a boxer before (nor, surprisingly, has he since), so I gave him all my previous fights on DVD and, sure enough, he became a boxing coach! He would identify what areas of my body I needed to work on. He was back with programmes that were 'ring relevant'.

Harry had already stated the need to improve my strength, not just to keep guys off me but to ensure I didn't suffer from holding and leaning. That is what drains a fighter entering the championship rounds. We had specific wrestling drills. Mikey enjoyed this. I bet he didn't do too much of this with Paulie O'Connell!

Harry came to watch us in the field. He liked the big elastic power bands Mikey would put over my hand and make me jab and punch. They became part of the Holy Trinity gym as their use improves punching power.

We would simulate three-minute fights in our exercises. He was preparing me for the last three rounds of a real fight. The championship rounds. That said, McGurn had no influence on boxing tactics, but he was an athlete and a powerful man himself so I respected his ideas.

Within a few months I became a different type of boxer. It made opponents' research on my previous fights largely useless. In sparring sessions I was able to hold guys off a lot more. I didn't have to box my way out of danger. I could lean on them. I could fling them off me. I could take them pushing me and hold my ground. I didn't have to move as much; I didn't have to run away. I could handle super bantamweights. Holding is a big part of the game if it is done properly. Walstad kept doing it and he would get five, six shots away off the back of it.

We worked so closely together that I became good friends with Mikey. He told me what the Irish rugby players like O'Connell, O'Driscoll and Reggie Corrigan said about winning and losing with equal humility. Basically, how important it is for Irish sportsmen to maintain this tradition. It was how we have always done it. I agreed. You win and lose with the same amount of humility.

★

In June 2008 Brian Peters offered me a world title fight against the WBA champion Celestino Caballero. It was just a month before the second fight of my reborn career, against Damian Marchiano. We were in the County Club. He presented the offer in writing.

Caballero is Panamanian. He was thirty-two years old and had been world champion since 2005. Two things crossed my mind: (a) Peters is trying to cash in on me one more time and (b) I am definitely not ready.

Caballero is five foot eleven, which makes him a giant at super bantamweight. There were only two stains on his record. Venezuelan José Rojas stopped him back in 2003 and fellow countryman Ricardo Cordoba won a convincing unanimous decision in 2004. Thirty-four wins, twenty-three by knockout, Caballero possessed all types of skills. He was a right-hander but fought a two-handed, almost unorthodox, style. He could brawl or he could box. This was a serious operator.

It was the right fight at the wrong time. I turned it down.

Peters stated in writing that he was not in agreement with my decision.

That November Caballero tore Steve Molitor apart in four rounds, unifying the WBA and IBF titles. The damage was done with a left to the body before a right uppercut put Molitor through the ropes. He got up and Caballero started to mess him up. The referee stopped it as the Canadian's trainer, Stephane Larouche, jumped onto the apron with his towel.

Afterwards, Molitor told the stunned Ontario crowd he felt 'tight'. I guess Caballero felt loose, then.

Cordoba picked up the interim WBA belt the previous September by beating Luis Alberto Perez. When Caballero unified the titles by beating Molitor, Cordoba was upgraded to WBA champion in his own right. The Panamanians were circling the super bantamweight division, taking out all comers.

I had started a new training regime. I wanted to see some results. This is what happens when you get knocked out – people see you as a soft touch. They know you are at a low ebb. I wanted to fight for a world title when I had a chance of winning a world title and not a second before.

Marchiano smiled. I smiled right back. Both our faces had these crazed grins. It would have been funny if we hadn't been hitting each other. Other fighters would understand. Sugar Ray Leonard gave that smile to Marvin Hagler and Roberto Duran when they came looking to brawl. Marchiano was keen to knock me out.

The Argentinian was a travelling salesman. In fairness, he came for a fight. He didn't have the power to do much damage but I was trying to avoid a war as I knew a serious opponent was on the horizon. My confidence was back. I had changed as a boxer. Defeat will do that.

Again, he'd been hand picked by Harry and Peters. They were getting me back boxing. He was brought up from bantamweight. I was following orders and hitting him at will.

This proved to be my last ever performance in the National Stadium. I've had far better nights down the South Circular Road but my final bow was enough to put a genuine smile on my face. I enjoyed it. I fought with my hands down by my side and put on a show. He kept talking in Spanish but I knew what he was saying.

He wanted me to walk on in. No thanks, pal. When he charged I gave him the smile, slipped his best shots and caught him on the move.

It became one of those very rare, comfortable nights in the ring. I let everything go. My body shots were flowing. Great combinations. Perfect timing. I had received a painkiller for my right hand to make it through.

Unless I walked onto something stupid, it was all mine for ten rounds. Harry had my complete attention. No risks.

Marchiano was trying to make me lose my temper. I won every round. Not long ago I would have taken the bait at some stage. Not tonight. Combinations. Body shots.

I didn't realize this was my final show in the Stadium but for a moment I slipped back in time. I'm just glad I ended it with a decent display. One final boxing lesson in the old sweat box. Eighteen years. The left jab is never for show. So many memories. Robert O'Connor. Terry Carlyle. Molitor. The great Peter Perry. Unbeaten. End of an era.

'My game plan is always to box,' I tell RTÉ's Joanne Cantwell afterwards. 'Put a show on. We have learned since the Martinez fight not to get hit!'

I am getting stronger. I keep that to myself.

There was talk of going to England to fight Rendall Munroe for the EBU belt. Efforts were made to tempt him over to Dublin but Frank Maloney was having none of it. The King's Hall in Belfast was mentioned but after speaking to Mel Christle about it we decided against provoking the stir that a brain scan would cause in British jurisdiction. Kiko Martinez would have been the mandatory if I'd defeated Munroe.

Going back up to featherweight to challenge for the WBC title against Oscar Larios was another possible route, but I'd have needed at least a year before considering a move up in weight.

I'd believed that the Valentine's Day contract had put to bed our financial disputes but Peters refused to let up. He sought a reduction in my fight fee of almost 40 per cent and said that my complimentary ringside ticket allocation would be reduced from twelve to six. These were for my family and close friends. Nothing is more important to me than family and Peters knew this. There was also a suggestion that I would not be the headline event on his next card, yet in November I was back on top of the bill in Breaffy House.

When I started working on the RTÉ boxing panel for the Beijing Olympics, something I really enjoyed, all of a sudden he reminded me of our management contract. So he was my manager again!

I was due to fight in a few weeks' time, but for most of the training camp I had no idea who my opponent was going to be. It was initially the Mexican Eduardo Garcia but Peters got rid of him a few weeks out. We kept training away with a different spread of sparring partners. Choi was back in, and he could do almost any style, and the unbeaten young featherweight Ryan Walsh came over from England. So we were ready. Harry also came up with a new way of wrapping to protect my right hand. We did it every time I sparred or hit the bags. I was feeling like myself again.

Finally, it was decided I'd fight Cristian Faccio, a confident little bull from Uruguay. He was the type who liked to get in close to do damage. He was also searching for redemption in County Mayo having fought for the WBC bantamweight title the previous June in Tokyo. Hozumi Hasegawa handed him a second round TKO.

There were no changing rooms in Breaffy House so we had to use an apartment and then come down across the outside of the arena. It was November 2008 and freezing. Sleet, rain and snow as well. I had to be carried around the back of the hotel. Big Al Gannon earned his keep that night.

Davy Fitzgerald is ringside with new highlights in his hair! I love Davy's company. We have similar personalities. I carried his hurleys and spare balls for five years at the Poc Fada competition. This is an event up in the Cooley mountains in County Louth where many of the great hurling goalkeepers attempt to 'poc' the ball the furthest.

Martin Donnelly claims he has me on tape kicking Davy's sliotar ten yards further up the course. I know he is calling my bluff. I did kick Brendan Cummins's sliotar backwards. The Tipperary man still prevailed.

Davy is a two-time All-Ireland winner with the Clare hurlers; a super bantamweight goalkeeper for the Banner's epic victories in 1995 and 1997. Now he is managing the Waterford hurlers. He might wear his heart on his sleeve but Davy Fitz is a clever man. He is someone I have bounced stuff off over the years. Davy is a believer.

I have learned from fighting shorter opponents that you must wait for the angle, take the shot and get out. By the seventh I am dominating and Faccio is tiring. I look visibly stronger (there are finally some defined muscles) as several months in my private boot camp with Mikey McGurn is beginning to yield results.

I let Faccio come inside, I get hold of him and fling him back out. He tries to come in again and I rattle him with the jab. I can do either now.

Thirty-eight seconds into round seven we both throw right hooks to the body. Clunk. I am seeing stars.

'Wha' the . . .' I turn away. That couldn't have been a punch as he was too low down. We have bashed skulls. The pain is horrendous.

'Accidental,' says Emile Tiedt.

Blood immediately starts flowing down my face. Benny is up on the apron trying to fix me up. Emile wants us to continue. 'Let's go!'

The blood is in my eyes. I am dabbing it. Fuck, I am blind. There is a lifetime to the bell. I get him in a head lock. I need to stall. 'Let him up!' Emile insists.

I desperately need Benny to stop the bleeding. A cut man's trade is as old as boxing itself. Benny King is one of the best in the business at stemming the flow of blood. Harry has seen him work miracles.

Faccio sees his golden opportunity and starts firing everything he has in the locker.

I hold him again. I'll grab on to this fella for two minutes if I have to. Emile is losing patience with me. We break.

Even in this grave situation, my hands are still down by my side. It is just the way I always liked to box. A better fighter would have knocked me out by now. I have blurred vision. I can see shadows. More importantly I can't see his hooks. I have to do something before he finds the hammer blow.

I come back at him with all types of different shots. Overhand right, left uppercut. If they stop this I want everyone to be convinced I was in control. Or maybe I can knock him out. It's a bloodbath. I roughly fling him off me. Yeah, I'm stronger. He is lighter than Mikey. I slap him across the ring but I am fighting blind. This is some kamikaze shit. Fighting with just my reflexes. Blood in my eyes. At least Faccio isn't trying to knock me out any more. Another left uppercut stuns him. The crowd roar. Makes him think twice about coming inside again.

The bell goes to end the round.

'Benny, I can't see.' I can barely talk, there is so much blood in my mouth.

Emile is going to end the fight if Benny can't patch up the wound.

'Go away, I can stop it,' he pleads with Emile. But the job is taken away from him. There is commotion at ringside.

I'd been cut open a few times in fights. There was a bad clash of heads against Adrian Valdez in 2004 but Freddie Roach had been in enough corners to staunch the bleeding and keep me going. It was a manageable wound. I have been busted open plenty of times sparring. The worst was the rip above my eye in Terry Fenwick's gym in Sydney against Somluck.

The Cristian Faccio collision was the worst possible scenario. No fighter is happy with a bout being stopped due to a gaping hole in their head. Even if they are miles in front.

I am beginning to panic. People in pubs all over Ireland think I have lost. The crowd are thinking the same. So do I. Jimmy Magee isn't exactly sure either. Another defeat on my record would be a disaster. 'I can go on,' I say.

But I can't. There is blood everywhere. The fight is stopped. Peters tells me it will go to the referee's scorecard.

'What? This is ridiculous. Fuck! I'm okay!'

'You should be delighted,' whispers Harry. The cautious coach as ever.

But Peters and Harry have remembered what Benny and myself have forgotten: Irish rules. If the fight had been in Britain, or several US states, the decision would go to the guy who can fight on. In that case, Benny would have been forced to work a miracle. Thankfully, Emile Tiedt is a sensible referee, who knows his business.

Under Irish rules, an accidental clash of heads after four or more rounds means the fight is decided on points. Emile explains this to the other corner. Faccio is bollixed whether I carry on or not. They complain. Emile explains again. Emile is an imposing referee. The crowd, fearing the worst, start booing. There would have been a riot in Dublin by the time Mike Goodall got to make the announcement.

'The referee's scorecard reads 70–65 to the winner . . . Bernard Dunne!'

A cheer. The place kind of celebrates. I don't. It was a vicious cut and hurt like hell. Joanne Cantwell is in the ring to interview us. I'm disgusted, but calm down. It's not the end of the world and I am feeling good again. Later, back in the changing room, Dr Joe McKeever stitches me up without an injection. Seven stitches. No painkilling injection, nothing. I wail like a banshee. Dr Joe is still my doctor but never again without a shot, Joe. When I look in the mirror I see two scars. Eleven stitches to remind me of my detour down to Breaffy House.

My self-confidence was not badly shaken by the Kiko Martinez experience. It was the public who really needed convincing. They were just starting to believe in me when the carpet was pulled from underneath them. This happens in boxing all the time. The recently dethroned American Kelly Pavlik looked unbeatable at super middleweight, then he went up to light heavyweight and was torn apart by an aging Bernard Hopkins. After struggling to come back down in weight, that air of invincibility was gone and Sergio Martinez took his middleweight belts off him. Mike Tyson? See James 'Buster' Douglas. People don't want to hear about your weight issues or disputes over money. That is why I was determined to keep the constant conflict with Peters out of the public domain. People don't care. You live and die by what you do in the ring. That's why an off night is so hard to forgive in boxing. People stop believing. They believe only what their eyes tell them.

The Irish public seemed to be tentatively behind me again. We were building momentum. Word was spreading that I was coming back. Again, RTÉ played a massive part in all this.

The harshest of critics, he or she who sits on the bar stool, still doubted my ability or whether I had the heart to dig deep when it really mattered, but they were willing to support the cause. Two trips to Castlebar showed me that. I needed to get back to Dublin.

'World title fight next year,' said Peters without much pomp and ceremony after Faccio, but in the same breath he kept the Rendall Munroe EBU title shot on the table. There were plenty of offers coming in.

I would have got a shot at the world title as a contender if I'd beaten Kiko but, of course, I get one anyway. Everyone likes to fight you once you have been knocked out halfway through the first round. They think you're a busted flush. The Point has reopened as the O2; a spanking new arena that deserves to host a world title fight.

I am stronger. It feels like the right time.

★

Ricardo Cordoba was the new WBA champion and looking to come to Europe for a pay day. His people liked the idea of Kiko Martinez but they couldn't reach an agreement. The fight was offered to Munroe and Frank Maloney. They said no. Next, it came to me. I said no problem. It would be a pleasure to have the Panamanian come visit. They only knew what they had seen of me in the ring, but I had my secret weapon in Mikey. Cordoba's manager Richard Dobal and Peters reached an agreement: €200,000 got him to Dublin.

Mikey McGurn really did put his heart and soul into his pet project. I would like to think it was because he could see the vast potential for improvement. He never looked for a penny off me. He just dived in head first and helped me get into the shape required to fight competently for a world title.

The rest was up to me.

A month out from the Cordoba fight, Mikey took a week off from his contracted job with the Ospreys in mid-season for what he described as 'five days of over reaching'. I would describe it as a glimpse into hell. Little did I know I would be going there for real when I fought Cordoba on 21 March. It was three sessions a day for five days. Fifteen sessions in total. At one stage I swear he was trying to kill me. He was definitely enjoying it.

The idea was to drive me until I could do no more. He wanted me to learn how to cope when suffering from massive fatigue and then learn how to fight under such conditions. I was on the floor an awful lot. Mikey had made me get back up. He turned me into a machine.

I remember the fifteenth session on the fifth day. It was like the bell for the last round of a fight that I couldn't win.

'I don't think I can do this, Mikey.' I really meant it this time. I wanted the ground to eat me up.

'You can do it. Once you start, you will do it.' I was too fucked to curse at him.

I warmed up and flew through each task.

All I could say afterwards was, 'Thanks.'

Nothing else would come out. But there was plenty inside.

12. 'It's ours – It's all ours'

Defeat was in the air Ali alone seemed to refuse to breathe.

Norman Mailer, *The Fight*

No mas.

The great Panamanian welterweight Roberto Duran quits, early in the
eighth round, against Sugar Ray Leonard

I don't even recognize the sound coming out of me. It is a deep-set
roar.

Whoooof – now that is the sound of my right glove skimming past
Hubert Earle's chin.

'I near got you there, ref.' I give the Canadian a little tap on the
backside. The smiling Neilstown boy is caked in blood. Earle can only
chuckle.

You crazy fuckin' Irishman.

At least he knows I'm okay. His chin just avoided my right hook by
an inch – I threw it after the bell. I had to give them something –
Cordoba, Earle and the crowd – because all they can see is my mess of
a face with cuts that have me half blind. I rage against the dying of the
light. I throw it for the 9,037 people staring at their shoes in the O2
and the 600,000 tuned in at home or within the drink-stained walls of
pubs all over this island on what must seem a never-ending day of
sporting drama.

Another few seconds and Earle would have had to step in. Everyone
presumes the game is up.

Ricardo Cordoba should be heading back to the changing room

with a big fat cheque tucked into his shorts, having just knocked me out.

I was dropped twice in the fifth round.

Want to know why a boxer is always told to keep his hands up? Sixteen punches in succession. In seven seconds. I block fourteen. One, two, three, four, five – this was a killer blow but I ducked – six, seven, eight – this gets through my left arm but I take it – nine, ten, eleven, twelve, thirteen, fourteen – he is tiring – fifteen, sixteen are token gestures. The bell. I defiantly swing out my right, along with the roar; it comes very close to catching Hubert Earle, who only dived between us to ensure Cordoba didn't land number seventeen. It is more a gesture than a punch. I know Cordoba has stopped and is moving away. There is a look of disgust on his face as he slumps back to the corner.

Fuck you, Cordoba, I'm not done with you yet. My smile disappears as soon as I turn away. 'Fuck that.' I am disgusted. Harry slaps my tummy. I am in the trenches again, but I am lucid. There is no other option but to slug it out. They say I am a beautiful, technical fighter but I am also Brendan Dunne's son. Eddie Hayden's nephew. If you are coming at me you'd better knock me out because if you don't I'll come back at you.

Every fuckin' time. Now, this is what I call a war.

When I was fifteen I began thinking seriously about boxing as a career. When Ricardo Alberto Cordoba Mosque was fifteen he fought his first professional fight against Hussein Sanchez. He fought twice more in 2000 and eight times in 2001 including two twelve-round bouts. He was already known as 'El Maestrito'.

The English translation is 'The Teacher' or 'The Master'. He was schooling opponents. I was still 'El Rasher'.

In 2009, still only twenty-four, Cordoba is nine years a professional with a hugely impressive record in the Central American boxing stronghold of Panama where the weak get weeded as teenagers.

Three early battles with Roinet Caballero led him up to March 2002, when he was paired against the undefeated (6–0) Nicaraguan William Gonzalez, who was four years his senior. Cordoba stopped him in the tenth and final round.

Willy Gonzalez earned every cent of his wages for the three weeks he spent in Holy Trinity leading up to Cordoba. Gonzalez would do whatever he was told. He was fast, hit hard and could take punishment. He told me exactly what Cordoba didn't like and produced a flawless impression every day. Some sparring partners work, some don't. We also had an unbeaten Italian in named Alberto Servidei. He could adopt most styles. They were both brilliant for me.

Willy would stop mid-round to explain Cordoba's every habit. A Spanish kid in the gym named Jorge would translate for us and hung out with him after hours to keep him happy. Gonzalez had just lost by majority decision against the IBF bantamweight champion Joseph 'King Kong' Agbeko, my unhappy sparring partner prior to the Pickering fight.

Cordoba was the recently crowned WBA super bantamweight champion, having easily outpointed Luis Alberto Perez the previous September, and was now after a respectable voluntary before being forced to face the now mandatory challenger Poonsawat Kratingdaenggym for a second time.

Besides that controversial split-decision defeat in Bangkok against Poonsawat back in August 2005, the only other blemishes on Cordoba's exemplary record were two draws in his other ventures outside Panama. Both were in Germany against the Ukrainian tank Wladimir Sidorenko, a year apart in 2006 and 2007. Both Sidorenko and Poonsawat are power hitters and they caused Cordoba problems on the inside, but they couldn't stop him – both men could blow Kiko Martinez out of the water with their sustained power. All three fights had been for the WBA bantamweight title.

Cordoba had also comprehensively beaten Celestino Caballero back in May 2004, even putting him on the floor in the tenth.

This was a whole new level of competition for me.

I was a well-known name in the super bantamweight ranks but I was third choice for Cordoba's people. His manager Richard Dobal stated this was because Martinez and Munroe were seen as easier fights. It helped that the money was right as well. My fee was a drop down from what I received as European champion but I didn't care. It was like going to America, I was getting what I wanted at the time I wanted it.

The fight was announced on Christmas Eve 2008. I was already in training. I'd only stopped for two weeks after the Faccio fight and that was because Harry and Mikey made me take a rest. We'd known since November that this was coming.

I started working in St Matthew's twelve weeks before the 21 March fight date. I set up camp in Turf Lodge with nine weeks to go. Same routine: weights and fitness with Mikey in the morning before boxing training in the evening with Harry. Alec Docherty continued to punish my body with the medicine ball.

Everything felt different this time. I was never bored. Never restless. I had a countdown to a world title fight. I loved that I wasn't rated by Cordoba. That is why he was giving me the shot. I'm just a boxer like him. Minimum risk. A stepping stone. I liked that.

There were no distractions. Pat Magee had no involvement while Peters was kept busy promoting the biggest event of his life. He was even working well with Harry on the recruitment of sparring partners.

Every morning there was a spring in my step. *This is great.* It was never about proving people wrong; it was about confirming what I'd always believed.

Myself and Harry would chat every day about little details. There were good and bad days. I always pushed myself. If we did something new on the pads I would want straight in the ring to simulate it in a fight scenario to see if it worked. No instructions for the sparring partner: I didn't mind getting hit to try out something different. Simulated or body sparring only frustrates me. If Harry tells a guy to jab, I want him to hurt me if I fail to slip it. You only learn if you get punished.

I knew what was coming. Harry and my dad both said he was a beautiful boxer. But Harry watched every Cordoba fight he could lay his hands on and he was delighted with his style. He would sit me down to watch certain rounds against Perez, Sidorenko and Poonsawat.

On Sunday mornings the family would gather, as usual, in Neilstown for breakfast and Dad would have seen the same DVDs. He was repeating what Harry said. I knew the two of them well enough to tell when they were just trying to fill me with confidence, which they were, but they also encouraged me to sit through the Poonsawat and Sidorenko bouts. So, when no one was about, I did. I started to understand what they meant.

Harry also cornered me one night with another DVD in his hand. It had one word on it: 'Kiko'.

'You need to watch this for one reason, Bernard.'

The third knockdown. If I had covered up there was a chance I might have survived, but I tried to punch him off me. I squirmed in my seat. I knew what he was saying and it helped to see it again. Imagine being attacked by a vicious dog. Your hands become useless against his gnashing fangs. You will get torn to shreds.

'You didn't back then, but you have the strength to hold off that kind of onslaught with your arms now. Don't fight when under this kind of pressure against Cordoba.'

We climbed into the ring and practised covering up as Willy Gonzalez unloaded.

The Martinez fight would be top of Cordoba's research list. We were sure he would try to end it fast.

George Kimball wrote as much in the *Irish Times*:

Cordoba, for his part, is by habit a slick-boxing counter-puncher who prefers to let his opponent take the lead, hoping to capitalize on the other fellow's mistakes. This had portended the possibility of an Alphonse-and-Gaston scenario in the run-up to Saturday's title fight, but at Friday's weigh-in Miguel Diaz, the Argentina-born cornerman who had been imported to work with the Cordoba faction for the Dunne fight, revealed that despite the Panamanian's handlers' insistence that they had not relied on videotape of Dunne's prior fights, they had in fact thoroughly deconstructed footage of the 2007 Kiko Martinez debacle and had made a conscious decision to test Dunne's chin early and often.

The Barry McGuigan/Eusebio Pedroza comparisons were unavoidable. Another Irishman challenging the Panamanian world champion. Cordoba's manager Richard Dobal played along: 'Sure he's spoken to Pedroza, he's spoken to [Roberto] Duran, he's spoken to [Celestino] Caballero. They mentor young fighters in Panama and see it as passing on the mantle from generation to generation.'

Both small boxing countries, they had their icons in touching distance and we had ours. I had spoken to McGuigan, Carruth and Steve Collins.

I didn't read any newspapers leading into the fight but I was aware nobody was giving me a chance. The Irish media didn't think I could compete at this level.

Still, some of the questions at the pre-fight media conference were ridiculous.

'Are you prepared to go twelve rounds?'

'It is a twelve-round fight so, yes, I have trained for twelve rounds.'

Miguel Diaz had worked my corner in America as a cut man. He was amazed by the line of questioning directed towards me by Irish journalists and said as much. He was part of the welterweight world champion Miguel Cotto's team. Now he was with Cordoba. Diaz had watched me banging away at the torsos of Manny Pacquiao and Israel Vazquez on a daily basis. He correctly assumed that I had improved in the past seven years. He said I deserved a world title shot.

I never claimed to be the greatest but I knew I could handle anyone on my day. The press no longer believed this. I always tried to speak to the media unless it was disruptive to my preparations. I fed the beast. They helped me achieve what I wanted and to get my message out there. It was a quid pro quo. When they wrote I was great it didn't change my outlook, so when they had a go at me it didn't change much either.

Being in America, especially around Sugar Ray and Freddie, gives you an idea of how to deal with reporters. I listened and learned. The boxing media need decent shows or naturally they become cynical.

Cordoba arrived in Ireland on 10 March. He trained out of the National Stadium. Bernardo Checa is a Panamanian who trains out of John Breen's gym in Belfast. The Cordoba team hired him in as a translator and cornerman. Afterwards, word got back that Cordoba was in the best condition of his life. I wasn't in too bad shape myself. On the morning of the weigh-in I ate an omelette. My weight was perfect: 121¾. Half a pound heavier than my opponent. I knew he was experienced but Cordoba still had a boyish look about him. I had too many scars to look like a kid any more.

★

21 March 2009
The O2, Dublin

The rugby match in Cardiff is unavoidable that Saturday afternoon. I watch it in my hotel room and, like everyone else, I get excited by the last few minutes as Ireland beat Wales 17–15 and complete the Grand Slam for the first time since 1948, but I am too focused to get carried away. The joint appeal of the two events becomes apparent when I look through the window and see all the green jerseys streaming down to the O2.

The Irish outhalf Ronan O'Gara is a sportsman I can relate to. He might miss a kick at goal, even an easy one, but he has to put it out of his mind and go again because the next moment needs his full attention. As the place kicker, the whole team relies on him so he understands the pressure of individual sport. If I have a bad round and get hit hard, I must recover and forget about it so I can focus on the next move, the next three minutes. I have huge admiration for the mental strength O'Gara has developed over the years – he keeps coming back – and I can relate to the fact that practically every opponent is physically stronger than him. But he always finds a way to stamp his personality on games.

The big Welsh forwards went after him early in the game. Looked to rough him up more than usual. He recovered and when Ireland really needed him, he delivered. His drop goal was the winning of the game – he celebrated but quickly got ready for the next play.

I think how perfect it is that these two events are occurring on the same day. We probably won't see the like ever again. Jimmy Magee tried to piece it all together as pandemonium was developing in the ring. March 1948 and March 2009. Rugby and boxing. On 23 March 1948 Belfast's Rinty Monaghan became the undisputed flyweight champion of the world when he beat Scotland's Jackie Paterson. On 13 March 1948 Ireland won their only Grand Slam in rugby. On 21 March 2009 the second Grand Slam was captured by Brian O'Driscoll's Ireland. And now it was my turn to deliver. I push all that stuff to the back of my mind. I turn off the television and lie on the bed. I can relax. I have waited all my life for this so why should I be anxious.

I am exactly where I have always wanted to be.

Irish people might not expect much from me, but that is largely down to what they have read in the papers. Most people believe what they are told. I don't blame them. They have the Kiko fight etched in their memories.

There are a few believers.

Three weeks before the fight Mikey McGurn started showing me charts of my improved strength in comparison to when we started, but I didn't need proof. I could feel it. I was a stronger man and I was actually lighter, with less body fat. We had come a long way in a short time. Mikey believed I could win.

He really should have gone to Cardiff for the Grand Slam decider. Half his Ospreys team were on the pitch playing for Wales and he had coached all the Irish players. But he stayed in Dublin.

He told me later that he'd got a taxi from Ballsbridge to the O2 that evening.

'Going to the fight, yeah?' asks the driver.

'That's right.'

'Dunne doesn't stand a fuckin' chance.'

'Really?'

'Yeah, sure, he can't take a punch at all. Yer man Kiko . . .' (Kiko, in fairness, is a fairly catchy name.)

Mikey was bulling. He stayed quiet.

The taximan misread the stony silence as encouragement to keep going.

By the time they got down the quays, Mikey had had enough. 'Anyway here will do. Make sure you tune in now.'

Shane Horgan and Denis Hickie are also in the building – three rows from the front. Until very recently, both were an integral part of the Irish rugby team but Shane is just back from injury and Denis retired. They should be in Wales, too, but they are here.

My fight usually begins with the walk but it starts before that tonight. As the challenger, I am first out. There is a long corridor from the changing rooms. A white sheet enhances my frame to twice its size for the crowd. The drums are rolling just a few feet away.

Jesus, this is high-tempo stuff. The place is rocking.

I look to my right and there is Ricardo Cordoba. He is shadow boxing about twenty metres away with his cornermen around him. The *Omen* theme begins. He looks up and I just start roaring at him.

'Let's fuckin' do this! I'll see you in the ring, son!'

He shouts back but his words are drowned out by 'The Irish Rover'. The sheet drops and the crowd drag me into the heart of them. My family is all here. This is what I was put on the earth to do. This is the defining moment of my life. I feel stronger than I ever have in my life. I am ready.

I see Paul McGrath. Paul is shy and minds his own business but the man has an aura. All the regulars are around him. All the people who have been on this trip since 2005 when I stopped Jim Betts at the Stadium with a rib tickler in the fifth.

I climb into the ring and wait. The *2001: A Space Odyssey* music has Cordoba dancing into the arena. He is such a laid-back customer. He enters a big room of people spitting abuse and there he is singing away to himself.

'Amhrán na bhFiann' sounds different than ever before. It is not just lashed out by some pop singer. It is sung properly and it sends shivers down my spine. Everything about the place is different than before, and not just because of the refurbishment. The whole occasion carries more weight.

Harry's latest mantra: 'Relax in the first round. Pick your shots. Let him reveal to you how he wants to approach the fight.'

We had a good idea what he would do. He would try to frustrate me with his southpaw jab and when I lost the rag and retaliated, he would end it quickly. But we were ready for that. Willy Gonzalez was the crash-test dummy to counter the jab. It opens up everything unless you go underneath it or slip it. Make him not want to throw it so often.

I was just looking to come across his jab with overhand lefts. Nullify a boxer's jab and he will have to alter his fight plan. That puts doubt in his mind.

Eleven seconds in and I shake him with my first proper shot. A left slap stoops him over and puts him across the ring.

Holy shit, I can hurt this guy. I just did. A surge of confidence. The crowd is gone. The corner is gone. I hear nothing.

I can win this fight.

I am looking to dip to my left and catch him with hooks to the body every time he sends out that straight right. Right uppercuts to the body as well. He doesn't like them. I hold my ground in the middle of the ring and just try to time everything. If you walk into Cordoba you will get picked off all night. Still, his reach is superior and he lands two crisp right jabs towards the end of the first round. The crowd are going so insane that their noise breaks into my consciousness, but it is too early to feed off that emotion.

Cordoba doesn't pile on the pressure. He gives you space to work. The same can be said of Hubert Earle. The referee lets the fight flow. Sure, there are a couple of things going on. Low blows and a few early headbutts. Nothing unusual.

With seventeen seconds remaining we are holding. I feel comfortable. Mikey McGurn is stronger than this guy and Mikey had been hanging out of me for six months now. I can handle this. He breaks and hits me a body shot just on the bell. I can't breathe for ten seconds but I have got what I need from the opening three minutes.

I can hurt this guy.

'Good round,' says Harry.

In the second my head movement has him missing a lot of clean shots. I am constantly moving so he cannot see what's coming back. Everything is about getting low and driving across with a body shot or right uppercut. Coming up and over and letting his long, languid strokes sail over my head.

I slip midway through the round. It punctuates the noise levels. The silence is louder than the roars.

I send in some dummy right hands – something else we discussed during training. They are working, too. Harry and my dad did a great job picking Cordoba apart. We are grappling. Lean on me, Ricardo, no problem; I can lean right back. This wasn't in the videotapes now, was it?

Harry: 'Next three minutes. Win the next three minutes.'

Round three. I keep slipping off his right jab. Something is going to break here. I have several options and I'm going to take one of them at the next opening. He hits me on the back of the head as we hold. I flex my shoulders and cross my arms, loosening up. *I have something for you, son.*

I back up to a neutral corner. He thinks he is stalking me. I get low and rise with a right to his body before unleashing a left hook that connects cleanly with his chin. Cordoba stumbles backwards across the ring. There is nothing to stop him and he eventually crashes into the lowest rope.

This boy is gone, I'm thinking. His eyes are glass. He gets up. He has twelve seconds to survive.

I lunge with a right. He grabs hold of me. No room to unleash one. Smart boy. He pushes me up against the ropes. He hits me after the bell and legs it back to the corner. The place goes absolutely bananas.

'BER-NARD. BER-NARD. BER-NARD.'

Everyone is suddenly a believer. It has been a long day for the Irish public. One heart stopper was enough. The O'Gara drop goal. The Welsh penalty falling short at the death. The Grand Slam, but only just. Everyone must have presumed the stress was over and they could work away on the world record attempt for drink consumption. Then I go and bowl Ricardo Cordoba over in the third round. Heads swivel to the big screens that were never taken down from this afternoon. Smokers come back inside to see what the commotion is.

Even the bar-stool boys are back on my side again.

I always knew Dunne could do it. He is a real technician.

Yeah, we have been with him from the get go.

We have indeed.

I am on my stool making eye contact with Harry. The place is still hopping when I go back out for the fourth.

Here begins the longest night. I am confident I can take his best shots. I can see them coming.

With a minute and forty-three remaining we clash heads. A cut opens above my left eye. I'm not sure if it was intentional but this is a well-established Panamanian weapon. I have blurred vision and he sees the blood. He charges in. This calms everyone down. The crowd are tuned into every blow at this stage and they notice the sudden swing in momentum. The sight in my left eye is restricted for the rest of the fight. Against Faccio I fought blind for less than two minutes. I couldn't see Cordoba's swooping lefts from midway through the fourth.

I just want back on my stool so Benny can fix up the cut. With a few seconds remaining, I hold my ground and exchange blows. Just a reminder that the first three rounds really happened and that I'm not the Bernard Dunne you have done your research on, Ricardo. On the bell we look straight at each other. No smiling.

Benny does his job. I will have more work for him in three minutes. I will have plenty for Harry to be doing as well.

I was trailing on all three scorecards. The judges – Ted Gizma, Tom Miller and John Poturaj – were not buying into the spirit of the evening. They were too busy counting Cordoba's punches. The crowd failed to sway them. They may even have done the opposite. Even so, I was amazed when I found out. But the judges' scorecards didn't matter where we were going.

We are entering the inferno now. We are past the point of no return. At the start of round five I sneak in a left hook that puts Cordoba down. I back into a neutral corner, waving my hand in celebration. *A slip? Fuck off!* Hubert Earle mistakenly waves his hands to indicate no knockdown. (Jimmy Magee thought it was a signal to stop the fight and screamed as much to the nation – nice try, Jimmy.) I can see it in Cordoba's eyes. He isn't hurt but he is fuming. I am unlucky as he will not be caught so easily again. He comes in hands held high, spreads his legs in a wide stance, hunches low, and begins to work behind a relentless right jab.

The fencing stops. The technicians down tools. Cordoba has been dropped twice. A fighter of his quality, a world champion, has professional pride. Ego. He has been hurt when he didn't think he could be. He has been told I have a glass jaw but it won't break. There is not supposed to be this kind of power in my punches. He was sure I would tire by leaning on me. And he has been told all this by Irish people! He must be thinking it was all a big con.

The fight suddenly becomes feral. We go to war. Harry can only breathe in deeply and say a prayer. My dad's chin slumps into his chest. Looking at my history, he knows this is going to end badly.

A chat with Harry from a few days ago, before we came down to Dublin:

Remember, he has all types of shots.

Then Sunday breakfast as the savages scoff all the bacon in front of me:

One thing I will say about him, son, is his range of shots. He can do most things.

They were telling me not to find this out the hard way.

Three right jabs snap my head. A straight left and right hook to the ear puts me down.

There is one minute fifty-five remaining in the fifth. I am dazed but not confused. I am compos mentis. I get up, walk to a neutral corner and signal to Earle that I am okay. Standing eight-count.

Cordoba piles in.

I hear two voices. Dad and Harry.

Move! Move!

Hands up! Hands up!

I move in close and get some clean shots off but so does he. I am brawling, but he quickly reverts to the Panamanian playbook. He has a beautiful repertoire of shots and, finally, the man that was clobbered by Kiko Martinez appears in front of him.

I'm thinking, *Let's do this! One chance at glory. One chance at history. One chance at . . .*

At what? I have no idea where I am or what I am doing. Am I signed to America Presents or Sugar Ray? Is this the Wildcard or CIE shower room?

I am knocked out.

In the space of two, maybe three seconds, so much happens. I look up and there's my mam. What is she doing here? Where is here? She couldn't look at me.

I remember where I am. The Point Depot. No, it's the O2 now. My mammy has her head buried in Daddy's chest. I am looking straight at her. Why isn't she watching the fight? Mam never watches my fights. She can't bring herself to do it. But it still strikes me as unusual that she has turned her head away. Oh no, that can only mean one thing. Her little boy is on the canvas.

Sweet suffering mother of Jesus, Bernard!!!

Is this it?

Is it over? I was trading shots again, wasn't I?

Ah, for fuck's sake, will I ever learn?

Is my chance gone? What will I do now? Am I going to become a fireman? I never made it to the Olympics. I lost the European title in a flash. I have failed to win a world title.

Jesus, I could have won this fight. All this work and I am beaten again. Maybe everyone was right. Boxing is over. Bernard Dunne. Contender. Nothing more.

All this in a few seconds.

Cordoba thinks he has dealt with the skinny Irish upstart – a handy pay day.

Harry tells me to get up. Everybody tells me to get up.

I even tell myself. 'Get up, ya fucker.'

And I do. One foot, then the other. It's my stubborn nature, honed over all these years. It is the umpteenth round of sparring in the Holy Trinity with Harry shouting away at the back of my mind. It is all that work in the field in Palmerstown. Halfway through the session and I am exhausted. But I know I can keep going. Thousands of squats tell me it's automatic now. I climb back to my feet in one movement.

In an instant I am back under the bright lights. I nod at Earle. I have been through harder than this, Ricardo. I know I can go again. He marches in. No more slick combinations – this next onslaught is from the back streets of Santa Maria. This is Ricardo banging away at one of the thousand other contenders who want to become Panamanian champion. He comes now to destroy me. He is the rabid dog and I am about to get knocked out. So be it.

I threw two tickets to Mikey, knowing Seán Boylan would be sitting beside him. That was his fee for six months of incredible conditioning – he asked for nothing else. The two men prepared the Irish International Rules team to play Australia.

'Mikey, he is getting stronger,' whispered the Dunboyne herbalist.

'It looks that way, Seán, but we don't know.'

Boylan knew. He knows better than anyone when a Dub is out on his feet. His boys have ruined enough days for us. Yeah, the Meath man can see more than most. It meant a lot to have men of the stature of Seán Boylan backing me.

There is a three-knockdown rule in WBA title fights. I'd been down twice. Cordoba comes thundering in with thirty-nine seconds left on the clock.

I try to hug him. He breaks free. Wild swings. If one catches me it is all over. The long right jabs are controlling everything. He backs me up to the ropes so I cover up. Drop my guard and he will knock me out. I remember watching the third knockdown against Kiko. I close up shop.

I survive.

Round five ends. I am fine. First things first. Breathe. Benny is working the multiple gashes.

'Stay off the ropes and get your hands up.'

'I can't see, Harry.'

'Look, it doesn't matter. Stay low. He is fucked. He is cut as well. Move side to side.'

Harry loses his train of thought for a split second. He looks shocked. Then he almost smiles. He realizes his fighter is fine. Better than fine, I am buzzing. I have just survived an unholy beating and now I have an immediate chance to atone.

Harry: 'Three-minute round coming up. Can you win it?'

Nice and simple. 'I can.'

I raise my arms and flick an imaginary switch above my head. I want the crowd to know I am back. Sorry about the last three minutes, folks; promise it won't happen again.

An almighty sound bounces off the ceiling and lands in the ring. I am in Dublin. I love this city. I can hear them all. The Irish are screaming for Panamanian blood. Fuck me, this is a rush. It is all instinctive now.

Cordoba has never heard a guttural Irish roar before. It is not like any other. We don't get to shout like this very often.

Like any boxer who had just dropped their opponent twice in the previous round and seen him saved by the bell, Cordoba knows to fly at me, but he is forced to check his assault. Harry accidentally spills water in the corner. A full bottle of it. Very clumsy, is Harry Hawkins. He needs to clean it up. He is very sorry. It takes a few seconds.

'Let's go! Take it out of the corner,' shouts Earle.

Cordoba knows the crowd cannot help me but he sees I am not hurt. Most boxers smile when they are suffering, others are betrayed by their eyes or posture. I wasn't hurt. I just look at him. He heard me shouting at him at the end of the fifth. Now he understands what I was saying.

Here I am. I refuse to hide. If I run he will give chase and throw everything at me. *Push him back! Keep tight, stay low.* His corner are roaring at him to attack but my refusal to back off makes him cautious. He remembers the third round when he should be remembering the fifth.

If you get into your opponent's mind you have him. By the end of the sixth I had my tent pitched inside the head of Ricardo Cordoba. He is remembering those nights in Bangkok, Stuttgart and Hamburg when he was denied the status he feels is his birthright. Greatness. He will not be the victim of a home-town decision as he had against Poonsawat and Sidorenko. He believes he must knock me out.

It was still all about timing. That's why he suited me so much. I can counter a guy's punch all night long. It is why I got so far as a boxer on, to quote McGurn, 'prehistoric' physical training.

Out comes his right jab, in comes my overhand left. Pow!

I just keep chopping away at the base of the tree. I pull him into a head lock and lean down. I repeat the process until Earle snaps at me. I give him a big left hook. I put him into the corner. I can see the cut above his right eye now. It is bleeding.

My right hand feels good tonight and that's unusual; I prove as much before finishing round six by sticking him with left jabs.

'The Fields of Athenry' begins. Everyone is singing.

Harry: 'Get low. Bang the right hand and left hook.'

The game plan is holding. Gonzalez and myself had worked on it over countless hours in the gym.

Round seven. Cordoba gets through with a good left hand. The crafty bollix belts me with his head. He is beginning to counter my low stance with sweeping right uppercuts. I stand tall and walk into the right jab. I have to change up slightly. I seem trapped in a corner but my head movement avoids two big shots and I come out with a straight right and some body shots. He doesn't like them.

Back on my stool, Harry is flapping his towel like you would down the beach to generate more air. I believe there is nothing between us on the scorecards. According to the judges I am way behind.

Round eight. I'm going to make this guy miss. I'm going to outsmart him. He is a kid. I am 'El Maestrito' now. He belts me with another headbutt. I lean on him at every opportunity. Eventually, Earle warns me, but it is worth it. I remember how heavy that used to feel. Straight after the warning I bring all my weight down on the back of his neck. The Boxing Union of Ireland officials at ringside have dropped any pretence of impartiality. 'Come on, Bernard!'

Round nine. Boxer versus boxer again and I match him for skill. I refuse to walk in. Just before the bell I catch him a gem of an overhand right. Top of the glove to the top of his head. He takes it. We touch gloves after the bell out of respect and to show we are both unhurt, but as soon as he turns, he rubs his swollen face. My right eye is busted open. He is amazed that I am still coming.

Round ten. Cordoba goes for broke. I nearly don't survive the initial onslaught. He throws 114 punches but it is a mistake. Like me, his cornermen have not done their sums correctly. Two of the scorecards have him at least three rounds clear while the other has him ahead by one round.

Mistake or not, I was just hoping he tired soon because I couldn't take much more punishment. I refused the offer of another brawl. I just gave him the round. My turn next.

This is boxing at its most brutal. He hurts me with a body shot. He goes for broke but I catch him a great left hook. Timing. It breaks his rhythm. He throws two aimless shots after the bell in frustration.

Cordoba has fought hurt many times as a kid. That's how he made it out of the packed Panamanian gyms. He can mask his pain from an untrained eye and keep reeling off combinations. But I know immediately that Cordoba is finished. So does Harry. And so do his corner. Those 114 punches were all he had left, but the ringside judges and the crowd don't suspect.

Harry is sure of it. He tells me to go after him. I just want to win the last two rounds. Make the judges' decision difficult. My right hand is hurting by now, but I'm feeling good.

The crowd punctures my consciousness: BER-NARD! BER-NARD! BER-NARD!

I can hear them now. They aren't calling me Ben Dunne any more.

Round eleven. I let it all come out.

With a minute fifty-one remaining I catch him a decent shot and then belt the back of his head. We touch gloves. I'm not sorry.

He is like a different fighter. I feel the same. Fucked, but the same. His combinations feel like powder now. They are not travelling as far and they have less impact.

I am watching for openings. I send in a left. It shakes him.

We come in close and I get off another left hook. It hurts him badly. He holds on tight. No headbutt this time. We are on to something here. There are eighty-two seconds left.

'Break!!!' yells Earle. Cordoba is wobbling. There is a lull in the crowd. They are tiring as well. They don't see it. Nobody sees it yet. Nobody but me.

Left hook. Left jab. Right hand. They all land. There is a delayed reaction as Cordoba steps a full metre away before he starts to stutter backwards. I leg it after him. The place erupts. The next two rights don't really connect but he is off balance and going down anyway. Timber!

I turn and jog to a neutral corner. Just like the old days. A simple Peter Perry mantra. Don't have the referee wasting his count by telling you where to go.

Cordoba takes the mandatory eight. Near the end he grimaces and digs deep. He can barely lift his arms.

On forty-nine seconds there is a left hook in the post for Ricardo Cordoba. I step in, I step out. Bang. Down he goes again.

I retreat, arms raised. He clambers back up onto jelly legs. Every boxer's worst nightmare is now his reality. Two knockdowns and thirty-two seconds to survive.

I jog over to the corner to meet him. I am acting purely by instinct. A left to the chin. Another cracker. He is out on his feet, ref. But he is the world champion; Earle has to let him continue.

Only seventeen seconds remain but I am not rushing it. I am well ahead. (I cannot believe the scorecards afterwards.) I am in cruise control, convinced the double knockdown has won me the fight. Sensing the bell, I am content to let the twelfth round be my victory lap. I throw out two jabs.

Harry knows better. He is pounding the apron: 'Keep punching him!' I do what my coach tells me. The power in my legs from all those squats is still there. I get low and rise with a right, followed by the left hook that nearly takes his head clean off. I slip, so I go down with him, but it doesn't matter.

With one second remaining, the fight is over. The bell can't save him from the three-knockdown rule, regardless of whether he gets up. He isn't getting up. It should have gone down as a straight KO but the record books have it as a technical knockout, probably because Earle waved his arms immediately. But we all know the score.

There are two children in the ring. The big one from Clare has a beard, the other from West Belfast a few grey hairs. Martin Donnelly is on his knees praising the gods while Harry Hawkins is punching invisible clouds. Some sight.

When I get big Martin off me, I motion to my family: 'Get my dad in here.'

Cordoba is still down. With Peters in tow, I try to get over to him. Earle asks us to give him room so we hold off. My dad appears and lifts me sky high. Two little Dublin men on top of the world. We did it, Da. We did it. I close my eyes. How many times have we acted out this moment when messing in the kitchen?

Peters is still on my back. I turn to him – he tries to lift me up: 'Look,' I say, 'regardless of everything that has gone on between us, thanks for getting me the fight here.'

I jump up on the ropes. The place erupts.

My big brothers Willie and Eddie are in for a massive double hug. The photographer Dave Maher has to tell me Pamela is here! I am careful not to get any sweat on her. I know better. I kiss my wife. She gets to kiss a world champion. Then my ma and Deborah. My family are all in the ring now.

I try to reach Cordoba again as they put him on a stretcher. Harry pulls me away. I turn to the crowd again – over to where snooker world champion Ken Doherty and Shane Horgan and Denis Hickie and McGrath are.

Davy Fitz gets into the ring, shooting me with his fingers for pistols – the Clare gunslinger. 'I told you you could do it, boyo!'

He did. High up on the Cooley mountainside.

I am tiring now. I still have blurred vision. I need water. I speak to Miguel Diaz from Cordoba's corner. Mel Christle is freaking out about Cordoba. I calm down, kneel in my corner and say a prayer.

I need to sit down.

Harry tells me Cordoba is fine. I stand up for Mikey McGurn. Just the sight of him makes me work muscles I didn't know about six months ago.

They take Cordoba off to hospital so the WBA presentation is done without him. I am the seventeenth Irish world champion.

Marty Morrissey asks for my thoughts. All I can think is that the world is ours. Ireland has a champion of the world. Bliss. 'It's ours – It's all ours,' I tell him. 'I said during the week [leading up to the fight] if there was one comment I could make it was "believe". And I believed I could win this world title. I have sacrificed so much. I have dedicated so much of my time.'

I give Cordoba his due for the damage he did in the fifth round. I lay praise at the door of Mikey McGurn. I mention Peters and Hunky Dory for bringing the fight to Dublin. And Martin Donnelly for being Martin Donnelly.

'There are two people that completely have faith in me. My dad and Harry Hawkins. These guys never, ever . . .' I nearly lose it.

Harry says a remarkable thing next. 'Fantastic. No one deserves it more than Bernard Dunne. And I must say Brian Peters deserves a world champion for the promotion he put on here tonight. It has been fantastic. Everyone will agree.'

Peters wanted to sack him a year previous and Harry still says that.

'I had the bollix in my house for nine weeks – he wasn't going home without that belt! I would really like to thank Kiko Martinez for putting us where we are . . . We learned a hard lesson.' Hawkins is enjoying this!

Marty: 'Bernard, you are now the world champion, what's next on this amazing journey that we have shared with you?'

I can't resist.

'Well, I'm going to go home to see my kids. We are going to see *Lazytown* at two o'clock in the Olympia. And Happy Mother's Day to every mother out there.'

It was Sunday morning.

Marty interviews my mam. I butt in.

'At one stage I remember looking over and she had her head in my dad's lap . . .' I'd meant to say 'chest'. I try to save it but only make thing worse: '. . . and it wasn't sexual. Definitely wasn't . . .'

Marty wraps it up: 'Ladies and gentlemen, Bernard Dunne – world champion.'

We are all in stitches.

I seemed in good spirits but I started to crash as soon as I got back upstairs. Just the natural comedown from the adrenaline rush, I thought. I kept slipping in and out of consciousness. Somebody kept slapping me. Then I heard the medical guys saying they needed an ambulance. 'Quickly!'

For who, I wondered.

My family was getting worried as well. I was definitely on a downward spiral. I refused to go anywhere until Dr Joe McKeever examined me. Joe arrived with a few injections and put me on a drip. He kept talking to me and after about an hour I recovered. The fact that I was world champion perked me up!

We went out to Jury's in Ballsbridge. I was in bits but Peters insisted I stop in and make a short speech. I told Al: 'Don't let anyone grab me.' One or two people at that time of night can't help themselves. My hands were like balloons. One lad started crushing my hand and Pamela had to save me. She just grabbed him off me. She could see me wincing in pain.

Cordoba had been the 1/3 on favourite. My mates made a fortune off me knocking him out. Except for Big Mark, who threw a tenner on a knockout in every round from one to ten; his account ran out of money for the eleventh. He would have got better odds to pile it in on a straight knockout. Some mothers do have them.

Telling the world on live television after the fight that we were going to see *Lazytown* the following day probably wasn't the smartest idea. We timed it to get to the Olympia late but as we walked in the four of us were swamped by well-wishers. The security had to come out and bring us inside.

RTÉ couriered the fight DVD out to the house on Monday afternoon. All my mates came over to watch it. Five or six of us jumping around like we didn't know what happened. Great craic.

'Fuck it, let's head into town,' someone said. I'd been too sore to go out Sunday night. I told Pamela I'd be one hour. I was still exhausted. My face was wrecked and I was sore everywhere but I soldiered on for the lads' sake.

We headed into Temple Bar.

I got out of the taxi and walked over to Oliver St John Gogarty's. As I get to the door, the bouncer puts his hand on my chest. Waving his finger, he goes, 'Sorry, what happened to your face?' Now he really was taking the piss, I thought.

I played along. 'Ah, just doing a bit of boxing over the weekend.'

I reach for the door but he puts his hand on my chest again. 'Sorry, not tonight.'

I can only laugh.

None of my mates are smiling and none of them are bantamweights and they have all done a bit of boxing. They stay calm. At this stage, two Gardaí come walking by and ask what's happening. They grab me. 'We'll just lock Dunne up now!' They turn around to your man. 'Buddy, you taking the mickey?'

The bouncer realizes he has done something wrong but he doesn't know what. The manager is out. 'Sorry, Bernard. Come on in.'

'Look, I don't want to argue but I'm not coming in. I really just think it's disgraceful that you stop somebody because they look like this. I could have been in a car crash for all he knows. I just think it is wrong.'

I wouldn't mind but my brother works for the guy who owns the place.

There is pandemonium in the Auld Dubliner across the road.

'Bernard! Come over here! We'll give you a drink.'

We ended up in Coppers. You ask someone where to go for a late pint in Dublin city centre without any airs or graces and Copper Face Jacks will be suggested. You just follow the trickle of drunk people. I bumped into Brian O'Driscoll and Rob Kearney and settled in until the early hours. Good session. It was nice to share the moment with the rugby boys as well. I got home at about half seven the next morning but it was so worth it.

I didn't move outside the house all week. The door bell was worn out eventually. The press, family and friends. I did what I could for everyone but I was shattered.

Twenty-nine years old and a world champion. Jaysus, some going. Some hangover. Then I look at the belt and the haze clears.

I'm not one for using bad language but all I could think was, 'Fuck me, I did it.'

The Grand Slam rugby team was getting a civic reception in the Mansion House on the Sunday afternoon following the fight. The City Council said to us early that morning that we were to go down as well. Then word comes through that we were not to go down. I got a phone call from Marian Finucane to do an interview on the radio. She said live on air that I was getting a civic reception. I had to tell her that I wasn't. I had no problem with this but the RTÉ switchboard lit up. The council were back on trying to make it a joint reception, but we had promised the kids we were going to see *Lazytown* so I wasn't going to disappoint them.

A few weeks later I got two civic receptions – both were in Cork, strangely enough. I might be the first Dub to be honoured twice in Cork! We were also invited up to Áras an Uachtaráin to meet President Mary McAleese on 7 April – that was a great day out for my family.

I thought I had made it. Surely, the next few steps would take care of themselves. I was wrong again.

13. Promoters Know Best?

On the evening of Tuesday 18 August 2009 we finished training still not knowing who I would be fighting in five weeks' time. The O2 was booked for 26 September and I would be defending my world title against either the mandatory challenger Poonsawat Kratingdaenggym, widely considered the best super bantamweight in the world, or a voluntary of our choosing. Poonsawat shouldn't even have been an option. Fighting him would obviously not be in my best interest – at least not in my first defence as world champion.

I left Brian Peters a voicemail saying that I wanted to know now, and unless he called me back within the hour I would not be turning up on Thursday for the press conference to announce my opponent officially. Five minutes later he was on the line. The title defence would be against Poonsawat.

Two days later myself and Harry were backstage at the O2. We still hadn't spoken to Peters face to face. He was sitting in front of the media waiting for us to join him. We had decided to direct both barrels on Pat Magee. Harry and myself would make a statement pointing out how Pat had brought us to this situation by signing up Poonsawat. I told Rosie to go up and get Peters or I was leaving. He came backstage. We told him what we were about to do. He was against it on the grounds that mentioning Pat Magee's name would only give the Belfast promoter credibility or a platform or whatever.

The whole thing stank to high heaven.

We went along but really we were being played. We knew it. We just couldn't do anything about it.

This, unfortunately, is boxing.

The ugliest side of the sport is not the brutality, it is the mental torture inflicted upon fighters by those who have never so much as swung a fist at their own shadow. The fight game is riddled with all sorts of characters, good and bad. There are shifty managers, wise old chief seconds, cut men, con men, punch bags, lifers of all shapes and sizes. Bees to honey; flies to shite.

But it is the promoters who pull it all together. They are the necessary evil.

Along with the managers, they are the ones that control boxing and it is these people who will leave a sick feeling in your gut. If you let them. Nobody, however, including me, is immune to their influence.

Life changed yet it stayed the same. After beating Esham Pickering I had been recognized most places I went but it was a fleeting type of celebrity status which meant nothing to me. I was well known in Dublin anyway. After beating Ricardo Cordoba I became a world champion. It was different. People remember where they were when it happened. Irish sports fans have that never-ending day etched on their memories. I get a surge of pride just thinking about it all.

Yeah, life changed, but only because more people wanted a piece of me. The public relations fraternity came chasing. The mainstream media too. At home things were also changing because Caoimhe and Finnian grew a little every day.

I tried to balance everything but, most importantly, I was still just a boxer. I realized there were opportunities to do other things when it all ended. I was never going to linger in the game but I was unaware of how rapid the fall from the highest peak would be. The plan was to stay on top for a while and then scale gently down the other side. Maybe have a few respectable defences before aiming for something really special. Get stronger. Perhaps return to America and get involved in a big-money unification fight.

These were my aspirations now I was on top of the world. The problem with being so high up is it becomes easier for others to pull you back to earth.

On 30 April the Holy Trinity boxing family threw us a party up in the Balmoral Hotel to celebrate winning the world title. It was a proper Belfast bash – they had the fight replaying on a big screen and it was great to mix my Dublin crowd with all the people I had got to know so well during the training camps in Turf Lodge over the years. The groups had only ever met on fight nights so I was always a little distracted.

Pat Magee and John Rooney were there. There was a charity auction for a pair of my gloves in a glass case. Magee paid £550 for them and in a grand gesture presented them to Harry Hawkins on the night.

Harry was there, 'Sure I can just take a pair off you!'

'Beware of Greeks bearing gifts,' I told Harry.

It was the last time we would joke about the ongoing rivalry between the promoters that were intertwined in my career.

Pat Magee, John Rooney and Harry had been managing and directing Brian Magee since he turned professional in 1999. Harry was the trainer and Pat Magee the manager of record. It was long established that Pat wanted a piece of the Bernard Dunne pie. He had done little to hide it. Having been there at the outset, when he introduced me to Panos and Frank Maloney, he wanted back involved once I became European champion. The presence of Brian Peters did little to put him off.

That's all well and good but he had no television deal and no established boxing venue. Sure, he could probably deliver both of these but he had never done so. That was always the bottom line.

Pat made his first move when Kiko Martinez was the mandatory European challenger. He brought in Denis Hobson, Ricky Hatton's promoter at the time, to help facilitate the process of moving me away from Brian Peters and RTÉ. They wanted to transfer me to satellite television.

It would also have assisted Brian Magee's attempts to climb back up the ladder. Like all promoters/managers, Pat was trying to build a stable. It didn't work mainly because Kiko beat me and Peters refused to back off.

Pat Magee held on to Kiko in case a rematch could be arranged but Rendall Munroe ended that plan. Peters also made it clear he would not do business with Magee or Rooney again.

None of this mattered to me.

What did concern me was that on 4 May 2009 Pat Magee had informed Harry Hawkins that he had signed up Poonsawat – the WBA mandatory challenger and current interim champion – with a mind to force Peters's hand once again.

Magee had sent Charles Atkinson – a Liverpudlian trainer with long-standing links to Thai boxing – over to Bangkok as his representative to secure the option on Poonsawat. Atkinson met with Galaxy Promotions, headed by Niwat Laosuwanwat and his English-speaking son Terry, and a representative contract was signed with an initial payment of just $9,000. That meant that when 'Team Magee' was celebrating with us in Belfast on 30 April, Atkinson was already in Thailand talking to Poonsawat's people.

Peters and Magee both claimed to agree on one issue: fighting Poonsawat in my first defence as world champion would be a mistake.

There are several ways the mandatory can be put on hold in this situation. He can be paid to go away for starters – this being the most common method used in professional boxing – or delayed with the promise of being next in line after the champion gets a pay day against one or two voluntaries. These would be hand-picked opponents who are respectable enough to make it an interesting fight. Like I was for Cordoba!

The other options are to fight the next in line or vacate the belt.

It sounds like a complicated business but this is how it has always worked and if people are willing to get into the same room a deal can always be hammered out.

Pat Magee, just as he had been during the Kiko Martinez negotiations, was now the intermediary that Brian Peters Promotions was forced to deal with if the mandatory challenger was to be held off. Peters refused to meet him.

Here was our problem.

A lot of the arguments arose over the amount that Peters was willing to pay me. The marketing of my name was also still a problem. Endorsements are part of a professional athlete's earnings, especially as they become more successful, as success doesn't last for ever.

The main sponsorship deals in my career tended to go directly on the promotional event I was headlining, yet it was my name bringing them in. Peters would say it is six of one, half a dozen of the other as I was getting most of the profit. 'So how much are they paying you, then, Brian?' He would never tell. After Cordoba, my solicitor John Hogan recommended Dave McHugh of Tri-Line Sports Solutions to handle my commercial interests. Dave represented rugby international Rob Kearney and big-wave surfer Fergal Smith from Galway.

I worked with Dave for six months. This meant I could finally maximize earnings off the promotion of my own name, but it wasn't the end of the childish disputes.

Peters was always trying to get hold of my gear. Gloves, shorts, you name it. He always wanted something. After all these years you'd think he would have figured out how my brain works. Including this in a contract instead of asking me face to face for a memento would only irritate me. We had a ridiculous row before the Cordoba fight when he put on paper that my shorts were to remain the property of the promoter.

Ridiculous though it sounds, the fight was nearly cancelled over this. I told him he wasn't dictating what he could take off me. He insisted it stayed. I told him to stick his contract where the sun don't shine.

'But you have never given me anything,' he moaned.

'I give gear to my family. Go swing off a rope if you think I am giving it to you.'

Eventually I relented and agreed to give him my robe. It got robbed from the corner on the night. I was told of this on the way to hospital to see Cordoba. Myself and Pamela had tears in our eyes from laughing. It was priceless.

There was another twist. Some fella managed to get down to ringside posing as security. He got in touch with a friend of mine looking for an autograph, mentioning that he had the 'other fella's robe'. I got his number and gave him a call – he wanted me to sign stuff for his nephew. No problem. It turns out he was not a professional thief, he took it out of revenge for a perceived sleight.

The WBA badge fell off my shorts during the fight and one of Cordoba's cornermen grabbed it out of the ring. The guy who was posing as security was standing behind them so he asked for it. They were a little busy so they told him where to go. When Cordoba was down on the canvas at the end of the eleventh he nipped in and swiped the only thing in sight – Cordoba's robe. I don't know the guy's name. He had got hold of credentials and, as sporting history was unfolding, he pulled a fast one!

We'd tried to handle my first defence cleverly.

On 27 May myself, Harry, Martin Donnelly and Peters met in Dunboyne Castle. It looked like a deal could be done to put Poonsawat off at least until December and squeeze in a voluntary.

The O2 was booked for 26 September. My first defence as world champion was again to be televised live on RTÉ. I presumed it would be against either Jason Booth or Michael Hunter with Poonsawat held off. These were Harry's preferences. Both were respectable opponents with decent records. Hunter had already fought for a world title against Molitor and had previously taken the EBU belt off Pickering. In June, Booth beat my regular sparring partner Rocky Dean.

It would have been an easy sell to the public. First time back in Dublin I fought an Englishman. First time as world champion I fight an Englishman of genuine calibre. I would have been able to showcase my talent to a wider audience. It would have been a legitimate defence (the pair ended up fighting in October with Hunter quitting after five rounds – he never did recover from the Molitor defeat).

Then there was talk of a possible unification match against Caballero or Israel Vazquez, my old sparring partner from the Wildcard, while Tommy Egan had been trying to get me in against IBF featherweight champion Cristobal Cruz before the Cordoba fight was pulled together. This was suggested again.

I was champion and I wanted a big opponent. Harry wanted anyone but Poonsawat.

A few weeks later I instructed Peters, as my manager, to meet Pat Magee and sort it out. Do whatever needs to be done to satisfy him and Poonsawat's people. Sulking up in Meath was not going to sort anything.

He agreed to make contact the next day. Typical Peters, he changed his mind.

He refused to meet Magee, beginning four months of behind-the-scenes negotiations that would bring us close to an agreement on several occasions before it would all fall apart again. I thought the build-up to Kiko was bad but this was about to get worse. It dragged on through most of my training camp. This was down to the stubbornness of both Magee and Peters. On 4 July Pat shook Harry's hand up in the Balmoral golf club when Harry asked him for a guarantee to keep Poonsawat at bay for at least one voluntary. But it never happened. I don't know why.

Martin Donnelly strived to find a solution, but nobody could get Peters and Magee in the same room. On 12 July Peters sent his matchmaker Tomás Rohan along with Martin to the meeting with Pat Magee at the Carrickdale Hotel. At one stage Pat Magee agreed to take a certain figure back to the Thais to placate them for a few months.

Both promoters still say their intentions were to get me a voluntary. They each blame the other for it not happening. Poonsawat was the interim WBA champion. He could have been guided down another road. He wasn't.

It also soured Harry's relationship with Team Magee and he is no longer in Brian Magee's corner as a result. Harry trained Brian from an early age and was with him for thirty-five of his thirty-six professional bouts. When Magee's moment of glory finally arrived and he beat the Dane Mads Larsen for the European super middleweight title in January 2010, Bernardo Checa was running the corner. Harry deserved better.

Unfortunately the whole mess and lack of an alternative proposal meant the World Boxing Association insisted that my first defence be against the mandatory challenger. All that would have been needed to avoid it was for Galaxy Promotions to be kept happy for a few months, or even for Poonsawat to be put on the same bill.

Another option was to vacate the belt and move on. That was the boxing game, Peters told me. He still didn't get it. I am world champion. I have earned it the hard way. I am not giving it up to play the game. If you can't get me a voluntary, Poonsawat is the only option.

Like Harry, Peters was worried about Poonsawat. They warned me that he was very dangerous. Two more fights for another world title shot, maybe at featherweight?

No. I was not giving up my title without a defence. What would that look like? I wanted to retain the integrity of my achievement.

By the end of July Galaxy Promotions were dealing with Peters, as reported by eastsideboxing.com:

'We just had our first contact from Brain [*sic*] Peters promotions about the Dunne Kratingdaeng [*sic*] fight. Neither camp wants the fight to go to the purse bid, so we have started to negotiate with Brian Peters,' said Terry Laosuwanwat.

'What Galaxy Promotions are trying to do right now is to bring Dunne to fight Kratingdaeng in Thailand around the end of September.

'We have been informed Dunne can't take a voluntary defence anymore, he must face Poonsawat for his next defence. So we are now in talks to ensure that happens with both teams happy.'

I was never going to Thailand.

Having secured the Cordoba fight, Peters tried to get a voluntary through his previous contact with the WBA president Gilberto Mendoza. Mendoza is based in Venezuela and has dealt with every boxing promoter – from Don King to Bob Arum – since the 1970s. Peters pushed for some breathing space. He was given the same answer Mendoza always gives: sort it out amongst yourselves or fight the mandatory.

Peters had another plan. It didn't work out in my favour but certainly assisted his promotional company. He blocked Magee's route into the purse-bid process as the Thai's representative, as Magee wasn't a WBA licensed promoter. On 20 July Tomás Rohan went into the purse bids with two envelopes – one contained a substantial figure and the other had the minimum of $120,000 (just over €84,000). Rohan was the only bidder, so he presented the smaller sum. This naturally pissed Galaxy off and Pat Magee was duly frozen out of the process. Brian Peters the promoter secured the promotional rights for the minimum outlay.

Brian Peters the manager was becoming increasingly difficult to locate in all of this.

Galaxy was forced to deal directly with Peters and Terry Laosuwanwat was none too pleased with how it was working out, telling eastsideboxing.com on 12 August:

'We're in world boxing business for more than 20 years. We've been to many countries and worked with many world champions but we never worked with anybody as bad as this before. They want us to experience as many problems as possible before the fight. The contract doesn't allow us to arrive in Ireland any earlier than 22 September. That's just four days before the fight. We have offered to pay all our expenses if we arrived before that date, but they still say that they will only allow us come any earlier [*sic*]. That is ridiculous and dangerous for our fighter.'

There was still a window of opportunity:

Email From: Tomás Rohan
Sent: 10 August 2009 16:41
To: Harry Hawkins
Subject: Voluntary Agreement

Hi Harry,

In order to close this with the WBA and proceed with Bernard making a voluntary on 26 September we need Pat to sign a statement along the lines of the following:

'I Pat Magee, as the exclusive representative of Poonsawat Kratingdaenggym accept Brian Peters Promotions offer of $50,000 US for Poonsawat to stepaside [*sic*] and allow Bernard Dunne a voluntary defence. Bernard Dunne will then subsequently defending [*sic*] his title against Poonsawat Kratingdaenggym with Poonsawat Kratingdaenggym to recieve [*sic*] a purse of $140,000 for the bout.'

Once we have that in writing or on email from Pat we can close this off with the WBA and proceed with the voluntary and putting all the details of the stepaside arrangement on paper.

Cheers,

Tomás

On 14 August Harry and Peters were in the Citywest Hotel in Dublin for a charity boxing event headed up by Barry McGuigan. Harry called up Pat Magee but Peters wouldn't take the phone. Harry asked Pat what he needed to make Poonsawat back off for one voluntary. Magee said $50,000. Harry offered to personally guarantee $25,000 with the other half coming once Pat delivered something in writing from Galaxy. Everyone agreed.

I don't know why but it never happened.

(Magee subsequently began legal proceedings against Peters over alleged interference with his Poonsawat contract, but they found a way to climb into bed together after I had disappeared over the horizon. In August 2010 the court proceedings were shelved when it was agreed that Brian Magee would top the bill at the National Stadium to defend his European super middleweight title on 11 September and, wait for it, Kiko Martinez would be on the undercard fighting for the EBU super bantamweight belt. Kiko was calling me out of retirement for a rematch but I was happy to do my talking at ringside as part of the RTÉ panel.

On his new arrangement with Pat Magee, Brian Peters joked in August 2010, 'I would have given you the County Club if you told me this was going to happen a month ago. It's a funny old world.'

Pat Magee added, 'We've signed a confidentiality agreement.'

My suspicion is that money eventually united Peters and Pat Magee. That and the need to present RTÉ's new head of sport, Ryle Nugent, with a decent fight-card so they would continue to broadcast live boxing.

They still say they were acting in my best interest.

I say they are promoters who know no better.)

'We would have preferred a voluntary defence,' Peters said at the press conference on 20 August. 'But the WBA ruled against it and said we first had to look after Poonsawat. We'd talks with [Celestino] Caballero and [Israel] Vazquez, which shows that Bernard Dunne is up to fight anyone.'

The die was cast now so I wasn't going to moan. I never had a problem giving Poonsawat his shot – the problem was how the whole situation was handled and how nothing had been learned from the Kiko Martinez affair.

I faced the media:

'He has been sitting in the mandatory position for eighteen months. Let's fight him, put him to bed. He's always going to be there. But he has to come to my home town to take my belt in front of my fans. That's a tall order for any fighter.

'He's all action. I won't have to chase him around the ring, that's for sure. But I feel technically I can handle anyone in the world, and physically I've shown what I am capable of too. It is huge compliment that he is being referred to as Thailand's Manny Pacquiao. Pacquiao is the best fighter in the world, so hopefully those comparisons are not accurate.

'I hope to keep him on the outside. I've a three-inch advantage and I'm a better boxer than a fighter. Mentally, after coming back twice against Cordoba I know what I'm capable of.'

Poonsawat also delivered comments from Thailand:

'I've been waiting for this chance for a very long time but I've kept busy and I am very determined to finally get what I deserve. I believe that I will knock Dunne out inside seven rounds.

'I watched [the Cordoba] fight and both Dunne and Cordoba are good boxers but I'm not sure Cordoba was in the best of shape for that fight. I fought him before and I know he's not an easy guy to knock down. So either he came into that fight in poor condition or else Dunne must be a very big puncher.

'Clearly Dunne has a great fighting heart but I don't see him as a very skilled boxer. He proved against Cordoba that he has a big heart and maybe he is a big puncher too but we will see what happens next month.'

Further efforts were made to put Poonsawat back a few months but I had to start focusing on defending my title. I keep coming back to one fact: the two key men involved refused to meet face-to-face, but when it suited their interests and I was no longer around to top the bill they realized they needed each other. Funny, that.

According to the purse bids, I was entitled to only 55 per cent of $120,000 to defend my title. I had already explained to Peters that it

needed to be a substantially bigger pay day. He knew leading into
Cordoba that Poonsawat was the next step. In my mind, he should
have been working on the presumption that I was going to beat
Cordoba. You know, at least consider it, just in case lightning strikes.
That's what a manager does. A promoter weighs up the odds.

I believe he thought, like most people, I would be cleaned out by
Cordoba within five rounds. Our promotional contract had finished
and he never sought an extension. If he'd had any faith in my ability
to beat Cordoba he would have got my name on paper.

He had been in a position of strength. He could have got me for
pennies as I was only concerned with my crack at the golden chalice
– I would have signed almost any type of extension that promised it.
But now I was a free agent. He had to re-negotiate with a world champion. That was something.

I would have loved one or even two voluntaries and the opportunity to grow as a world champion. I had been in training since May. I
would have been back sooner but Mikey and Harry insisted on four
weeks' recuperation after Cordoba. In fairness, the effort I'd put in had
been horrendous.

Mikey felt there was another 30 per cent improvement in power to
come. 'We have only just scratched the surface,' he said. 'Other than
Paul O'Connell, I have never come across someone with such an appetite for the workload.'

I had taken a massive leap in six months. I firmly believed there was
more to come.

But now I'd have to get past Poonsawat to find out.

14. Thai Granite

From a distance, Poonsawat Kratingdaenggym looks like an adolescent boy,
deceivingly so. When I first saw him, my first thought was 'he's just a kid'.
That was from a distance though. When you're face-to-face with him, the first
thing you notice isn't a youthful appearance, but two mangled clumps of flesh
which somehow still function as his ears. He is seasoned, painfully so, and a
closer look at his face won't let you forget this. Fifteen years of torturous
training in boxing and Muay Thai along with the hundreds of gym wars
have weathered the twenty-five-year-old. Standing near him there
is no doubt — he is a fighter through and through.

Scott Mallon, Asian boxing correspondent for thesweetscience.com.

September 2009
Dublin Airport

(Heavy drum beat. Jingling bells. Thai flags are waving. Women
    screaming.)
Drummer: *Poonsawat!*
Chorus: *Wai-hai!*
Drummer: *Poonsawat!*
Chorus: *Wai-hai!*
Drummer and chorus: *Poonsawat! Hai-hai! Hai-hai! Wai!!!!*
Chalermwong Udomna walks into the arrivals lounge and is showered
    with flower necklaces and bouquets. His gloved right hand is
    extended so people can touch it. The Thai people with the flags
    treat him like an arriving pop star. He is a national hero to them.
Drummer and chorus: *Poonsawat! Poonsawat! Hai-hai! Hai-hai! Wai!!!!*
Sports photographers are snapping away, trying to coordinate the
    chaotic scene as only they can.

Two airport employees:
What the hell is going on over there?
That's your man Dunne is fighting.
What's his name?
Drummer: *Poonsawat!*
Chorus: *Wai-hai!*

Chalermwong Udomna fights as Poonsawat Kratingdaenggym. The
surname means Red Bull Gym – where he trains out of in Thailand.
Poonsawat, his nickname, loosely translates as 'Full to the brim with
prosperity'. He changed his name from Prakob Udomna to Chalermwong Udomna after consulting a Buddhist monk before our bout.
Chalermwong means 'honour for the family'.

So, my opponent Full-To-The-Brim-With-Prosperity Red-Bull-
Gym arrived in Dublin. Trust me, it is not a good idea to laugh at him,
but if I ever go to Thailand for the rematch I will be known as Rasher-
Holy-Trinity-Hunky-Dorys-Martin-Donnelly.

Muay Thai is similar to kick boxing. It is called the Science of Eight
Limbs as the fighters can utilize eight points of contact – punches,
kicks, elbows and knee strikes. Poonsawat set up his training camp at
the Muay Thai gym at Arbour Place in Stoneybatter, which is on the
north side of Dublin's inner city. The media session is captured on
youtube.com by someone in the gym.

'I'm guessing he is going to fight a lot on the inside,' says a distinct
Dublin accent from behind the camera phone as Poonsawat hammers
the pads.

'Dunne's a long-range fighter, isn't he?'

'He [Poonsawat] is going to bulldoze in on top of him.'

It was an impressive pounding of Anan Tualue's pads as his coach
was sent sprawling across the ring. At the end of the session, Poonsawat
switches to Muay Thai with a barrage of knees and kicks for the gathered crowd. They clap. He smiles.

The only benefit of Muay Thai, when it comes to boxing, is the use
of elbows should he ever be required to sneak in a few. But, more
importantly, he has developed the ability to generate an enormous

amount of power from close-range shots. He also seems fairly immune to pain.

You'll just have to trust me on this.

I know Poonsawat will be my toughest ever opponent. A ferocious puncher who can go for twelve rounds, he will not tire.

I remember Harry and Dad giving their opinion after watching the DVDs. Harry had watched them months ago and was adamant that we steer clear. 'This will be a tough, tough fight. You are going in against it, Bernard. Be under no illusions.' Dad kept fairly quiet. They both said I would have to stay out of his way. I was not that bothered by this as I take every opponent seriously. It is never easy to climb into the ring, no matter who you are fighting.

I had already forced myself to watch Poonsawat beat Cordoba on a split decision in August 2005. He was awesome. Cordoba held him off with some great shots and movement as Poonsawat initially struggled to figure out the languid southpaw style. And still a massive left hook nearly settled matters at the end of round two. Cordoba looked in serious trouble but the bell intervened. Our Panamanian friend was stranded on the ropes for most of the night. I had never fought on the ropes for twelve rounds. Cordoba landed his best shots and never stopped punching but Poonsawat just kept marching on in.

The boxing writer and photographer Scott Mallon was ringside in the Rajadamnern Stadium in Bangkok for thesweetscience.com:

Both fighters came out winging big bombs in round one with the taller, southpaw Cordoba using his jab and long, looping punches to keep Poonsawat from landing his own shots. For the first four rounds Cordoba held a slight edge and looked to be landing the harder punches. Bobbing and weaving and moving side to side, Cordoba held the edge in speed and made his Thai opponent miss from the outside.

Poonsawat did eventually manage to work his way inside where he began landing straight rights and left hooks to the body. By the fifth round the body punches of Poonsawat began paying dividends. Where in the first few rounds Cordoba was able to fight his way off the ropes, his punches were losing steam and the Thai was able to pin him on the ropes, unloading wicked body shots. Cordoba looked to be tiring and his punches seemed to be losing steam. A clash of heads in round six opened a nasty gash just above the right eye of Poonsawat. [*Good old Cordoba – this is a familiar weapon when he is in trouble.*] Blood flowed freely from this round forward, but his corner was able to stem the bleeding sufficiently and problems from the cut never materialized. By round seven Cordoba had caught his second wind and delivered a round-long barrage of punches, turning the tide once again. In round eight Poonsawat cornered Cordoba who at this point was content to fight with his back against the ropes. For the next three rounds both fighters evenly exchanged punches whether it was on the ropes or in the center of the ring. Poonsawat looked to be the stronger of the two, however Cordoba consistently beat the Thai to the punch. In the final stanza Cordoba turned up the pressure, stalking Poonsawat, desperate to make his final bid for victory but it was too little too late.

Two judges gave it to Poonsawat with narrow margins of 116–113 and 116–114 while the third, Luis Rivera, had Cordoba the clear victor, 118–111.

The lesson I learned from watching that fight, before both Cordoba and Poonsawat, was an old phrase Freddie Roach used when he couldn't dissuade me from mixing it.

'Be first, Bernard. You got to be first.'

Be first or be dead.

There was one blemish on Poonsawat's record – a defeat to Wladimir Sidorenko in July 2006 at the Ukrainian's home base of Hamburg. It was his only trip outside Thailand.

I watched that too, thinking I would find some weaknesses in defeat. I didn't. They were a similar type of squat machine that knew only one direction. Forward. Sidorenko was poxed to get the decision with a disgraceful 120–108 coming from the Swede Mikael Hook's scorecard. It was a unanimous decision, though, with the other two judges scoring it a more conservative 116–112 and 115–113. Sidorenko's left eye was welded shut by the time the referee raised his arm in the air. He is a tough little bastard and adopted the perfect tactics. He let Poonsawat walk in and then exchanged blows. I was never going to do that. Well, not after Cordoba. Not unless all else failed.

I needed to achieve two things: halt Poonsawat's relentless forward march and, in the meantime, survive some of his big shots.

For the first couple of rounds the plan was to move. Build up some form of a lead or at least stay close enough on points that I could catch him in the middle to championship rounds. Stay in the fight and trust my stamina.

I was in better shape for Poonsawat than for Cordoba, if that was possible. I certainly trained harder. I knew my limits but unfortunately so did Mikey McGurn. He pushed them further.

'You are world champion now – everybody will be gunning for you. If you stand still, you rust,' was the first thing he said to me as we met up for the start of our pre-Poonsawat training regime.

'We got to go harder. Are you prepared to do that?'

I was. I did.

With the money issues sorted out, on Monday 24 August myself and Harry began official preparations for my first defence of the world title. I started sparring with Holy Trinity's amateur champion Ruairi Dalton, while Harry and Peters searched for Poonsawat replicas. They came back with the roughest pair they could find. Olivier Lontchi is Canadian but of Cameroonian descent. He was unbeaten and a world-class super bantamweight. He lived up to his billing and we kept him for all three weeks. For the middle week Peters got us the French-Algerian featherweight Khedafi Djelkhir – he was of a similar mould to Poonsawat and had just won a silver medal at featherweight in Beijing. He knew only one direction. It was a tough few days. Four rounds moving side to side against Lontchi followed by another four trying to deal with Djelkhir pounding away on the inside. Back to back. I could never rest my right hand or ease off as these boys would dominate if I allowed them. They were told to rough me up – a dream instruction for sparring partners. It was a good camp. The two boys seemed to enjoy it as well.

On 10 September Pat Magee filed an injunction to the High Court in Dublin to halt the fight. With only two weeks to go, Harry tried to keep this away from me and went to a meeting with Martin, Peters and Rohan in the County Club.

After convincing us to say nothing a few weeks back, Peters wanted me to publicly condemn Magee. There was a press release, sent to Harry on Sunday 13 September, which stated:

Dunne adamant that legal threat won't affect preparations for Poonsawat

Bernard Dunne is adamant that the threat of an injunction to prevent him defending his World title won't disrupt the final stages of his preparations for his bout with number one contender Poonsawat Kratingdaenggym on the Hunky Dorys World Title Fight night at The O2, Dublin on the 26th of September.

Belfast man Pat Magee, who claims to represent the Thai challenger, has threatened to seek an injunction in the high court to prevent the fight from going ahead due to what's believed to be an internal dispute in the Poonsawat camp. However WBA Super Bantamweight Champ Dunne says the threat has only served to make him more determined to defend the title he captured with a sensational KO win over Ricardo Cordoba in March.

'Myself and my trainer Harry Hawkins are both disgusted that someone who we would have considered as a friend and boxing fan is trying to jeopardize my career and let's face it the careers of all the other Irish boxers on the card,' said Dunne. 'Ireland doesn't get too many World Champions and now I have a fellow Irishman saying that he's going to go to court to try and prevent me from earning a living.

'I don't understand what his problem is because he was quoted in the media recently as saying that he's not in the business of stopping people from fighting but now he goes and does this. I'm not sure what he's playing at but I'm not going to let it get in the way of me defending my world title. He's supposed to be backing the Thai so maybe it's all some kind of plan to disrupt my preparations and if that's the case then it's pathetic that he would have to stoop to that to try and give his fighter an edge.'

Promoter Brian Peters is adamant that Dunne's World title fight will go ahead as planned at The O2 on 26 September. 'It seems that there is an ongoing dispute between Pat Magee and the Poonsawat camp but I won't allow Bernard to be dragged into that row. I won the purse bid to stage the fight and the WBA have sanctioned the contest so it's full steam ahead for the show.

'Bernard has had another great training camp for this fight. He knows he'll have to be at his very best again because Poonsawat is a tremendous fighter and a lot of people seem to be tipping him to win but Bernard is a World Champion now and the extra confidence that's brought to his boxing can't be underestimated. There's no doubting that Poonsawat is one of the best in the world but so was Cordoba and Bernard Dunne at The O2 is a very, very hard man to beat.'

Harry showed it to me on Tuesday the 15th. I passed it on to John Hogan in Leman solicitors, who advised against putting my name to it. This was not my problem. It was between Brian Peters and Pat Magee. I wasn't going to be a pawn in their game. I refused to allow the statement to be released with my quotes attached. I was disgusted that this was still going on. That night I was so pissed off I stopped training after a few minutes on the pads, had a shower and went back to the house. Lontchi got the night off.

The day before that, Darren Sutherland had been found dead in his London apartment by his promoter Frank Maloney.

When I heard about it, everything stopped for a moment. I can't claim to have known Darren that well but we shared a few gyms together and I worked for RTÉ throughout his journey to an Olympic bronze medal only twelve months earlier. Darren should have won the gold medal. I think he would have sparked the Cuban in the final. I was amazed he lost to the Brit James DeGale. Some boxers are amateurs by nature, but Darren was made for the professional ranks. He had everything. A great puncher, a decent boxer and hard working. Dedicated. I firmly believed he was on course to becoming a world champion. He was a smashing prospect with four TKOs beside his name from four professional outings. It was a tragic week that just happened to coincide with the build-up.

I am a boxer and that is a very selfish pursuit. It has to be. When you're in training you can't be thinking about contract negotiations or your family or anything outside of the fight. I had a world title to defend. I put my head down and went back to work. There was nothing else I could do. On the Wednesday I went twelve rounds with Lontchi. I tired in the tenth. On the Thursday I broke his nose but the guy received treatment and got back into the ring. On the Friday we went four more rounds and cut him loose.

It was about tactics now. Me and Harry. It was a positive few days. Harry was able to shake off the strain placed on him by the Peters/ Magee mess and just focus on what he knows best.

On the Wednesday before the fight both sides gathered in Jimmy Chung's restaurant on Eden Quay in Dublin. A Chinese restaurant may have been slightly insulting to Poonsawat. Say I go to Bangkok and they bring us to an Italian restaurant, saying, 'Sure, it's all European, isn't it?'

There was very little of the usual pre-fight talk. Just a very polite Buddhist from Sakon Nakhon province in north-east Thailand. Fellas from Poonsawat's background have very few options but to become fighters, and Poonsawat was the toughest of the litter. He was brought up hard. He has black eyes, mangled ears and a grounding in martial arts. I had a height and reach advantage. That meant nothing. He had waited three years for another world title shot. Everyone was running scared. He had learned the lessons of Hamburg. The scorecards were irrelevant to him. He was there for the knockout.

Peters confirms that only 5,500 seats in the O2 have been sold, although he expects sales to increase now the GAA All-Ireland finals were over. 'It's impossible to compete with the All-Ireland,' he says. 'Yeah, things are definitely a bit quieter in the current economic climate. Average ticket sales are down everywhere even since March. It's going well, but it's not going to be a sell-out.'

A lot of questions at the press conference are about Darren.

On the Friday night I watch the *Late Late Show* interview with his father Tony. It is heartbreaking, but it in no way disrupts my preparations. I am focused on only one thing.

We adopt the same routine as before. We land in the O2 changing room about an hour and a half before the fight.

The fairytale has already been written. All apart from the ending.

Poonsawat stalks me from the outset. I am firing out the double jab and moving side to side but he is always there, constantly cutting off the angles. I jar his head twice in the opening seconds but he walks back in, hands held high. Chin well hidden down in his chest.

I don't see the first dig he lands, a left up the middle, but it rattles my brain. His delivery is precise. I won the round for the number of shots landed.

This will not be possible for twelve rounds.

Round two. He throws very short, powerful punches – plunging down with his right hand in a short chopping motion. Like a hammer. When he gets inside I tie him up but I still feel the stingers to my body. He doesn't require any space to get them away. His ability to generate power from close in is shocking. And his head is a rock. He bangs me with it. I thought I was cut. He zaps me with a jab. Jesus. I try a few combinations. He takes them and counters. He walks on in. I keep moving but he is always there. Into the last minute of the round, he hits me a big, descending right. And another. The power is immense. Do I run?

Instructions are constantly flowing from his corner.

When you hit a guy your best shots, step to the side to come back around again and he is still there in front of you it becomes disheartening very quickly. Harry is talking about not letting him inside. It's like swatting a fly and two seconds later it is back around your head. Poonsawat refuses to stop buzzing.

The fucker is used to elbows, knees and kicks being fecked at him as well. Jaysus, I need to make one of these punches feel like an elbow.

I have boxed in reverse for two rounds. I am conceding too much ground. I should be dictating the pace more. My hand speed is good. I rattle off decent combinations but nothing. He keeps on coming.

Lontchi and Djelkhir were the perfect sparring partners. Stamped with quality. But they are nothing compared to this. He is punching through my guard.

Thirty seconds into round three I realize something has got to give. I become embroiled in a few exchanges and then I set myself. Fuck this. I am going to hit this lad with everything I've got.

This is not the same mistake of old – I had no choice. Better to do it now, while I am at full strength.

I rattle off a three-punch combination. He fires three back. We do this twice more but one of his blows forces me into retreat. His corner goes silent.

The crowd begins chanting my name – in belief that another epic is about to unfold. They remember the third round against Cordoba. They also fall silent when he pivots his whole body behind short hooks.

It is the beginning of the end. I back up but a straight left and another right hook tee me up. A left uppercut is bang on the sleep button.

I can't see. Everything is foggy. I am bleeding out of my left eye. A white shirt with pink stripes catches my attention. My brother-in-law Alan, also one of my best mates, is wearing it. It gives me something to focus on. I snap out of unconsciousness and see Alan saying, 'Get up! Get up!'

That's how I knew I was on the deck.

I get hold of him but the punches don't stop so I let go. I could run. Everybody is telling me to run. I am trying to stay compact but he is punching through my gloves. He is not Lontchi.

I drop my hands and just reel off shots. The French referee Jean-Louis Legland is allowing the WBA champion to go down swinging.

Poonsawat invites me in and a short left sprawls me to the canvas again. Blood seeping from my nose. I get up.

I stand there for the last few seconds of a twenty-five-year career and swap punches with granite fists. A left hook to the temple ends it all. I collapse face forward. What a way to go.

Three knockdowns in one round. I know it is over. I am conscious. Harry jumps in the ring and turns me on my side. 'I'm all right, I'm all right.' That is not true but I only realize that later. A doctor climbs in and tries to put an oxygen mask on my face.

'I am getting on my feet!'

I get up, walk to my stool and sit back down. Dr Joe McKeever and Professor Jack Phillips are in my corner. Jack is staring deeply into my eyes (I looked through him, he told me later). I feel like someone has cracked an iron bar over my head.

My brother Willie comes up on the apron to check for our mam and the family. Poonsawat comes over and hugs me, shakes Da's hand and even goes over to Pamela. He is a decent fella. Everyone is telling me to get out of the ring. Marty asks if I want to do an interview. I say I do. I take a few seconds to compose myself. I realize it isn't all about me and I try to get this across.

'It is a tough time at the minute for the Irish people, especially the

Irish boxing people with the passing of Darren and just the Irish people in general and I wanted so badly this week to lift the mood. Just give people a bit of joy.'

That's all I can say, really. I am in no condition to be formulating my thoughts. My spirit is crushed.

Back in the changing room I look down at my feet and see them. The same pair of Adidas boots I'd worn against Kiko. I'd only ever worn them twice. I get them off my feet as quick as I can and fling them across the room.

Peters can have them as a memento, I think.

Big Al drives me to hospital. Pamela is beside me. They are all set up and waiting in Beaumont. I only need three stitches over my eye and convince them an overnight stay for observation is unnecessary by cracking some of my best jokes with the nurses.

What will happen to Poonsawat? Not many super bantamweights will go looking for him and why on earth would he come out of Asia again after his experiences dealing with Irish promoters and losing in Germany? He is a national icon in Thailand. He fears no man and has already gone to Tokyo and taken Satoshi Hosono's unbeaten record (that was a risk in itself, with one judge scoring it a draw), while in May 2010 he knocked out Shoji Kimura in round four. There is talk of Oscar De La Hoya's Golden Boy Promotions bringing him to America but not many established guys will risk fighting him. He may have to go chasing the featherweights, lightweights and beyond. If he devours the best Japanese and Asian opponents he may follow the path of Manny Pacquiao and start the climb up to welterweight, but at five foot four and a half inches that will prove very difficult. It would certainly put my defeat in a better light!

My guess is we will never see or hear from him again.

Poonsawat's a huge puncher yet he couldn't knock Cordoba out. I am not a huge puncher yet I knocked Cordoba out. Your career can change in an instant. That is what makes boxing so fascinating. You can't have an off night. Poonsawat, in fairness, wasn't an off night. He was an entirely different animal from Cordoba.

The manner of that defeat bothered me a lot more than my previous knockout against Kiko. I had very little answer to Poonsawat. He is a great fighter. Winning is all about believing you can beat your opponent.

That said, I wanted a rematch. I was even prepared to go to Bangkok. I have no idea what I would do differently. It was the only fight that I would have broken my heart training for again. Yeah, it would have been for personal pride. And no, I didn't think I could stop him. But I would have liked to try and outbox him. Go on, knock me out again. They were never going to give me another shot. Why should they? There was no rematch clause.

Boxing moves on very quickly.

I never really had a chance to enjoy my time as world champion. Just six months. That's still a regret.

Now I had to decide whether I was prepared to go again. Become a lifer. What was to be gained?

I had to decide if I was ready to try something else.

15. 'Thankfully, I've still some brain cells in my head'

If he had come back to me to fight again I would have cleared him on medical grounds, but I would have told him I saw the punch. A lot of people didn't see it and I tell you it was an absolute thunder clap. With a smaller frame like that you can't take those sort of blows no matter how skilful you are – from purely a head point of view if he was going to be exposed to bigger hitters that would be undesirable.

Professor Jack Phillips, Boxing Union of Ireland neurologist

I am standing at the podium in City Hall. I haven't said a word because of the standing ovation. It is the Tuesday after the fight, so my face is still battered and bruised. It has not fully sunk in that Poonsawat is back in Thailand with my WBA belt. I know the dream is over but I am not ready to wake up.

I had to drag myself out of bed this morning. It was a slog just to get dressed. I had no interest in leaving the house, never mind delivering the keynote address about Dublin becoming the European capital of sport in 2010. But I would have regretted not showing up. Bad timing, but hiding under the covers is not my style. Today though, I wish it was.

I am not in good form. My head hurts.

Still, I am surprised by the reaction. It is genuine and warm. That it comes from fellow sportspeople (even the journalists are clapping) means something as well.

I say my piece. I am out on the street for a photo shoot with Katie Taylor and the athlete David Gillick. A few old ladies walking by with their shopping bags stop to give me a hug. 'Ah, Bernard. Are you all right?' Usually a million funny things would come into my mind but I just smile instead. Not today.

Back inside, the media are circling. They ask about my future. They ask about the fight. I speak about Dublin. I give them nothing because I have nothing to give. I haven't even asked myself these questions yet.

On the drive home I cannot help but begin the process of reflection.

Boxing was never a job to me. Until now, that is. I was wearing wraps before I knew what kind of person I was going to be. I was sparring before I could read or write. I was a boxer long before I became a man.

The ring is a scary place for most people to find themselves. Staring down an opponent is a very difficult thing to do but I always fed off that fear. It was always fun for me. Even in the aftermath of Kiko and through all the problems with Brian Peters. Even boxing over in Breaffy House when our Point Depot nights were snatched away from us. (The Point exceeded anything I could have imagined – I still get a rush of adrenaline just thinking about it.)

Great times – all of it.

I loved performing in the National Stadium and returning as a professional was . . . well, I used to imagine fighting on the South Circular for a world title.

I fought in all types of places but the people who came to see me in the Stadium at first were hardcore fight fans. They knew what they were watching. Many of them had seen me as a kid and felt part of the journey. That kind of support played an important role.

You could see I was enjoying my last show in the Stadium against Damian Marchiano. It was written all over my face. I was sticking to the fight plan that night and I just boxed. I stood in the middle of the ring and picked him off. I know he was way down the pecking order when it came to the calibre of opponent people wanted to see but not long after we delivered what no one expected. It has to be a slow burn. To put an Olympic champion straight into a world title fight would defeat the purpose of building his profile as a professional. Boxing is about creating something piece by piece.

Now, still only twenty-nine years old, the joy was gone. Just the thought of going through all that effort again had become a chore. But I needed to be sure. I gave it a few months to let the pain take root, grow and die off. This needed to happen after Poonsawat. You can't just bury that kind of pain in a few days.

Freddie Roach let it be known that he would work with me after Poonsawat. Perhaps improve my armoury for what he presumed was a long road ahead. It was nice to hear that from Freddie. He didn't need to care any more, but he did.

By the end of November my mind hadn't changed, but I still wanted to hear what my options were.

Peters, of course, was hurting too, but we gathered in Dunboyne Castle for another meeting. It was to be the last. My manager and promoter. My trainer. Myself. And Martin.

I didn't have the heart for this shite any more. Around the usual circles we went again. There were pay days, I knew that, but I needed something more to get me back into the ring. Boxing takes so much out of you both mentally and physically for money to be the main reason to do it.

For me, the desire to become champion of the world got me out of bed every morning. For nine years. It's why I was able to start again after losing the European title. It carried me through the McGurn sessions. It's why I got back up when Cordoba floored me the second time.

Harry made it clear we would not be doing another tour of the backwaters. Peters suggested one tune-up fight in the Stadium but, generally, he agreed. Martin had very little to do!

Rendall Munroe was the EBU champion. Frank Maloney didn't want to bring him to Dublin and I couldn't fight in the BBBC jurisdiction, so it was never really on the table. Munroe is always in great condition but he is not a big puncher. I think he was made for me. He would probably say the same. I would have picked him off all night long. I enjoy southpaws. Cordoba proved that. Munroe would come on strong for twelve rounds. My conditioning was improving. Mikey was on the other end of a direct line ready to go again. It would have been great to see where he could have taken me. He is up with a young Armagh football panel now. The evidence of his work is already apparent. They just brought in a new hand-pass rule in Gaelic football. The players must use the closed fist. One night at training Mikey handed each player a pebble. 'That will keep your hands closed, boys.' That is Mikey McGurn. Good old Mikey.

As the meeting continued, I let my brain wander . . .

'So, maybe in March?'

Maybe I'll take a trip over to Anfield next weekend . . .

'Bernard?'

Everyone is looking at me. I had been staring out the window.

'What?'

'Munroe?'

'Yeah, sounds good.'

But I needed time to think about it. Harry was staring at me. Munroe would have been a boxing match. Boxing is what I'm good at. Wait, it is what I *was* good at. I'm not there any more.

The meeting went on. Beat Munroe and another big leap could be taken in 2011. A world title would come – either at featherweight or super bantam. I definitely would have had another shot, especially after Poonsawat. They would all be lining up to fight Bernard Dunne. Easy meat. Sells tickets. Says all the right things on television. There is nothing better than fighting a former champion – I have been in with a few of them. I could probably finally get into the MGM Grand on the Las Vegas strip. A tasty undercard maybe against Vazquez or Marquez or Caballero. I would be back on the road. Way out of my comfort zone. It would be a nice big cheque. Nothing more.

Harry was in Dublin coming up to Christmas so I brought him out on the beer. After a few pints we started laughing. We couldn't remember another time that we had done this despite living in each other's pockets these past few years. Never so much as a pint. No wonder I never listened to your instructions!

I knew some of my lads were in his ear. Encouraging me to get back on the horse. Their logic was simple: Bernard Dunne is a boxer at his peak. He should be fighting in 2010.

It is not Harry's style, never has been, to push me in a particular direction. He gives his advice when I ask.

I let Christmas then New Year come and go before making any decision about fighting again but the fact I was even having to think about it meant I didn't have the hunger to get back into the ring in a few months' time. I had never felt like that before.

Dad was himself. He simplified the issue. I could be sixteen years old or a former world champion, it made no difference to him. His advice was the same as ever. 'If you wanna box, son, box. If you don't, don't.' As a teenager I would sleep on it, get up the next morning and go for a run around the park. I would be in the gym later that day preparing for the next tournament. While others geared up for their nights out, I would be suffering. Sacrifice. A lifetime of it. I must have no regrets about my next decision.

I get up early on this February morning to go for a run. Hood up. I am feeling fresh. Clear-headed. My mind is made up before I break into a sweat. After about four miles I head for home and some break-fast with my three favourite people. My clan is in good spirits. Cartoons are blaring from the big-screen TV. Pamela is trying to get Finnian to stop bobbing and weaving so she can put some clothes on him. 'Use your jab, Finn. That's it.' Caoimhe is serving up gourmet food made out of Play-Doh. I sit down on the couch and start scribbling notes. Better start at the beginning.

I love telling people I'm from Neilstown. It's my badge of honour . . .

On Friday 19 February 2010 I invited the media to the Burlington Hotel to announce my retirement. Gerry Callan, the *Irish Daily Star*'s long-serving boxing correspondent, is unhappy. The press conference is clashing with the National Championships in the Stadium. It was never my intention but Gerry wants to have it out. So we do. Gerry means well.

Harry speaks.

'I do believe Bernard has made the right decision. In this game you need to have the hunger. You've guys from Thailand, South America, fighting for their breakfasts. Bernard is wealthy and healthy and that's important.'

The great Marvin Hagler lost by split decision to a dancing Sugar Ray back in 1987. Leonard refused to stand and fight (I never could perfect the art of running from an opponent during my time with Ray). Hagler was disgusted. He was thirty-one and already considered one of the greatest middleweights of all time. He moved to Italy and never boxed again. He walked away clean. This is rare. I don't know why Hagler stopped but I know the highs of boxing don't last for ever and I wanted out now, as close to the top as I might ever be.

I said years before that I would retire when I was thirty. Back then I thought thirty was old. I didn't want to become punchy and as yet I wasn't feeling any side effects. I have been hurt and not remembered things after a fight but they have always come back. From the end of 2006 onwards I'd been experiencing bouts of double vision, but it didn't really bother me. (It was a muscle imbalance in the eye. I had an operation to fix the problem after I retired.) I also didn't want to be the guy who hangs around the gym annoying young fellas with stories of the old days while they are trying to get in some quality rounds of sparring.

'I wasn't a journeyman. I went out on a world title,' I told the reporters. 'The worst I could have done now is go through the motions. I think I've made the tough decision. Thankfully, I've still some brain cells in my head. My health was never an issue but I did not want to be one of those thirty-five- or thirty-six-year-old fighters chasing the dream.

'I fulfilled my dream. Winning in the amateurs. Winning the European title. Winning the world title in front of my home crowd. That's what dreams are made of. I regret nothing. I loved my career, loved boxing. It's been a great trip for us, but I'd like to think I'm clever enough to say enough is enough.'

I was finished with it all – the constant bickering with Peters and the time away from my family. I suppose Harry was right; I needed to be fighting for my very existence to go again. After losing my European title I was willing to do anything to make the next step. I wasn't prepared to let it end like that. This time I had to look at the big picture. I thought a lot about Wayne McCullough and his career. If I was to go on it would have to be a long road and the complications of my cyst would eventually become public knowledge. I would lose the control I had exerted for long periods of my career, which in comparison to other boxers was impressive. I liked the idea of stopping at my peak. I suppose I'll never know if what came out against Cordoba could be repeated.

The sporting obituaries followed. It is weird to read about your own end. One or two columnists had a go and that's fine; I was not without flaws as a boxer and they are paid to go against the grain. Others gave me the credit they felt I was due. One line from Michael Foley in the *Sunday Times* stuck with me: 'He clung to his dream. That much alone made him a hero. When it came true he also knew when to let go.'

I liked that.

Lord knows, I nearly let go a lot earlier, but it was the beatings I took outside the ring that brought me to a world title. Coming so close to the Olympics and then having to sit in a Sydney pub watching it all unfold around me; that day in Jack Phillips's office as we looked at the tiny dot on my brain that I share with Rocky Balboa and so many other fighters. Endless waiting. Waiting for promoters. Waiting for brain-scan results. Waiting for the bus in LA.

America was difficult at times but those days in the Wildcard were special and exhilarating. I loved being able to test my bravery when Mike Anchondo and Nate Campbell and Willie Jorrin insisted I bow down and take my beating. I refused to relent without bloodshed. Yours or mine, pal? Up to you. You should have seen how angry I made them when I slipped their best punches and landed a left hook to the ribs. It hurt.

I want to be remembered as a stubborn fighter. I think I achieved that much. It felt like a good time to let go. I still believe that it was.

Later that night I was back on the *Late Late Show* with Ryan Tubridy. This is a good example of why I never considered breaking the link with RTÉ. They packaged my career into a television drama and when it ended I got to go on national prime-time TV to speak about it.

'When did you tell Caoimhe?' Ryan asks.

We were out walking the dogs. 'Daddy's not going to box any more, honey.'

'What do you mean?' replied my three-year-old.

'I won't be fighting any more.'

'Yes!'

To Caoimhe, retirement meant her daddy would not be going away so much. Those training camps seemed like eternities to her. When I came home for weekends she might remember I was sometimes irritable, distant even, if sparring wasn't going well or I was struggling to make weight. Boxing is a selfish pursuit. Caoimhe sees my retirement as her chance to follow me out the front door, climb into the back seat and be driven around for the whole day laughing and singing songs with her daddy.

The two of them understand what I am about nowadays. It is a normal life, even if it is sometimes weird to me. Someone comes to take a picture and they will step to one side. They are certainly not camera shy, though. Caoimhe will come into the studio and sit beside me when I am doing radio interviews. There is not a peep out of her. She just takes it all in.

Finnian arrived without complications but Pamela was in labour for twenty-three hours with Caoimhe. A stress birth in the Coombe Hospital. It was a nightmare; I was wearing a really uncomfortable pair of pants and had to sit around the maternity unit for the whole day. I couldn't leave even for a minute and my phone only had the one bar on. All you can hear is women moaning. I stayed the pace because leaving would be worse. Pamela's battle was the harder. The suction clampers were out and everything (that is why I can never complain at home about Poonsawat's digs). And a week later Pamela was nursing our daughter while I was up in Belfast getting spoon fed by Noreen Hawkins and doing what I love to do every evening. That's the type of father and husband I am!

Seriously, though, Pamela sacrificed for the both of us and never once asked me to stop boxing. She just stood by me – from LA right through to the end. When I was away in training camp the kids would come into our bedroom in the morning and I wouldn't be there. They got used to that. Finnian was surrounded mostly by women for the first two years of his life. He has changed so much even in the few months since the Poonsawat fight. I can see his personality developing. I have become a father to my son. Bringing him up the way I feel is right – the way my dad was with me. A boy needs a male influence.

I will never encourage him to box. To be coming from two generations of boxers, he doesn't need any added pressure. It has to be his decision and if he does come asking, well, we will help him out. I'll be happy either way.

My career as a boxer has opened up new paths away from boxing. It has given me the opportunity to have an influence on Irish life. That is my interpretation of fame. I had so many different charities approaching me that I decided to set up a website to coordinate them all: www.bernarddunnecharities.com. Every year we hold a celebrity soccer classic, most recently at the Tallaght stadium, and the proceeds are split between two of the charities. This year I was able to help the Motor Neurone Disease Association and CASA (the Caring & Sharing Association, which supports people with disabilities). Helping motor neurone sufferers was an easy decision because Jimmy Magee's son Paul died from the disease in 2008.

I get asked to give motivational talks. I spoke to the Dublin under-21 footballers before their All-Ireland final against Donegal. Jim Gavin is the manager and his brother Brían runs my local Irish-language centre – I am studying down there and take private lessons in the house. (I have a tricolour in the back garden. I want to be fluent *as Gaeilge*, in my own language. Both my kids will go to gaelscoil and I want us to be able to slag Pamela to her face without her understanding.)

I spoke to the young Dubs about focus. Don't forget why you are playing this game. Don't be distracted by outside influences. Someone who half knows you will inevitably stop you in the street to talk about the game. Have a few brief lines prepared, shake their hand and move on. Don't read newspaper articles about the game. Don't let any outside influences interfere with your preparation. Keep inside your own thoughts. Control what you can control. The crowd is irrelevant. It is the same type of pitch as the one you train on. Take it for granted you will concede scores. You can't change the last three points. You don't get to retake another wide. *Every ball is a match*. Just win the next ball. Be first, as Freddie would say. Focus on that. For me it was about controlling myself. For a team it is about controlling each other.

Dublin beat Donegal. It was not down to my talk – there were a few natural-born winners in the team. I could see that.

My link to the GAA was further enhanced by Davy Fitzgerald, who asked me to be a part of the Waterford hurlers' backroom team en route to the All-Ireland semi-final in 2010. It was a privilege to be in a dressing room with giants of the game when they captured their Munster title after a Dan Shanahan goal saw off Cork in the replay. Equally so, I was proud to be amongst them when they were beaten by Tipperary.

My first ever prolonged run of work for RTÉ was during the 2008 Olympics in Beijing (okay, it was not *actual* work). It was funny dealing with the different personalities on the panel. We were all boxers. We didn't always agree. Everyone had an opinion. But it turned into an amazing experience for all of us as Darren Sutherland, Paddy Barnes and Neilstown's Kenny Egan got amongst the medals. It would have been a nightmare if all five boys had gone out in the first round but everyone gave us a few moments to savour, including John Joe Joyce and John Joe Nevin. I was in every day. I really enjoyed it.

I had a go at the IABA earlier and I was right to, but I would love to be an Irish amateur boxer nowadays. The set-up is fantastic. The 2010 European Championships saw more Irishmen on the medal podium.

Katie Taylor was with us in the studio and she gave everyone a glimpse of her personality. You don't need to know anything about boxing to know what Katie Taylor is. Double world champion. Quadruple European champion. That just says it all. She is a machine. A natural sportsperson. She has also played international football and played in my charity match this year. She clattered into one of the men (who shall remain nameless). The ball broke in the middle of the pitch and they both went for it. Your man went about three feet in the air. Katie won the ball and moved it up the field. She's not your typical female boxer. I have seen plenty of female fighters in America and they usually look rough. Katie is a good-looking girl. She doesn't get the recognition she deserves while many of the people within Irish boxing who do know about her apply too much pressure. Many of them believe she has already won the 2012 Olympic gold. The acceptance of female boxing into the London Games means the sport's popularity is about to sky-rocket on a global scale. That is the power of the Olympics. It will help Katie up her game and I have no doubt she will become an Olympic champion if she performs to her potential and stays focused. It will take a great opponent to beat her. Why? Cracking right hand, her movement in and out – probably learned playing football – and her range of combinations. She is what women's boxing should be. What all boxing should be.

After winning the European title my career became as much about politics as about boxing. That is the life, once you are successful, and it can get very messy if you are beaten. I learned in America that this game is not just about what happens in the ring. You need to learn how to negotiate. You need to ensure personality is forceful enough to get what you deserve. Nobody will hand it to you. It was always a way of life for me and when people knocked me for coming home they didn't realize this. Every move I made revolved around boxing. Other fighters understand how deep that goes. Otherwise you can't expect to win the political battles every time. It is crucial to have the right people around you.

I still train. A habit of a lifetime. I go running at Liffey Valley Fitness. Lift weights. I don't shadow box until I get home. Don't want to be giving people the wrong idea so I spar with ghosts in my living room.

I know there will always be another fight to chase. There will always be another Munroe or Caballero that slips away. Or a Kiko – you could chase Kikos all your life. There will only be one Cordoba and, I'm afraid, just the one Poonsawat too. You could chase Poonsawats all your life as well, but what happens if one stops and turns around? I would probably stand there and trade punches again.

Maybe I will follow Brendan Dunne down to a gym some day and try my hand at coaching. Some natural kid can give me a piece of my own medicine by refusing to keep his hands up. Or maybe I will follow Dad out to the pigeon coop. I don't know. I create options for myself. I would like to manage a young fighter one day – guide him through the minefield. It would be the best way I could repay Harry Hawkins for what he did. Shoulder the burden for someone else.

I'm in no rush to jump back in. I know talent when I see it. I think I know what it takes. Talent. Personality. I prefer watching the lowest age grade possible now – they are not restricted by their style. I was restricted by my temper but never by my style – I always wanted to try something new. Double right hands against Pickering or the thousands of squats pre-Cordoba that allowed me to power in under his long arms.

Irish boxing is in a lull again. I was down working for RTÉ at Andy Lee's show in Limerick recently against Mamadou Thiam. It was nearly empty. The people who went out of curiosity will not be back. It was a dog poor show.

The middleweights are still there but it will be a few years before Andy Lee and John Duddy can spark interest again. For that they must climb into the ring against each other. Lee beats Duddy every time. Andy needs to speed up his hands but he is still young. He has time.

Time moves awful quickly, though.

I have done something special with my life; now I have to go live the rest of it. It is a big leap to take and there is no safety net. I could always go back down the gym when I got lost in my head. CIE. Holy Trinity. The Wildcard. St Matthew's.

I have always said I am more than just a boxer. Might as well go and prove it.

I am no longer a fighter, and that does not haunt me.

I let them all go.

It *was* ours, all ours. But we gave it back and we moved on.

Epilogue: The Early Hours

22 March 2009 – 3.30 a.m.
A hospital room in Dublin City Centre

In boxing it always comes down to the two of you. Every weakness, every chink in the armour eventually gets laid bare in the ring. Your best and worst personality traits are revealed. It is the survival of the fittest in its most physical form.

When I said immediately after the fight, 'It is ours,' I meant the people of Ireland, but in the darkest hour of that long night it was just Bernard Dunne and Ricardo Cordoba. Two stylists who went and got themselves tangled up in a brawl.

Now we are just two slightly built men – one a visitor, the other a patient.

I just had to go see him.

We dragged each other down to hell. I came back. His hell was these four walls. His hell would last for a very long time. He was trapped. His WBA belt now in possession of the man who sits before him. I escaped.

Never in Cordoba's wildest dreams did he imagine being stretchered out of that ring, with an oxygen mask strapped around his face, bound for Beaumont Hospital. It simply never crossed his mind. That's probably why he kept getting back up when his body screamed, 'Stay down!' His glazed eyes told me everything. There was no place to hide. My left hook was working beautifully and he knew all about it. To pull himself up in the third round was unbelievable. I caught him as clean as I had ever caught a man. In the fifth I got to my feet twice and fended off sixteen more punches. That moment changed me as a person. In the tenth he punched himself out. In the eleventh he got up twice, but he went down three times. The fifth and the eleventh will forever be my signature rounds. It was the left hook that sorted out matters in the eleventh. The first two knockdowns were follow-ups to another perfect blow, and still it took a vicious yet calculated third pummelling to finish him off.

This is boxing. Both men wanted the prize so much. To take Cordoba's title I had to inflict a gruesome amount of damage. I produced everything I had – I showed I could fight, I showed I could box, I showed I had balls, I showed how hard I could work and how badly I wanted it.

He had never been KO'd before.

It will change him for ever. But he knows this.

The Panamanian has a lion's heart.

He refused to say, 'No mas.'

Cordoba hails from a proud boxing nation. The Central American country that lies between Costa Rica and Colombia and separates the world's two great oceans is a breeding ground for pure boxers. He remains part of that dynasty. We Irish are forever linked with them through Pedroza and now Cordoba.

He is only twenty-four and can become a world champion again – if he gets through this horrid night. His bravery backfired badly. Most fighters refuse to venture outside their comfort zone. He did so three times before tonight, only to be punished three times by judges in Thailand and Germany. This time, though, it seemed like a sure thing. I was the voluntary. The tune-up for Poonsawat Part II. When you lose, everything goes away. Without the belt you become just another boxer again. At least Ricardo is still young.

So I follow him up to Beaumont. I ask for directions to Cordoba's room. The corridor is empty. There are two nurses on the ward. They tell me his heart rate and blood pressure had gone through the roof.

He is awake.

'Where is everyone? Where are his people?'

'He is alone,' a nurse replied.

That struck me as wrong. All his team had gone. I could only imagine what it would have been like if I'd got knocked out at the Arena Roberto Duran in Panama City after eleven savage rounds. You can bet the house that Pamela would be asleep on the chair beside me with Harry dozing somewhere out in the corridor. That's just the way it would be.

You are not paid to hate your opponent. It helps some fighters but I have never had to hate someone to hit him. That is not what boxing is about. That is why I always tried to avoid all the pre-fight bitching. I know it sells tickets but I boxed for fun, not from hatred. I always enjoyed hitting people in the ring and I was good at avoiding their attempts at retaliation.

But this night has gone past anything I have ever experienced.

Everyone in the O2 witnessed the remarkable, intricate exchange that we served up but no one – not the opposing corners and not the referee – nobody can feel the bond between us now. It was just the two of us that went through it. No one will ever know the effort it took from both of us. It defied logic. The moment went further than my wildest dreams. And they have always been vast.

Pride keeps you going, like it did for Cordoba, but that same pride will put you on a drip in a hospital. No one else loses but you. No one else feels the combined physical and psychological impact.

It feels good to be close to Ricardo on this night. He looks feeble. He is isolated – a long way from home. I still can't believe his people were not with him. Maybe they think he's sleeping – don't they know that's never going to happen? He is tough, but he is hurt too. Blood is still seeping from the stitching. An oxygen mask is still covering his face. They have given him some injections for the pain, at least. Losing the title is bad enough but being confined to this alien environment must be a living hell. The least he deserves is a few moments of my time.

I know his pain is the polar opposite of my joy. I hope my presence doesn't make matters worse but he is calm when I sit down. He understands why I have come to see him.

I hold his hand. He doesn't speak English and I don't speak Spanish but we communicate. I thank him for a great fight and for giving me the opportunity. We sit there for a few minutes together.

The bond between two fighters is unbreakable.

You win and lose with the same amount of humility. That is what being

an Irish sportsman is about. So, I sit in that hospital room with Ricardo
Cordoba and hold his hand.

We are back in the hotel – on this night it is the Clarion on the River
Liffey. Me and Pam. I am exhausted but I can never sleep. It is nearly
dawn. I am iced up but my head is throbbing and my hand is aching.
I can't take the pain any more.

I go downstairs to the receptionist.

'Howya, my doctor never gave me painkillers in the hospital. Have
you any?'

She doesn't.

'Have you any sort of drugs?'

She has nothing.

'Okay, where is the nearest chemist?'

She shrugs her shoulders. It is the night shift. She is foreign. She is
counting down the minutes before her relief arrives. She can't possibly
understand my predicament. Maybe if she saw the state of Cordoba . . .

I try to convey my pain with a look.

I give up. I ask for my car keys. The car was parked on the road outside
the front door.

I'll go in search of my own relief, but before I get to the motor a
taxi skids in front of me.

'BERNARD! Howya doin', son! Champion of the wuuurld!'

A Dub. He is hugging me before I can say anything.

Relax, buddy. Relax.

His name is Hugo Richardson and, sure enough, he is a brother of
a friend of mine.

'Just the man,' I say. 'Where is the nearest all-night chemist?'

'What do you need, pal?'

'Painkillers. I never got anything off the doctor. I am in agony.'

'Hold on a second.'

Hugo is a true Dub. He opens the glove compartment and it is
overflowing with tablets. 'Take what you need, you think will last.'

'You are a fuckin' saint, Hugo.' I grab a box of Solpadeine.

'No problem! Champion of the wurld, fuck me.' He turns and
whistles. 'Champion of the whole bleedin' wide wurld.'

Off he goes, back on his shift, driving down the quays towards the big hall where it all just happened. Where everything happened.

I take my medicine and sleep washes over me.

Next day when I come gingerly through the front door, my infant son Finnian is placed in my arms. His big sister screams in delight when she sees her daddy. Caoimhe doesn't see the fresh scars or the dark purple bruises, she just sees my eyes. Because they are her eyes as well.

Acknowledgements

I don't know where to start, so I will do what I have always done and jump in head first!

The Hawkins clan deserve a special mention for letting me become a part of their household. I want to express a particular depth of gratitude to Noreen, for making me feel like I was at home during those tough weeks in training camp. Terrence, Clare and Kevin just accepted me as one of the family.

Peter Perry and all those in the CIE gym who encouraged me from the first day I walked (or was it crawled?) in the door. That was also the day I fell in love with the sport of boxing and they are partly responsible.

Martin Donnelly for being a true friend and trusted advisor throughout every bump and sharp turn on the road. Martin is more than just a sponsor: he is a true patron of Irish sportsmen like me, while his constant support for the GAA remains unbreakable. I mentioned it in these pages already but Martin Donnelly is a great Irishman. The kind of guy you want to have in your corner should you ever get in a fight.

It is easy for a twenty-one-year-old kid to fall through the cracks in Los Angeles, but my American family (the Conlons) ensured that was never going to happen. It was just little things but those trips to Orange County, their unreal hospitality and tasty BBQs helped me to settle and made the whole California experience a memorable one for the right reasons.

RTÉ for their continued support. Thanks Glen, Jimmy, Darragh and the team.

Dave Maher and Sportsfile for capturing the memories that I can always treasure because of them.

Gavin Cummiskey for his hours upon hours of work and tolerating my sometimes jumbled-up mind (thank God for diaries!). Claire Bracken's reading of the early drafts is also appreciated.

Noel Kelly Management for guiding me towards this project and their continued work on my behalf.

Penguin Ireland's Michael McLoughlin and Brendan Barrington for all their work behind the scenes.

Freddie Roach and all the guys in the Wildcard Gym for helping me to develop as a professional fighter and for just being decent people in a foreign land.

Mikey McGurn for his selfless hard work and torture (approach this man with caution!). I appreciate my time with Mikey now that I don't have to do it any more.

Hunky Dory, Martin Donnelly and O'Neill's sports for the essential roles they each played in my pro career. Also, Merlin Motors for their support.

To Neville and all the lads over in Louis Copeland's of Capel Street, thanks.

I should mention the residents of Neilstown Avenue and O'Devaney Gardens, particularly my family: Mam, Dad, Betty, Willie, Eddie and Deborah. Thanks for everything you have ever done for me.

Mam, I forgive you for dropping me on my head!

From a very young age I had my dad, Brendan Dunne, and Harry Hawkins to turn to for words of wisdom. It was these two who experienced the sleepless nights leading up to my fights while I recharged the batteries. It was these two who never stopped worrying and strategizing about my opponents, allowing me to focus on getting into peak condition. It was these two that pored over the DVDs and then fed me the necessary information (when I took it all in I became very hard to beat). These two never stopped trying to improve me.

A special mention to my two best mates – Caoimhe and Finnian – for making life so much fun these past few years, especially every day since I retired.

And to my wife Pamela: thanks for putting up with me all this time. For never giving out when I had to go away for weeks on end for training camps while she had two young kids to mind. For putting up with my little moods when I was on diets or the week leading up to fights when I'd be a pain in the ass. But really for just being there when I needed you.

Finally, I'd like to thank all the people who came along for the ride, especially those who stayed with me even when I made you all drive down to Castlebar! The Neilstown people never stopped believing in one of their own. It was your belief that provided me with the inner strength to fulfil my dream.

Everyone in the O2 or watching on television on that crazy night in March 2009 will know what I mean: It really was ours.

Bernard Dunne
August 2010

Photo Credits

Index